CAMBRIDGE PAPERS IN SOCIAL ANTHROPOLOGY

No. 7

BRIDEWEALTH AND DOWRY

CAMBRIDGE PAPERS IN
SOCIAL ANTHROPOLOGY

BRIDEWEALTH AND DOWRY

JACK GOODY
AND
S. J. TAMBIAH

CAMBRIDGE
AT THE UNIVERSITY PRESS
1973

Published by the Syndics of the Cambridge University Press
Bentley House, 200 Euston Road, London NW1 2DB
American Branch: 32 East 57th Street, New York, N.Y. 10022

© Cambridge University Press 1973

Library of Congress Catalogue Card Number: 72-95407

ISBN: 0 521 20169 1   hard covers
            09805 x   paperback

Set in cold type by E. W. C. Wilkins Ltd
Printed in Great Britain at
the University Printing House, Cambridge

CONTENTS

PREFACE

The present volume takes a somewhat different form from previous numbers in this series. It was not our original intention to produce a volume of this shape. We had other contributions in mind and had discussed the main themes in a seminar we ran in Cambridge during the academic year 1970-1, whose members we collectively thank. But the theme outgrew the limited size of the publication, and we decided to publish our own rather lengthy contributions as two separate but interrelated essays, which were more widely comparative in scope than earlier essays in this series.

This policy had certain advantages since we could then concentrate upon Africa and Asia respectively. Moreover, we had often talked around the points we raise and found ourselves dissatisfied with some of the current treatment of kinship and marriage in anthropological and sociological writing. Certain themes of contemporary polemics, such as that turning on alliance and descent, seemed more profitably treated in a context that gave a greater emphasis to material considerations, a context that would enable us to deal with differences as well as similarities, with variables as well as constants. At the core of our analysis of kinship and marriage, therefore, lies a concern with the interrelationship of the productive and reproductive systems, particularly as these affect the position of women. Indeed it is the ability of women in many parts of Asia to acquire the same kinds of property as men (and often from men) that we want to contrast with the separation of the sexes that is characteristic of Africa — at least in the sphere of the devolution of the patrimony.

There are two conceptual/terminological points we would like to bring to the attention of the reader. Payments from the bridegroom or his kin for the use of the bride (given directly to her or else channelled through her father) have been called 'indirect dowry' by Goody; Tambiah refers to such gifts by phrases such as 'the analogue of brideprice which is transformed into dowry'. There is no disagreement about the nature of these gifts which should be distinguished from the bridewealth of Africa.

Secondly, while Goody refers to the mother's brother as a kinsman (at least where repeated marriage is absent), Tambiah calls him an affine. The use of these particular terms probably arises from the respective African and South Indian backgrounds to our research. We do not intend this should be a focus of polemic between us. Indeed, our aim is to by-pass, shortcut, even eliminate such arguments by calling attention to the nature of the property relations between the partners of a marriage and with the parents of each, i.e. to the interrelationship of marriage transactions and the devolution of property.

Finally, we would like to thank our colleagues for their stimulation, their criticism and their interest. Tambiah is especially grateful to Edmund Leach for his valuable comments and suggestions, particularly those relating to the sections of his essay about Burma. Tambiah's essay contains numerous words from the classical Sanskrit, Pali and modern Indian, Sinhalese and Burmese languages. The orthography adopted follows accepted conventions of romanization but omits all diacritical signs.

Cambridge, 1972

J.R.G.
S.J.T.

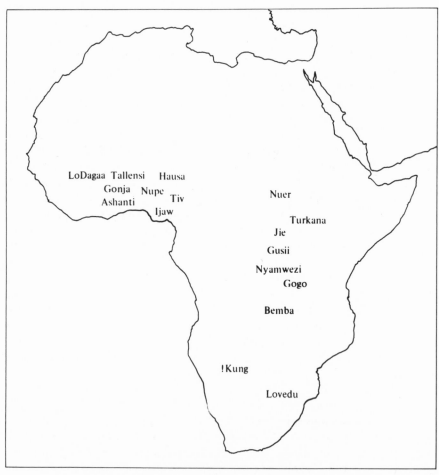

Location of peoples discussed

BRIDEWEALTH AND DOWRY IN AFRICA AND EURASIA

JACK GOODY

Both bridewealth and dowry involve the transmission of property at marriage. Whatever 'symbolic' aspects mark these transfers, they also have their economic functions, not primarily as intermediaries in a purchase, but as ways of redistributing property. Hence they must always be seen in the context of the wider movement of property and its exploitation for productive and other social purposes. Viewed in this way, these differences in marriage transaction have to be linked with other aspects of social organisation, particularly the economy.

There are three aspects of the institutions of bridewealth and dowry which I want to discuss, namely, their correlations, distribution and classification; all three are inextricably involved and logically one ought to begin with the last.

The categories used by most writers (and which turn up in the *Ethnographic Atlas*) are the following: bridewealth, dowry, bride-service, gift exchange, token payments, sister exchange and absence of gifts. We may put in crude diagrammatical form what is often assumed to be the relationship between these major forms of marriage transaction as follows:

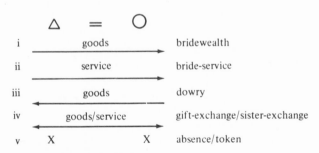

Fig. 1. Marriage transactions

A little thought suggests that this scheme, and particularly the 'opposition' between dowry and bridewealth, is quite misleading. The first discrimination to make has to do with dowry, rather than bridewealth, for there are circumstances in which the two are confused.

Dowry can be seen as a type of pre-mortem inheritance to the bride, bridewealth as a transaction between the kin of the groom and the kin of the bride.[1]

1

But in a good number of societies in Europe and Asia, the marriage prestations are made by the groom or his kin, and are consequently often classified as bridewealth (or brideprice). But the ultimate recipient of these gifts is the bride and not her kin. It is true that the gifts from the groom sometimes go first to the girl's father, who may indeed take a cut (in this respect there is a continuum); but the bulk goes to the bride herself and thus forms part of a joint (or sometimes separate) conjugal fund rather than a circulating societal one. Rather than employ the misleading term bridewealth (or brideprice), which has been used for example to translate the Sanskritic word *asura*, I would refer to such transactions as 'indirect dowry'. Mayne refers to *asura* as 'marriage by purchase'; it is difficult to reconstruct the institutions that existed alongside the laws of Manu, but clearly part of the transaction went to the bride herself (1892: 80 ff.) and so was more nearly akin to dowry.

BRIDEWEALTH

Even if we confine our discussion to the passage of goods or services from the kin of the bride to the kin of the groom, there are many significant differences among these prestations; the term bridewealth has been used to cover a set of transactions each of which has very different implications for social structure. However, this range of institutional variation and its economic implications have been obscured by a loose application of so-called exchange theory to marriage. That marriage in simple societies involves an 'exchange' is a somewhat vague notion that has often confused the analysis of social systems. The extreme case is the exchange of 'sisters', formerly practised in parts of Australia and Africa.[2] Here the term has the precise dictionary meaning of 'to be received as an equivalent for', 'to give and receive reciprocally'. From quite a different standpoint the virtually universal incest prohibition means that marriage systems necessarily involve 'exchanging' siblings for spouses, giving rise to a reciprocity that is purely notional. But in most societies marriage is mediated by a set of intermediary transactions. If we see these transactions as simply implying immediate or long-term reciprocity, then the analysis is likely to be blurred. If we assume immediate reciprocity,[3] whether with regard to women or property, then the two sides of the equation have to balance by definition: assumptions about the 'value' system follow from assumptions about the nature of the exchange. The tautology is even more apparent in systems of generalized exchange, where the reciprocity is notional. The analysis is further limited if one regards the passage of property simply as a symbol of the transfer of rights, for then the nature of the objects handed over (the *traditio*) is of little importance. What matters is that some object has been publicly transferred in order to establish the woman as a wife and the man as a husband. Neither of these approaches are wrong; both are inadequate. For they tend to lead to a neglect of the differences within those payments described as bridewealth (or indeed dowry,

2

though here the problem is somewhat different), and consequently to a neglect of the relationship of these differences to the rest of the social system, in particular the economy. I refer not only to the problem of the indirect dowry, which accounts for much so-called bridewealth (or brideprice) in Eurasia. In addition, there are important distinctions to be made in terms of the size of the payments, its material content, the personnel involved in the giving and receiving and the use made of the objects received. We also need to consider three other factors, whether the payments are returnable at death or divorce, whether they are fixed or variable and when they are payable.

I can put the point in more concrete terms by comparing the 'marriage payments' among the LoWiili and the Gonja of northern Ghana. The Gonja payment consists of a minimal amount of 12 shillings and 12 kola; it is small by any standards, though it is supplemented by courting and greeting gifts to the future bride and to her parents; and nowadays the expenses of the wedding itself have increased considerably. Among the LoWiili, the transactions flow in the same direction; there is a small payment of 350 cowries which is said to be all that is needed to 'legalize' the union. In addition payments amounting to some 3 cows, 1 goat and 20,000 cowrie shells should be made during the lifetime of the marriage, the last of these at the time the bride joins her husband. If they are not forthcoming at the right time, the bride's father (or his kin) will try to persuade her to return home until the husband meets his obligations.[4] Among the Gonja the transactions are non-returnable in the case of divorce; among the Lowiili, all are returnable.

There are two sorts of implications that arise from these differences. One has to do with the kind of rights in the bride that are acquired by the transfer; 'marriage' is not an undifferentiated concept and these rights are distinctly variable. The other concerns the relationship between the bride or groom and those who provide or receive the payments. The accumulation of property required for the transactions may well delay the marriage of the individual on whose behalf they are made. Such may be the case whether the transactions are part of the process of devolution (as with dowry) or part of the reciprocal process of bridewealth whereby the receipts for women are paid out for men.

Size of payments

Let me deal first with the question of the size of payments related to rights. In Africa, the relative size of payment is in a general sense linked with the quantum of rights transferred. In systems of matrilineal descent groups, where rights in a woman's procreative powers remain in the hands of her natal lineage, the amounts are comparatively less than in other societies.[5] Indeed the actors themselves recognize the connection between a substantial bridewealth and agnatic descent; 'one constantly hears the comment in Nyasaland that "with us a son doesn't inherit because we don't *loola* (the local form of *lobola*) our wives"'. As Mair points out

3

these statements do not mean that those who abandon high bridewealth necessarily abandon paternal filiation (1953: 73), but such a change does seem to be associated with a modification (or a difference) in the organization of kin groups. Indeed, H. Schneider sees social organization in East Africa as having been influenced in the opposite direction by the increasing accumulation of bridewealth. The number of societies in which there are matrilineal descent groups and a bridewealth consisting of livestock is 'statistically quite insignificant' (1970: 145). On the other hand, with the appearance of such a bridewealth, we find the levirate, virilocal marriage, important patrilineages and the disappearance of bride-service. 'Ultimately marriage becomes almost undissolvable' when we reach a figure of twenty head of cattle or their livestock equivalent. The Turu of Tanzania have travelled along this road, further than the Iramba and Mbugwe but not as far as the Gogo. 'That some significant long-term shifts are or were occurring in these societies is apparent. Central to the change was the tendency to accumulate livestock. It may even be that the growth of segmentary societies based on livestock is one of two major directions towards change in traditional Africa, the other occurring among relatively poor people without livestock – being a move in the direction of states' (1970: 146).

It should also be added that with matrilineal descent groups the payments are not always low. Among the LoDagaa the opposite appeared to be the case; the greater the emphasis on matrilineal groups, the higher the payment (Goody 1970b: 451). In this context the insistence on high payments seemed to be related to a reluctance to allow women to marry out (into the groups giving less emphasis to matriliny) and a reluctance to allow women to leave the natal home. In other words, it was a payment to discourage bride-removal; or to put it another way, to encourage initial farm-service on the part of the husband. Women are used as bait to attract the economic services of men.[6]

In bilateral societies in Africa, the payments also seem to be low.[7] This is certainly true of the Lozi of Zambia, and in West Africa low payments are associated with a certain type of centralized state, of which Gonja is one. Although this group of states, which includes the Hausa and the Mossi, emphasizes paternal succession to office and has dynasties based upon the agnatic line, the organization of descent groups is very different not only from acephalous 'tribes' like the Tallensi and the Nuer but also from centralized states like the Zulu and Ashanti. Some of these states have been influenced by Islam and hence tend towards the dowry rather than bridewealth (e.g. Hausa and Nupe). In addition the wedding itself may involve some further expense. Weddings are also associated with the Islamic tradition; indeed these *rites de passage* tend to receive more ceremonial elaboration in dowry systems than elsewhere, for they celebrate the establishment of a conjugal fund.[8] In Nigeria the amounts involved are increasing under modern conditions and have become a substantial factor in the groom's calculations. But although the amounts have increased, the payments are of very different character from the bridewealth of East and South Africa.

4

Use

I refer here to the use and destination of the transactions. Money spent on wedding expenses, like money indirectly contributed by the groom to the endowment of the bride, serves different ends from the circulating pool of resources we speak of as bridewealth. Bridewealth is not to be consumed in the course of the celebrations, nor is it handed to the wife; it goes to the bride's male kin (typically brothers) in order that they can themselves take a wife. Indeed it involves a kind of rationing system. What goes out for a bride has to come in for a sister. If the payments are small, the egalitarian distribution of spouses could be disturbed.[9] As Wagner remarks of the Luhya, the transfer of marriage cattle primarily serves as a regulator of marriages and not as a means of increasing the father's wealth.[10] To achieve this end an important aim is not to let the amount received fall below the effective rate. Of the Gusii, Mayer remarks, 'Every father fears being left in the lurch by finding that the bridewealth which he has accepted for his daughter will not suffice to get him a daughter-in-law; therefore he is always on the look out for any signs of a rise in the rate, and tends to raise his demands whenever he hears of other fathers doing so. This means in general terms, that *individual* cases of over-payment produce a *general* rise in the rate all round' (1950: 19).

Clearly the balancing can best be achieved if the items have little exchange value outside marriage transactions. Such is the case with cattle in the savannah areas of Africa. Of the Lobedu, Kridge writes that: 'cattle coming in as bride-price are not supposed to be used for any other purpose than marriage for, unlike the Zulu who kept large herds, constantly replenished in the old days by raids against neighbours, most Lobedu families do not possess cattle except for short periods of time' (1964: 160). In pastoral societies, such as the Zulu, livestock have of course a critical part to play in subsistence and are but rarely exchanged for other items of value (no more than is land in many agricultural societies in Africa). In farming economies, they are usually stores of wealth. While lesser objects can be exchanged into cattle (usually among kin), it is more difficult to change out, except through sacrifice. If cattle transactions are largely confined to marriage, then the dependence of the groom on a similar transaction is overwhelming. This is so even if the payments are freely exchangeable (like cowries, hoes or iron bars) but large in terms of the individual's capacity to accumulate, an index of which is their size relative to the average yearly income per head. In this case a man is again highly dependent upon 'sisters' for bringing the wealth and 'fathers' for distributing it. The effect is to reinforce the authority of the father and emphasize the tie with the sister.

The role of the father is clear. The authority of the older generation is linked to the extent to which the young are dependent on them for marriage cattle or the equivalent. The dependence will extend in some measure to all contributing kinsfolk, which may include maternal as well as paternal kin.[11]

JACK GOODY

The givers and receivers

This point concerning the range of contributors raises another difficulty about the assumptions behind the diagrammatical representation of marriage transactions given in Fig. 1. It turns out to have the same sort of failings as many 'models' (read 'diagrams') of cross-cousin marriage (XCM); it lets one man or woman stand for the sibling group, or worse still, the entire kin group. If we increase the number of roles laid out in the model (the failure to do which is a defect of much discussion about the mother's brother), we see where the problems arise.

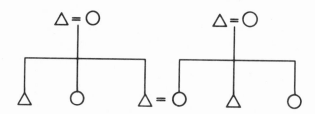

A few more roles are now included, but even this increase would be insufficient to permit a proper examination of bridewealth transactions in some African societies; for the Nuer, we would clearly have to introduce many more roles in the same and senior generation to ego, both inside and outside the patrilineal descent groups of the bride and groom. Indeed for some societies it has been argued that marriage sets up certain kinds of debt which can only be repaid at the next generation, by means of a return of spouses (XCM), or by remitting a proportion of the bridewealth received for the daughters of the marriage, or possibly by the sister's son's seizure of the property of his mother's brother (see M. Harris 1968), though in this latter case the compensation would appear to be travelling in the wrong, or anyhow the reverse, direction. In all these cases we have to include further roles and further elements of the network of transactions, if we are to understand the pattern of marriage prestations.

In sum, transactions in the same direction may be destined for different social persons. In Africa, bridewealth does not go to the bride, but to her kin; we recognize this when, rightly or wrongly, we speak of terms of compensation or recompense (Radcliffe-Brown 1950: 50), or even bride-price; it is wealth for, not to, the bride. On the other hand, dowry, in the usual sense, does not go to her kin, but to the bride herself, sometimes to the husband (at least for safekeeping) or even to both spouses jointly. Bridewealth and dowry then are very far from being mirror opposites. Indeed, the mirror opposite of bridewealth would be groomwealth; and of bride-service, groom-service. But there is little to be put in these two boxes by way of actual cases, except perhaps the payments for the 'borrowed man' of the Menangkabau of Sumatra (or, from one point of view, the *urugubu* of the Trobriands of Melanesia).

6

However, it is also necessary to remember that in Africa the payment was usually the responsibility of much more immediate kin; of the Hehe, Brown (1932) writes that in practice a man did not look for assistance to relatives more distant than his father and his mother's brother, and the same can be said of the majority of African peoples; the range of contributors and recipients is characteristically narrow, usually limited to members of the unit of production (the farming or herding group) but often to the unit of consumption, the children of one mother. This unit, whose existence is dependent upon polygyny (at least in its serial form), is of central importance in the fission of domestic groups (Fortes 1949; Goody 1973a) and in the establishment of new productive units, as well as in the more subtle solidarities of human life; and it also forms the focus for the distribution of male property under what Gluckman has called the 'house-property complex'.[12] In many cases the same group serves as the focus for the allocation of bridewealth between males and females. That is to say, the sister's bridewealth is used for the brother's wife. But even outside the group of uterine siblings, the mutual dependence on bridewealth may lead to the institution of 'cattle-linked siblings', as practised by the Lobedu, where the continuing debt of the brother to the sister allows her to claim his daughter as a bride for her son (MBD marriage). In this case prescriptive matrilateral cross-cousin marriage is to be seen as a continuation of the relationship between siblings at the succeeding generation rather than as an aspect of the affinal relationship between lineages.[13] Here it is clearly associated with the type of bridewealth payment and the cattle-linked sibling. The ideal is for every man to marry a daughter of the actual woman with whose cattle his father obtained a wife. The sister in question has the right to demand a son of her brother to be her daughter's husband; each is said to be 'born for' the other.

If bridewealth is both high and held within a small domestic unit, how are the inequalities of childbirth evened out? For in the family lottery a balanced combination of males and females will appear in much less than 50% of the families that have children (and there are often very high proportions that do not).

It is clear that in no case is a family with an odd number of children going to be in balance. Of those families with children, over 50% will fall in this category. With regard to families that are balanced in terms of numbers, one half of all two child families will be in sexual balance and 6/16 of the four child ones. In other words, not a large proportion of families are going to display the balance desiderated by many town-dwellers in western Europe and equally by those requiring a balance for the purpose of bridewealth or sister-exchange.[14] What strategy does one adopt when one has daughters but no sons? One answer is that in polygynous societies, a man continues to hope. And in extremity a man may sometimes use the daughter's bridewealth to marry a wife in order to bear a son.[15]

The influence of marriage payments on family composition is made quite explicit in Elechi Amadi's novel, *The Concubine*. 'Wolu, Madume's only wife, bore him four daughters – a most annoying thing, despite the dowries (i.e. bridewealth) he knew he would collect when they got married. But who would bear his name when he died? The thought of his elder brother's sons inheriting his houses and lands filled him with dismay. But there was enough time to marry another wife and the problem did not bother him unduly. Moreover, his daughters' marriages would provide him with the money for another wife'. Here we have illustrated an inheritance system that excludes close women in favour of distant males, which as we shall see, is connected with the bridewealth system. On the other hand, the position of women under such a system is in some ways better than under one of dowry; for the disabilities of daughters in terms of the patrilineal transmission of property and office are mitigated by what they bring to the family at their marriage. Their bridewealth can be used to obtain a wife for a brother, and in some societies even their father can employ that property to marry himself another wife, as in Madume's case. Such a strategy is based upon polygyny, and the example illustrates clearly the situation in which a man may seek another wife in order to supplement his holding of children. As a result of polygyny, the problem of imbalance is always a temporary one for any male. Nevertheless the present composition of the family (the existential family) must bear upon people's decisions about marriage. The second of two brothers may have to delay his marriage while waiting for bridewealth cattle. This delay may make him more likely to enter into a 'consensual' or 'alternative' union, where these exist; or in more recent times, it may make him more likely to leave as a migrant labourer. In other words the lack of a bridewealth payment could lead to similar kinds of action to those found under Eurasian conditions and dictated by the shortage of land, that is, the second son entering into a filiacentric union or leaving the countryside to swell the growing population of the towns.[16] Equally the father of several daughters, while traditionally he would have found difficulty in Africa in utilizing his assets to hire labour, could use them to help pay for farming parties; alternatively he can afford to be generous towards a kinsman who wished to marry his daughter, e.g. in a mother's brother's daughter marriage, and who might possibly come to live with him. The surplus of wealth is not difficult to deal with; it helps compensate a couple for the deficit in males who would have provided some insurance in old age. The surplus of sons is less easy. Here, a man may have to borrow bridewealth from near agnates more fortunately placed. He may secure such a loan by mortgaging the bridewealth of his future daughters, as when a Lobedu who had no sister would go to a maternal or affinal relative, or to a friend or even a stranger who had cattle, saying *'Ge no khuru* – I have a knee', in reference to his procreative powers, thus pledging himself to send an as yet unborn daughter in marriage (Krige 1964: 162). Or he may have to save out of current earnings, which means increasing production or lowering consumption. There is rarely any difficulty in Africa, even today in many places, in finding extra land to bring under cultivation. With a stable population the surplus of sons may itself lead to a distribution of existing land within the lineage, the additional sons in one family being balanced by a deficit in others. But one could also proceed by cutting down expenditure, especially on sacrifices. An alternative at the present day is for a man to engage in wage labour in order to acquire the necessary capital; just as women in an urban situation may acquire capital through selling sex in order to free herself from the marriage bond.[17]

But the relationship between high bridewealth and labour migration goes beyond the problem of the disadvantaged son. In Northern Ghana it is peoples with a high bridewealth payment that have the highest rates of labour migration (Table 1).[18] Among the Konkomba, wealth gained in wage labour is used for marriage payments (Tait 1961: 31). But the Konkomba are a particular case, having mortgaged their own women by a tight system of infant betrothal for girls; if they want to marry young, they have to import wives from outside.

This propensity of bridewealth systems to lead to male migration into the towns has an interesting corollary in dowry systems. Where considerations of status and honour dictate that a woman has to acquire a certain measure of property before she can get married, the opposite kind of migration may result. In many parts of Europe, young women moved into the households of other people in order to become domestic servants until the time for their marriage came along. Once

Table 1. Marriage transactions and migration in Northern Ghana (from 1960 census)

People	Total pop. in Ghana	Enumerated in non-natal regions	% Migrants	Marriage payments
A. Acephalous				
Konkomba	110,150	13,860	13	High(7)
Frafra(1)	242,880	26,580	11	High
Kusasi	121,610	13,870	11	High
Builsa	62,620	7,260	12	High
Kasena(2)	78,210	16,860	21	High
LoDagaa(3)	239,230	30,460	13	High
B. Centralized				
Gonja	62,700	4,880	8.0	Low
Dagomba	217,640	23,960	11.0(5)	Low
Mamprusi	58,710	3,300	6.0	Low
Wala	47,200	5,850	12.0(6)	Low
Vagala(4)	2,230	20	0.9	Low
Degha(4)	8,830	390	4.5	Low

(1) Includes Tallensi, Nankanse, Namnam.
(2) Includes Isala, Awuna.
(3) Includes LoWiili, LoBirifor, LoDagaba, Dagaba.
(4) Commoner groups within centralized states.
(5) Of the 'Dagomba' population, nearly half live in the towns of Yendi and Tamale (including Tamale rural).
(6) The bulk from Wa town.
(7) Marriage was sometimes by exchange, though more usually by child betrothal.

again girls from households with surplus females were likely to move into households with a corresponding deficit; servants, Berkner has argued, were to some extent children substitutes (1972). But women also moved into towns, in order to accumulate property for their dowry. In this connection, the intriguing suggestion has been made that the late marriage age of European women, combined with the necessity of accumulating property for their marriage, may have been a significant factor in both the supply and the demand for goods in the early stages of industrialization in western Europe (Hajnal 1965).[19]

The balancing out has an interesting link with the age of marriage. It has been argued that dowry delays marriage. When the daughter takes her portion, the familial enterprise has to be partly dismembered, whereas the marriage of men affects the fund in a similar way only if the property has to be handed on to the next generation at the time of the marriage.[20] Friedl describes one situation of the 'delayed daughter' in rural Greece in the following terms: 'Besides the property costs of the dowry, a farmer loses the labour of his daughter both on the farm and in the household. If he has no farming son who can bring in a wife, or has only a young son who will not be ready to marry for several years, and a single daughter, this cost may be considered great enough to delay the marriage of the girl. If a man has one daughter left at home and a wife who is ill, this may again delay the girl's marriage, for the cost of losing her services is too great. Finally there is a psychic cost to the parents, particularly to a mother, at the marriage of a daughter. She loses the companionship of a friend, confidante, and working partner. Since, among the more prosperous farmers, girls marry increasingly late i.e. between twenty-five and thirty, mothers have many years of continuing co-operation in the house and fields with grown daughters, and the wrench of of parting is seriously felt. They commonly speak longingly of how much they miss their absent daughters' (1963: 122).

Where substantial bridewealth changes hands, the opposite effect occurs. As Mair points out, 'When cattle payments are made, the marriage of girls tends to be early for the same reason that that of men is late − that a girl's marriage increases her father's herd while that of a young man diminishes it' (1963: 56). Among the Chagga and Luhya, men chafe at the delay, girls at the speed.

Just as with dowry, there are other factors affecting age at marriage that operate in a contrary direction. In dowry systems, a man may want to confirm an advantageous match as soon as possible, and hence a girl, and possibly the boy, may be betrothed while they are still children. The Brahman rule of pre-puberty marriage has been attributed to the concern to fix the partners of the woman permanently in a hierarchy of castes (Yalman 1963); the same argument would apply to other considerations of status. In bridewealth systems, a man may be in a hurry to see his sons beget descendants, while a girl's marriage may be delayed if the mother is still bearing children. Nevertheless, there is an interesting link between economic calculation and the prevalence of plural marriage. Polygyny, which is so widespread a feature of African marriage, is made possible largely by the differential marriage age, early for girls, later for men.[21] Bridewealth and polygyny play into each other's hands. Though there are high rates of polygyny in Africa even where marriage payments are low, the two institutions appear to reinforce one another. It should also be noted that in Burundi, where marriage payments are low and the age of marriage roughly equal for both sexes, polygyny is rare (van de Walle 1968: 206).

I have examined certain variables involved in marriage payments made by the groom and his kin to the kin of the bride, especially the relative size of the payments, the personnel involved and the use to which the goods are put. There are three other outstanding factors to consider, namely content, returnability and variability.

Content

One main division here is between perishable and non-perishable goods. Clearly the former are less likely to form the basis for the on-going series of transactions we regard as intrinsic to 'bridewealth proper'; they are more likely to be found as contributions to wedding expenses, to be consumed in the course of the ceremony itself (e.g. Forde 1951). They may of course be stored in the form of debts, but it is a debt specific to the bride's kin and therefore implies the particularized kind of exchange of spouses found in those forms of marriage that prescribe continuing transactions between a pair of 'groups'. If we set aside the exchange systems of certain acephalous societies in West Africa, it seems doubtful if these types of marriage, which include prescriptive bilateral cross-cousin marriage, as well as the probably non-existent patrilateral form, are ever found in Africa, at least as 'elementary' structures.

Non-perishable goods that occur widely in African marriage payments are livestock, shells (cowries) and metal objects (especially hoes). All these are objects of fairly generalized exchange, though large livestock has certain inherent limitations, especially when it comes to 'exchanging down' (Steiner 1954). But bridewealth transactions are above all typified by the very substantial cattle payments made by the patrilineal peoples of the savannah country in Eastern and Southern Africa, as well as in the sub-Saharan region of West Africa. Here the transfer of cattle in marriage is linked to the acquisition of a wife but above all to the production of children; hence the strength of those commonly quoted sayings, 'bridewealth is childwealth', or 'the cattle are where the children are not'.

In this area, cattle are not only a store of value; among pastoral peoples they constitute the basic means of production. As a result, cattle in bridewealth play a similar role to land in dowry (e.g. in Ceylon) except that being mobile and more easily divisible, the possession of livestock does not lead to quite the same pressure for status preservation and endogamy as occurs in systems of intensive farming. 'Fields on the hoof' are also a less steady source of livelihood than the soil. Moreover, the dependence on others for defence against raiders, for the protection of pastures and for the replenishment of herds struck by disease, tends to lead to a greater reliance on the insurance offered by kinship ties and hence a greater 'corporateness'. 'A spring blizzard', writes Ekvall of Tibet, 'can leave the pastoralist with no herds at all — making him a virtual pauper without "fields"' (1968: 31). His survival depends upon his ties with others.

Returnability

The returnability of payments in the event of the dissolution of the marriage is clearly linked to their use (and hence their size and content). Payments involving the transfer of rights in the fertility of the woman (rights *in genetricem*) are likely to be spread over a period of years and to be completed only after the birth of children. Similarly, the premature dissolution of the marriage means that payments usually have to be repaid; since repayment would disrupt the economy of the woman's natal household, she will be persuaded to rejoin her husband or enter into a new marriage. High returnable payments of this kind lead to a pressure on a woman to remain a wife rather than return to live as a sister. Consequently they tend to be associated with the situation whereby a widow remains 'married' to her husband's kin, either as a leviratic spouse or as an inherited widow.[22] Whereas the kind of 'terminal separation' described for the Gonja (E.N. Goody 1962; 1973) is to be associated with the low, non-returnable payments, where the residence of a wife is of no 'material' concern to her kin.[23]

Variability

Bridewealth payments are often fixed amounts; this is so for the Kipsigis and Gusii of East Africa, and it is the case for many West African peoples. On the other hand the Luo vary the standard rate and the Nuer permit haggling in the byre. But in both cases there is a close connection between the marriages of men and women. For standard payments seem to fluctuate in relation to the cattle population, so that an increase in the herds does not lead to cheap marriages. While the bargaining process usually works out in such a way that only one marriage can be made from one herd at one time (Mair 1953: 6).[24]

Standard bridewealth has an effect quite opposite to dowry, which is intrinsically variable. For it means that, other things being equal, a cat or a commoner may look at a king. In terms of property, one man or woman is as good as another. Hence the system permits heterogamy (for which out-marriage is a prerequisite), while the dowry on the other hand inhibits such dispersion of marriage partners, even though property may be used to compensate for the absence of other attributes.

But bridewealth is not always fixed; there are some variations that depend on status. LoDagaa chiefs who emerged as the result of the white man's government, built up large holdings of wives, though they certainly did not send

12

to their in-laws the full amount of the bridewealth; they delayed payments after the first, and their in-laws were afraid or unable to press them for the remainder (Goody 1969a). As far as the daughter's of high-status men are concerned, they tend to get marked up rather than down, as was the case with the daughters of Ashanti royals (Rattray 1927). In both ways the upper status groups gained (on the swings as well as on the roundabouts, as givers as well as receivers). Such tendencies are no doubt universal concomitants of status differentiation, but they played relatively little part in traditional Africa. In acephalous societies like the LoDagaa, such differentiation as existed arose with the advent of chiefs; among the Ashanti, the mark-up was small and the royal daughters even took slaves as husbands. On the other hand selection is certainly playing an increasing part under modern conditions, especially as traditional payments and services (where such things persist) tend to get transmuted into cash which is usually derived directly from the groom's earnings. In this process of computation, there is plenty of room for bargaining, and hence for the introduction of inequalities. In present-day Africa, the fact that like does tend to marry like (and to demand that like be reproduced in their offspring) tends to reinforce a new type of stratification, a system that one may be tempted to designate as class. But this is undoubtedly a new development.[25] And whereas bridewealth transactions seem formerly to have varied (if at all) with the status of the girl, nowadays it is the status of both partners (a 'match') that is involved.

Finally, in view of the later argument, it is essential to stress that in economic terms bridewealth has a levelling function. An extreme case is that of the Lobedu, of whom Krige writes, 'The society is remarkably egalitarian and there is no concentration of wealth in the hands of the ruling group. Nor would this be easy in a tribe in which the limited resources in property (in cattle) are used primarily for, and are constantly being converted into, marriage alliances' (1964: 157).

By entering into marriage alliances, bridewealth achieves a double dispersal of property. Not only do cattle pass in the opposite direction to brides, they also bring in additional children who will divide whatever remains. Even where differentiation occurs, polygyny dissipates. It is 'an extraordinary fact', writes Polly Hill of a Hausa economy already differentiated by plough farming, 'that the average acreage of manured farmland per working-son actually shows little variation as between Groups 1, 2 and 3. . . It is certainly clear from these figures that many sons of rich farmers are bound to inherit relatively small acreages' (1972: 181). Thus, despite the existence of 'a fair degree of economic inequality', there is no 'peasant aristocracy', no differentiation one can call 'class'. While the poor, on the other hand, are 'not institutionally trapped by their poverty' (1972: 188).

We are reminded here that one important aspect of bridewealth is its relationship with plural marriage. It has been argued that polygyny is found where women make a substantial contribution to productive activity, especially to cultivation. And that a measure of their contribution is the bridewealth that is paid for them at marriage. The argument is oversimple. Women's domestic roles are more complex than the theory allows and in any case polygyny occurs throughout Africa, even where marriage transactions are 'token' in quantity. However, diverging devolution, especially when it involves dowry, is strongly linked with monogamous (and polyandrous) marriage, which leads to the formation of a kind of conjugal estate (by limiting the number of marriages) and militates against its dissolution (by limiting the number of heirs). Such funds have an individualizing character. It is difficult to make more than one match of this kind, though subsidiary non-property unions are always feasible, with hand-maidens, concubines and the like.

The absence of bridewealth

I have mainly discussed bridewealth in the African context. But there are a number of societies in that continent where bridewealth is absent, or anyhow low. Large bridewealth is primarily significant in cattle-keeping societies of the savannahs. It is of less importance (or absent) in matrilineal societies (which tend not to be cattle-keeping, see Aberle 1961), in Muslim areas (where more is invested in wedding expenses and in dowry) and in some state systems such as the Barotse kingdom of Zambia, the Hausa of Northern Nigeria, and the Gonja and Mossi states of the Voltaic region.

Moreover, in some societies which have bridewealth payments, provision is also made for marriages without bridewealth. So before we examine bridewealth as a variable between societies, let us look at the effects of variation within one social system. And before we discuss these institutionalized alternatives, let us look at the problem in a wider context.

While I was working among the LoWiili in 1950, a near-neighbour of mine was the headman of Nayiili. His daughter was a good-looking girl who had reached the age at which girls usually get married. One day I asked a distant agnate why she had not yet done so. I was told that the headman wanted her to bear a child before she got married so that it belonged to him. If an unmarried girl (that is, a girl for whom the critical bridewealth payment has not been made) bears a child, that child 'belongs' to the mother's father and is a member of the latter's patrilineal lineage. Such a child is known as a 'housechild' (*yirbie*) and is not, I think, looked down upon. Indeed, I knew 'housechildren' who had achieved very important positions in their lineages. In due course (as I have illustrated elsewhere), the sister's son, or rather his children, would be completely assimilated since he would call his mother's father 'father' and his children would therefore call him 'grandfather'. I do not know if this difference in manner of recruitment continued to be recognized after the first generation for any social purpose, but I believe not; the recollection disappeared. The unmarried sister's son, recruited by the maternal tie, became part of the agnatic structure of her patrilineal descent group. In these cases no bridewealth was paid and the daughter's child was affiliated to her father and incorporated in his patrilineage. Pre-marital illegitimacy' therefore presented no great problem for the LoWiili. There was no illegitimacy in the strict sense, since the offspring became members of their mother's patrilineage. Indeed, a few heavily incapacitated women might stay all their lives in their natal compound, never having been sought as marriage partners, and they would breed children which would be attached to their natal lineage.

Not all societies are so accommodating. Among the patrilineal Sumburu and matrilineal Ashanti, a girl could not bear acceptable children before marriage (or before the puberty rite). In earlier times, such children are said to have been destroyed, irrespective of sex. But given the early age in marriage, pre-marital illegitimacy could not have presented much of a problem. Most girls married around the age of puberty. In both these cases it seems to have been the premature opening of fertility rather than the absence of a father that constituted the offence.

In other cases, a man could legitimize such offspring (as with mantle-children in medieval England) by subsequent marriage to the mother. The children would then be legitimate offspring and members of the paternally recruited kin group to which the father belonged. In few, if any, cases in Africa was there any major problem of illegitimacy and even in the contemporary situation in towns, we do not find the great mass of unwanted children that filled the foundling hospitals of Western Europe in the seventeenth and eighteenth centuries.

Finally, in this continuum of affiliation, are the offspring of women who have been married in the fully acceptable manner. In patrilineal societies, they belong by definition to the unilineal descent group of their fathers. Nevertheless, they have some rights in the mother's patriclan which in certain instances, could lead to residence with maternal kin. If this shift became permanent, it could lead to the formation of an 'attached' lineage (as among the Tallensi), or to the gradual incorporation of the kind we have earlier described for the children of unmarried mothers, or (at the other end of the spectrum), to residence, without attachment or incorporation, as we find among the LoDagaa. The obvious result of this last alternative, with its determined attachment to clanship, is multi-clan communities rather than the mono-clan settlements of the Konkomba or the Tallensi. Among the LoDagaa, such continued attachment to one's clan is seen as directly related to bridewealth payments.

In matrilineal and bilateral societies, where payments are generally lower, affiliation does not present the same problem. In the first case, and often in the second, marriage transactions have less effect upon the affiliation of the children, or at least upon their membership of the major descent groups. In bilateral societies paternal affiliation is often determined by genealogical paternity (the assumed genitor is the legal father) and the children are linked to paternal and maternal sets of kin, though the ways in which they are linked may vary widely. In matrilineal societies, the conjugal relationship is irrelevant for matrilineal purposes, though the husband/father is often important from the personal and even the interlineage standpoint.

Let us now try and gain some insight into the function of bridewealth generally by looking at those societies which have legitimate forms of marriage with and without bridewealth, namely, the Nyamwezi of Tanzania and the Ijaw of Nigeria. Abrahams has recently summarized information on the Nyamwezi in his volume in the *Ethnographic Survey of Africa* (1967). To marry with bridewealth is known as *kukwa*, and this form of union involves the allocation of both uxorial and genetricial rights to the husband. He is entitled to compensation in the case of adultery and he both receives and pays the bridewealth for his sons and daughters. To marry without bridewealth is described by various terms (e.g. *kubola*), and such marriages were traditionally initiated by elopement. In such instances, the husband has no genetricial rights and only limited uxorial ones. The children may be taken by right to live with their mother's people at about eight years of age, and it is the maternal kin who have the rights and obligations regarding their bridewealth. A husband may bring a case against an adulterer, but he is not himself entitled to compensation. Note that the children of such a marriage have a somewhat inferior status to those born of bridewealth unions; they have no right to inherit from their father and only take a major share of their mother's brother's property if he has no 'bridewealth' children of his own (1967: 44-5). However, it is possible to convert the inferior marriage into a superior one by a subsequent payment, which includes a sum for 'rearing'. In both types of marriage it was formerly common for the groom to spend the first part of his married life at the home of the bride's father.

A similar situation is reported for the Ijaw, but bridewealth marriage appears to be less common and more equal in status. Writing of the Okrika section, which includes Bonny and the Kalabari, Williamson writes of the two important types of marriage, 'yà, which is usually translated as "big dowry", though of course if refers not to a dowry but to bride-price and *igwà*, "small dowry",' (1962: 55). The essential difference associated with these payments is that in the first case the children belong to the husband, i.e. are counted as members of his family and his 'house', and inherit from him, whereas in 'small marriage', the children belong to the mother's house and inherit within it. The wife may also continue to live with her natal family even after the marriage, which is considered to be much less stable than the rather rare 'big' variety. A third form of marriage is to an Ibo woman, for whom a smaller payment will bring full genetricial and uxorial rights.

What light does this throw on the role of bridewealth? Clearly in these societies bridewealth has the function, firstly, of securing the affiliation of a child to its father's kin group. This kin group need not necessarily be a unilineal descent group such as a clan or lineage. The Kalabari House recruits mainly through women and does not attempt to change this link into an agnatic one (as we found among the LoWiili). Alternative forms of recruitment do indeed imply a modification of the unilineal structure, though such deviations may be regularized by the system of classification, that is, by the kinship terminology.

Secondly, the question of affiliation is tied in with that of inheritance and responsibility for bridewealth payments.

Thirdly, non-bridewealth marriage means less conjugal, more consanguineal control over the bride, and is hence associated with less enduring marriage (higher divorce rates) and with less compensation in the case of adultery.

Given these differences within societies, it is to be expected that matrilineal and bilateral (or alineal) societies will tend to have lower (even token) payments as compared with those where patrilineal descent groups play an important role. Among the 'bilateral' societies with token payments are those centralized states that have been influenced by Islam, and others that have included a number of disparate groups within a single polity. In these polyethnic states, marriage trans-actions (which occur between all elements in the population where marriage is heterogamous) tend to be reduced to the lowest level of any of the groups participating in the regular exchange.

DOWRY

Having considered bridewealth and the variables involved in such transactions, we now return to examine the contrast with dowry. We have seen that bridewealth passes from the kin of the groom to those of the bride; it forms a societal fund, a circulating pool of resources, the movement of which correspond to the move-ment of rights over spouses, usually women. But dowry is part of a familial or conjugal fund, which passes down from holder to heir, and usually from the parents to the daughter. It is thus part and parcel of the transfer of familial property, but a process of transfer that includes women as well as men; that is, male property is transmitted to women as full heirs, semi-heirs or residual heirs. Consequently dowry belongs to a type of transmission I have called 'diverging devolution' (or 'the woman's property complex').

While recognizing that 'female inheritance' and dowry 'sometimes shade into each other', Yalman tends to stress the 'extremely important' differences between the two. For example, he writes: 'These differences arise because female inheritance and dowry have two different purposes. The former is *merely* a reflection of the general *descent ideology* of the Kandyans that sons and daughters both inherit in the same fashion. Dowry, on the other hand, is the result of a bargain and has a specific intention: that of linking the daughter – hence her family – with a particularly desirable son-in-law' (1967: 175, my italics). The difference exists, but it is one of timing and flexibility. Yalman's interpretation of diverging devolution shifts the frame of reference from ideology to manipulation, the former being applicable to inheritance, the latter to marriage. My own interpretation involves both levels; female inheritance is clearly associated with a 'bilateral ideology', but I would argue that it also reflects a general interest in preserving the status of offspring of both sexes; dowry too carries both these implications.

We have seen that bridewealth is not simply an item in an exchange system (everything is this); it entails the dispersal of wealth in exchange for conjugal

17

rights and duties, at least where polygyny is allowed. The more women you receive, the more wealth you give. Nor is this loss made up in the receipts from marriage transactions in the next generation, since the offspring will tend to be equally divided between males and females, which will lead to a balanced series of trans-actions within the generation. If the wealth employed consists in a distinct set of objects which circulate in their own cycle, the distribution of wives will be very closely related to the distribution of 'sisters' (or daughters, if generational transfer is allowed); in this case, and especially when generational transfer is forbidden, bridewealth acts in favour of the equal distribution of women; it is a substitute for sister exchange, a form of sexual rationing.

If, on the other hand, the objects involved in bridewealth can be acquired by other means (e.g. by productive as well as reproductive activity), then the system will not be entirely closed. Nevertheless, the higher the bridewealth the more closed it will be, and in any case a premium will be placed on non-variability in payments (see Ardener 1962).

Dowry does not involve any similar kind of rationing of women; indeed from the standpoint of our initial diagram, women and property appear to be transferred in the same direction, so that the more, the wealthier. The reason why the system does not in fact work like this is revealing. Dowry transactions place a premium on the matching contributions of the spouses. What women and men bring, either in concrete dowry or in inheritance chances, vary, although among conjugal pairs these tend to match.

The actual working of the type of marriage depends upon the social strata of the bride and groom; the higher the strata, the more elaborate the match. There are many accounts of this process, but to bring out the features of such an arrangement among the nobility, I refer to the great Irish epic of *The Tain* and to the way in which the legendary wars began with the pillow-talk of King Ailill and Queen Medb, comparing their respective endowments. The matching of Ailill and Medb, object by object, beast by beast, quality by quality, is simply an exaggeration of a general characteristic of dowry, its tendency to vary with the status of the bride and groom.[26] As we have seen, in bridewealth systems, standard payments are more common; their role in a societal exchange puts pressure towards similarity.

The role of the dowry in European society in more recent times is delicately portrayed in Giuseppe di Lampadusa's great novel, *The Leopard*. The future of an impoverished aristocratic family is assured by the engagement of the Sicilian Prince of Falconeri with the daughter of Don Calogero, a representative of the rising bourgeoisie, to whom the Prince became attracted both by 'the physical stimulus of a beautiful woman. . . and also by the (as-it-were) numerical excitement aroused by a rich girl in the mind of a man ambitious and poor'. By this match the Houses of the Saline and Falconeri were saved and yet changed, as on a political level they had been by the success of Garibaldi and his militants: 'The major interests of the Kingdom [of the Two Sicilies] and of his own class, his personal priveleges had come through all these events battered but still lively'. Parallel to the main theme there runs the story of a peasant wedding, where a dispute over an almond orchard is settled by the enforced marriage between the grandchildren of the siblings who had quarrelled. In the latter case the marriage (FZD) involved the retention rather than the acquisition of property, in other words, a close rather than a distant union. As such, it contravened the prohibited degrees of the Catholic Church, and special dispensation had to be sought, a not uncommon event for we are told of 'the frequent marriages between cousins in recent years due to sexual lethargy and territorial calculations'. In both cases property was the key to the affinal transactions, though other factors such as the bride's beauty and the bridegroom's grace 'managed to veil in poetry the crudeness of the contract'.

One point we need to recognize, at least for stratified systems, lies in the differences that may occur between the marriage transactions of rich and poor. This is especially clear in India, where dowry is often associated with high status. It is this that Yalman means when he associates different patterns of 'descent' (filiation) and inheritance with differences in 'concepts regarding the position of women' (1967: 130). For the rich 'actively controlled the property rights of the daughters', while the labourers did not. The daughters of the rich take their 'portions' of the estate at marriage (and therefore do not 'inherit', leaving the remainder to the sons), while the poor have 'too little to make dowry settlements possible' (p. 136) but let daughters take their share when the property is redistributed at the parents' death. It is this difference that gives rise to what Yalman sees as a leaning towards patrilineal 'descent' in the former case and bilateral 'descent' in the latter. Hence also the equation rich = dowry = arranged marriage.

The relationship between diverging devolution and stratification is not confined to rural societies. In discussing the accumulation of wealth by English merchants in the late seventeenth century, Grassby notes that while trade and thrift were important, many business fortunes were made through marriage. Between 1600 and 1624, 8 per cent of London Aldermen rose through marrying their masters' widows or daughters and there are no signs that this practice declined after the Restoration (1970: 102). 'Merchants, like landowners, sought profitable marriages for themselves and for their sons; birth and death rates played a major part in extending or dissolving family estates. Frequent remarriage and premature deaths benefitted some families and left considerable sums in the hands of widows and daughters' (pp. 102-3). Defoe defended commercial marriages, attacked by some as a form of prostitution, because a dowry could be used as a means of raising credit. However, 'most marriages took place between families of corresponding status and wealth, and therefore tended to widen the gap between rich and poor'.

In countries around the Mediterranean, wealth was even more closely retained within the existing status groups. In Spain men and women found it less easy to raise their socio-economic status by marriage, since legal rules existed preventing marriage outside the status group; until 1783 legislation also existed regulating the offices and trades deemed to be fit for the different estates (Martinez-Alier 1972: 100). This division was embodied in marriage because like married like; class endogamy was 'the manifestation of a hierarchical view of society' (p. 117). Lineage, legitimacy, honour, were all involved, but property remained central to the marriage system, which depended upon parental control and the emphasis on the pre-marital virginity of girls; the only escape was by institutionalized elopement.

While property is the major factor in the affinal situation, it is clearly not the only consideration, since pedigree, beauty and circumstance also enter into the calculation. For example, in the quarter of San Carlo in Bologna, Tentori reports how a rich girl who had an illegitimate child might get married, despite the emphasis given to pre-marital virginity: 'la cosa si accomodava con la dote'. If she were poor, the problem was more difficult.[27]

As in the case of bridewealth, there are a number of important variables to be taken into account when discussing dowry. In the first place, there is the origin of the dowry i.e. whether it comes from a girl's parents (or her siblings if the parents are dead), or from her husband and his kin. The second alternative I have spoken of is 'indirect dowry'. An example of what I mean by indirect dowry is given in Lewis' account of marriage in the North Indian village of Rampur. He notes that it is customary to spend large sums of money on weddings; even at the risk of going deeply into debt. The main outlay of the groom's father however is not for the expenses of the actual festivities but for 'ornaments for his daughter-in-law'; one individual had bought three pounds of silver and eleven ornaments for her. In addition to this, 'the father of the bride spends more money than does the groom's father' (1958: 162); he too provides money for the dowry, the main recipient at marriage being the bride, who also receives dresses from her father's sisters and her father's brother's wives, as well as gifts from her mother's brother.

What I have called indirect dowry is more common in North India than in South, where dowry proper, in some parts a landed dowry, prevails. This system of marriage transaction carried certain different implications for social organisation. Just as inheritance, as distinct from dowry, delays the break up of the estate of the bride's natal family, so indirect dowry leaves that estate intact (though it doesn't prevent a dowry transaction) while requiring a major contribution from the family of the groom, a contribution which again represents an early call on inheritance prospects.

Secondly, there is the question of the control of the dowry, whether it remains entirely under the control of the woman, under the jurisdiction of the husband or forms part of a community of property on which both partners can draw. Clearly it is likely to be returnable in the case of divorce, since it is an endowment upon the woman; whatever managerial functions the husband may carry out, the destination of the dowry is the bride herself. For example, among the Tibetan

Indeed the contrast becomes even stronger when we separate off the major Eurasian societies.

In other words these major Eurasian states are characterized by dowry, or by diverging inheritance, while Africa is characterized by bridewealth, or rather by the absence of dowry; though some state systems there have token transactions, none have dowry, except where Islamic law prevails.

In trying to explain this situation, I would start with a comment of E.J. Krige upon Leach's analysis of her material on matrilateral cross-cousin marriage among the Lobedu of South Africa. There is no evidence, she suggests, for his suggestion that the Lobedu have a 'kind of Kachin structure in reverse', with a 'strong tendency for the wife-receiving group to rank the higher'. For, she explains, 'In endogamous unions in one Lobedu royal group both husband and wife may be members of the same lineage. Lobedu society is, moreover, not a stratified society though the royal lineage enjoys great prestige' (1964: 164). While I would want to dissent from the denial of stratification, certainly the hierarchies of African states have a different base, and hence a different character, from most Eurasian ones.

The different base I refer to is an economic one, though it has political and social implications. If we limit the discussion to the states of Africa and Eurasia, we find major differences in the systems of agricultural production. In pre-colonial Africa, and indeed in much of Africa today, agriculture is carried on by means of the hoe, the axe/adze and even the digging stick. Until recently, nowhere did we find farming carried out by means of the plough, nor yet with the aid of the techniques of large-scale irrigation which played such an important part in the early empires of the Asian continent, and whose 'hydraulic civilizations' have been seen by some writers as the basis of a particular type of political system, Oriental despotism (Wittfogel 1957).

The kind of differentiation that advanced agriculture allowed was clearly much greater than that permitted by the hoe, even when farming was supplemented by income from trade and the control of trade, and by the kind of booty production that marked the internal and external slave trade in many parts of Africa. Since population densities were low and since the acreage any individual could cultivate by hand was strictly limited, land was not usually in short supply. Men were not differentiated to any great extent in terms of their holdings of land, that is of the basic means of production in an agricultural society. The situation is now beginning to change with the expansion of crops for sale and the introduction of the plough. In a Hausa village, Polly Hill recently recorded variations of an average of 19.5 acres for 17 better-off farming units (Group 1), 8.4 acres for 45 units of Group 2, 4.2 acres for 68 units of Group 3 and 2.8 for 41 units of Group 4, though the average acreage per working-man was more nearly comparable, ranging from 5.3 acres (Group 1) to 1.5 acres in Group 4 (1972: 62). The traditional picture is one of relatively equal holdings, at least in acephalous ('tribal') societies. Among the LoDagaba of Northern Ghana, the average size of a farm was 9.82 acres (Goody 1956: 30), and the variance was small, if one took into account the size of the farming group. But farm size depended not so much on the size of one's holding (a concept which makes only limited sense under shifting cultivation), but upon the size of one's household.[31] A large household means larger claims. Consequently elders had somewhat larger farms than younger married men and in centralized societies control over labour enabled chiefs to have larger farms. For example, among the Bemba, land was plentiful and the average farm size was 3-4 acres. On the other hand the Paramount's farm amounted in 1933 to a total of 18 acres (Richards 1939: 289, 387). Even in a centralized society in Africa, the variance is not great; and perhaps of greatest significance is the fact that there were no 'landless labourers', no 'rural proletariat'.

Contrast with traditional Africa the kind of differentiation found in a village in medieval England or in present-day Asia. In discussing the former, Postan divides the inhabitants of a village into three groups, which depend essentially on their holding of land. 'The difference between land titles, like the differences in personal status, though important, did not greatly influence the economic evolution of the village or create enduring distinctions of economic or social status in village society. These distinctions depended much more on the actual sizes of holdings and on the quality of the land and the use to which it could be put' (1966: 616). The division he makes is a tripartite one, between top-rank tenants, middle rank tenants and smallholders; the first held a virgate or more, the second between a quarter and a virgate (i.e. 12-15 acres of arable land), and the third group under a quarter virgate; the average for eight estates in the thirteenth century gives the proportional distributions of these groups as follows: 1, 22%; 2, 33%; 3, 45%. Only a smaller proportion of the top rank could be described as rich peasants. 'There were always a large number of smallholders, a small group of village *kulaks* and an intermediate mass of middling peasants' (p. 628). The same differentiation existed in the English village of the Middle Ages as in the Russian village of the late nineteenth century (Dunn 1967: 15) and as exists in contemporary India.

In India today, land-holding is only one of a number of aspects of social differentiation, but it is of critical importance in social life, giving rise to parallel kinds of landlord–tenant relationships. In Lewis' study of the north Indian village of Rampur, he found that twenty-five of the families owned less than 4 acres, while twenty-nine possessed between 4 and 10 acres. That is, 69% held less than 10 acres, 21.6% between 10 and 20, and 8.8% more than 20 acres (1958: 100). In rural Ceylon, rice lands are the chief index of wealth in the community; 'the social hierarchy is related to the limited supply of rice lands' Yalman (1967: 56). There is a large body of men who own none but who have to go in for shifting cultivation, a form of production which has totally different consequences for social organization, being essentially more egalitarian (e.g. there are no permanent rights in these *chena* lands). Again, we may take Smith's general statement about landholding in Japan. 'Typically they show in each village a few large holdings, somewhat more middling holdings, and a great many small holdings, with some large holdings bulking many times the size of some small — ten or twenty times was very common and even a hundred or more not unknown' (1959: 3).

As we see, differentiation was not only national but was reflected in wide variations in landholding between members of the same village. Upon these differences status largely but not exclusively depended. Consequently it became a strategy of utmost importance to preserve those differences for one's offspring, lest the family and its fortunes decline over time. One way of maintaining one's status might be by limiting the number of heirs who would share in the heritable property.[32] However, it was a matter of preserving the status of daughters as well as sons. Sons might inherit all the productive capacity but daughters had to be assured of a marriage that would provide them with the same (or better) standard of life to which they were accustomed. They had to be endowed with property to attract a husband of the same rank, though other factors such as beauty and lineage, and even the location of the property entered into the match.

The implications of the endowment of women, of which dowry forms a part, are many. In an earlier article (1969b) I discussed some possible associations that could be tested by means of systematic comparison using the *Ethnographic Atlas*. There I suggested that when women were receivers of property from males as well as females in the form of dowry or inheritance, special attention would be given to the marriage (and other unions) into which they would enter. Particularly in the case of an heiress, her partner is likely to be prescribed or otherwise arranged for her; and in any case, a girl's marriage will tend to be made within the particular social group to which she belongs. In this way, her status, and the family investment in it, will be preserved. One index of the concern over the marriage of daughters is control over their virginity. Hence it seemed probable that the prohibition on premarital sex would be linked with diverging devolution. For the same reasons, so too would endogamy and other forms of in-marriage, such as union with the father's brother's daughter (FBD). All these three variables were tested and found to be positively associated with diverging devolution (at the $P < 0.001$ level). Monogamy was found to be correlated in a similar manner, as were types of kinship terminology which mark off full or half-siblings from other kin ('cousins') of the same generation. Both monogamous marriage and kinship terms had the effect of isolating the conjugal dyad and its offspring. The Dravidian terminologies of South India do not have this effect, since sibling terms are used to designate more inclusive categories and are associated with prescriptive cross-cousin marriage. But it is the case that in many societies in Europe and Asia, even where unilineal descent groups are present, sibling terminology is not applied to all a man's clansfolk of the same and even alternate generations, as is so often the case in Africa. As we shall see, this different usage implies a less 'corporate' kind of kin group in Eurasia, cut across as they are by the distinct conjugal funds established at each marriage.

I also tested the association of what I called 'alternative residence':— for example, the case of the Russian *primak*, a son-in-law who is taken into the house 'as an heir' when there are no sons (see Dunn 1967: 74). Finally, I examined the relationship of diverging devolution to political and economic factors, finding it strongly linked with large states, with complex forms of stratification, and with plough and intensive agriculture, all at the $P < 0.001$ level.

The contrast between dowry and bridewealth systems, if I can use these terms to point to sets of interrelated variables, now appears to expand. From the standpoint of inheritance, dowry systems are inherently bilateral, since they distribute relatively exclusive rights in a manner that does not link property or patrimony to sex; it descends in a diverging way. If property diverges between members of both of both sexes, then it can never be wholly contained within the boundaries of the unilineal descent group, or even within the group of siblings. Let me first deal with UDGs. In Africa, land is often inherited within a lineage or clan. When this happens we can specify a certain tract of land as 'belonging' to a particular group whose members have access to the uncultivated sections of that territory. The land passes by inheritance between members of the group, whether it is defined by matrilineal or by patrilineal descent. The same applies to other property, when the system of inheritance is 'harmonic' with the system of descent. Using an ambiguous term in a very restricted way, we may speak of such descent groups as 'corporate' when inheritance takes place within them, though clearly greater importance is to be attached to this designation if the property so transferred is the basic means of production, that is, land in an agricultural economy, livestock in a pastoral one.

In using the word 'corporate' to describe a group I do not even imply that its members hold equal rights in common property, though this may be the case with ritual possessions. I only mean that productive property normally devolves within the group. In other words the mode of inheritance and eligibility to group membership (e.g. 'descent') are 'harmonic', and are recognized as such by the actors. As a consequence of this recognition, members of the group will constitute a chain of potential heirs. A true corporation, the members of which hold equal rights (or contemporaneous ones rather than the sequential rights involved in an inheritance chain), seems comparatively rare, unless we are thinking of a domestic group of a strictly limited size. Maine's attempt to apply the concept of the corporation to larger groups (e.g. clans and lineages), while valuable from a moral, jural and political standpoint in understanding collective responsibility, presents some problems on the economic front, even when we are dealing with the forms of ownership found with shifting cultivation. But such groups are at least 'corporate' in the sense that reserves of land are often held jointly and the devolution of property takes place within its boundaries.

On the other hand, the transmission of property by diverging devolution means its passage outside the unilineal descent group. The group cannot be 'corporate' in respect of the property so transmitted, since it passes to children of both sexes. Or rather, the estate can remain intact only if all marriages take place within the group. In other words, the group can be corporate and closed (endogamous) or non-corporate and open. But even in the first of these cases, the sibling group is still split as far as property is concerned, since marriage within is rarely permitted and never enforced. Under diverging devolution the 'incest taboo' on brother–sister marriage effectively prohibits the continuing cohesion of the estate attached to an elementary family, the nearest alternative to dispersal being (in a patrilineal system) the attempt to bring back what has been divided by inheritance or dowry by means of marriage to the father's brother's daughter or another close cousin. I do not mean to suggest that all close marriage has an economic function; such a proposition would be quite untenable. In the case of 'institutions' as widespread as 'the marriage of cousins', no one explanation, or category of explanations, can possibly be expected to satisfy all conditions. This is especially true of cross-cousin marriage which, as has often been pointed out, may specify categories rather than genealogically related individuals. Nevertheless, actors often describe certain forms of cross-cousin marriage in terms of conserving property and status, or simply the ties between siblings. This feature is given prominence in Yalman's analysis of prescriptive cross-cousin marriage in South India. 'Brother and sister must be separated, but their offspring must be united' (1967: 374). It is also critical to our discussion of cross-cousin marriage in Northern Ghana, where 'the unification of the split siblings' may or may not be a matter of inheritance (J. and E. Goody 1966: 349).

Marriage within the sibling group does occasionally occur, and under interesting conditions. It is often assumed that such marriages take place only within certain royal families, of which the Egyptian is the best known example. But Middleton's recent summary of the evidence on close marriage in ancient Egypt shows that such unions were not in fact confined to royalty but were found in other strata within the population. Certainly during the period of Roman rule there is strong evidence that brother–sister marriages occurred with some frequency among commoners. Why? His explanation runs as follows: 'These consanguine marriages among commoners were probably used as a means of maintaining the property of the family intact and preventing the splintering of the estate through the operation of the laws of inheritance' (1962: 603). And these laws of inheritance, as in other societies of the ancient Near East, explicitly transferred to women, either in inheritance or in dowry, part of the estate of their parents.[33] In other words, in-marriage was specifically related to the existence of diverging devolution, a type of transmission which transferred property both to sons and daughters and hence diffused that property outside the 'exogamic' unit, or rather outside the range of kin with whom marriage was forbidden.

The results of this are clearly brought out in E.L. Peters' examination of the reasons for the failure of the Bedouin of Cyrenaica to apply the Islamic law of inheritance, which allocates male property to daughters though not in equal proportions to sons. In this case, the most significant property is livestock, though land plays a significant role in the economy.

'Males acquire their proprietary rights to mobile property and land by transmission through males. Women are not permitted to inherit. Bedouin are aware that in dispossessing women of inheritance they are contravening the law, but to do otherwise would result in an uncontrolled alienation of property from the corporations in which ownership is vested. Bridewealth sees the transfer of property from one corporation to another, but the transfer is controlled. Since women are free to be married by men outside their natal corporations — and nearly half their marriages are of this sort — then if they inherited as wives and daughters, an uncontrolled run on corporate resources would ensue. This would be serious enough if only mobile property were involved, but if land was threatened in this way also, the entire basis of corporate life would collapse. Therefore, the lack of legal status of women as heirs to property is, among the Bedouin, to be related not only to the status of individuals as heirs, but to the nature of the property owning group. This group is a corporation of males clustered together on the basis of what is conceived of as agnation' (forthcoming).

The difficulty the Bedouin have in applying the Islamic law of inheritance also crops up with dowry, which is part of the same process of intergenerational transmission. When land or cattle are involved, the property of the group is split at each generation. Even where the basic means of production are not transmitted, each marriage will entail some reorganization of the family estate. The raising of a dowry in money or other movables may require sacrifices on the part of the parents or the brothers; the family fund will suffer some diminution.

This feature of dowry relates to a point made by Leach, Yalman and others, especially in the context of Ceylon, that in Asia the boundaries between patrilineal, matrilineal and bilateral systems are often shaded. Of course to some extent this is true within Africa. Not only do differences exist between nearby and generally similar societies like the Tallensi and LoDagaa, as well as, more obviously, between the kind of UDG found in segmentary societies (like the Tallensi) and in many centralized societies in the same general area (e.g. in Ashanti). But in a number of centralized societies such as the Gonja and Hausa of West Africa we find groups with more limited functions, which has led us to refer to them as dynastic descent groups. While in societies like the Ijaw, which provide for alternative modes of entry to kin groups by means of a big and small marriage payment, a considerable degree of flexibility enters into the question of recruitment.[34] Nevertheless, there tends to be more flexibility (to use a value laden word) in many Eurasian systems, a flexibility which is associated with specific features of the social organization and is not random.

Unilineal descent groups in Africa are more corporate not only because inheritance takes place within them. They are also less differentiated in an absolute sense because of the system of agriculture and of land holding. We have already seen the range of holdings that may be found in a plough village as compared with the relatively homogeneous conditions under hoe cultivation. This differentiation may occur within as well as between descent groups. In

China gentry and commoners could belong to the same local lineage. According to Hu Hsien Chin, the *tsu*, or common descent group, was descended from one ancestor who settled in a certain locality (1948: 18). Since it included all the families descended from the common ancestor, 'it comprises various social strata: the wealthy and the prominent as well as the poor and the lowly, for the fortunes of individual families vary' (p. 10). This inclusiveness led to groups of enormous size which included landowners as well as gentry and officials. One writer remarks that 'The intraclan differentiation of gentry and commoners and the domination of the latter by the former are well-established facts' (Kung-Chuan Hsiao 1960: 330). He goes on to describe how those members of a certain Shantung clan who had no wealth or eminence did not attend the semi-annual rites and the ensuing feasts, nor did they have charge of the ritual land. As well as providing leadership the rich also extended charity to their fellow lineage members, so that the wealth of the group depended upon the prosperity of its most successful individuals. The solidarity that arose from these ties of clanship, cross-cutting social and economic differentiation, made them particularly useful to the imperial government as a means of rural control.

The lineages Barth describes among the Swat Pathans are differentiated in a less radical way, and the children of brothers are often held together over the generations by the marriage of their children (FBD marriage), a system which destroys the 'corporate' character of the lineage in respect to its marriage arrangements. Genealogical ties remain a focus for local groupings much larger than the stem family or local line. While the genealogies of such groups may have a formal resemblance to those that are used as reference systems by many African societies, the group of 'lineages' to which they refer differ in a major respect.[35] In most of traditional Africa, the elementary families or sibling groups that constituted the basic units of production were little differentiated in terms of the ownership for the means of production, land. For it was rarely a scarce resource (one could usually shift), rarely subject to exchange, and in any case, the holding of uncultivated land was frequently under the control of a community or kin group.

Differential land holding did not mean a great deal when there were not the techniques for an individual to exploit more than a hoe would allow. Land might be reallocated among kith or kin according to need rather than ownership. In addition the absence of the plough or irrigation meant that systems of advanced farming, providing a significant and utilizable surplus, were rarely found. As a result, differentiation within the kin group in terms of land-holding and status was relatively slight, though in centralized states political office brought its own rewards.

African lineages, then, were relatively 'homogeneous' in contrast to comparable groupings among plough or other intensive agriculturists of Asia (though intensity of production is again a relative concept). The pyramidal, ramifying model of the lineage, frequently an actor model, indicates not only span but often a broad equality of socio-economic status.

Under the extensive farming systems of Africa one found, of course, poorer and richer farmers, the gap between whom is increasing under modern conditions, as Hill has emphasized for Hausaland (1972).[36] But the difference between the two, where they were not to be attributed to exogenous factors, depended upon labour and that of one's dependents, kin or slaves. The conditions for landlordism rarely if ever existed; land did not differentiate the population, either within or between clans, into gentry, kulaks, poor peasants and serfs. Consequently the strategy of not letting one's daughter marry 'beneath her' in terms of landed property was hardly at issue. Nor was it necessary to endow a daughter with land or other major goods (though she was often given household gifts) in order to maintain her position. Bridewealth passed between males, and was sometimes differentiated by the status of a bride or bridegroom. But by and large marriage payments were part of a pool of circulating resources, enabling brothers (real or classificatory) to take brides with the wealth brought in by their sisters.

Finally there is a third and related way in which diverging devolution tends to make UDGs less 'corporate'. Diverging devolution places great stress on the downwards transmission of property, upon the preference for children as against siblings. Indeed, dowry seems to divide the siblings from one another as far as property is concerned; even among brothers marriage often means an allocation of resources which carries the further implication that the divided property will continue to go downwards rather than sideways. Again there are important differences between Africa and Eurasia in this respect, although many African societies (especially those with the house-property complex) also stress downwards rather than lateral transmission.[37] Even the so-called 'joint family' of Hindu law was subject to constant division as the result of downwards transmission. While undivided joint property may sometimes have passed down in the manner of universal succession described by Maine in *Ancient Law*, the usual Hindu system of inheritance excluded brothers, precisely because the property had already been 'divided'. Hence inheritance was filial and not fraternal. Though the 'divided' brothers still belonged to the same kin group and sometimes to the same labour group, they were not now entitled to inherit their brother's property; and it is this lack of 'corporateness' of the joint family, kin group or village community that accounts for the great frequency of 'fictitious' heirs, through adoption or through filiacentric unions, that characterizes Indian society.

The point I am making here goes back to earlier suggestions. For example, Leach argues that we may have two categories of society in which 'the principle of unilineal descent is all important, but it plays an entirely different structural role in the two cases'. He distinguishes between the category into which most of the African lineage systems seem to fall (as well as the non-exogamous lineages of Islamic Western Asia). 'In this case the on-going structure is defined by descent alone and marriage serves merely to create "a complex scheme of individuation" within that structure. In contrast, there is the category of those

30

societies in which unilineal descent is linked with a strongly defined rule of "preferred marriage". In this latter case "complementary filiation" may come to form part of the permanent on-going structure, but to understand how this comes about we need to consider economic and political factors as well as the kinship structure in isolation' (1961[1957]: 123). Looked at from one standpoint, Lévi-Strauss was making a similar point when he distinguished between the elementary and complex forms of kinship, the former including the systems of preferential marriage of Asia and the Pacific, the latter the bridewealth systems of Africa (1949: 577), a complex form of generalized exchange based upon the credits obtained by circulating women. The point is also touched upon by Yalman when he calls attention to the danger of transferring (West) African notions of unilineal descent groups to the Indian sub-continent (1967: 367) and again by Buchler and Selby when they point out the importance of distinguishing between the analytic tools required for the study of societies of the 'African' and 'Asian' type (1968: 135). But none of these authors attempt to explain these regional differences. For we need to look further than differences in 'descent' and 'affinity' if we are to arrive at a satisfactory understanding; we need to examine the nature of the economy itself.

If one is concerned to understand kinship in the context of the economic and political framework, then it is necessary to place less emphasis on descent and affinity *per se* and more upon the property transactions which are involved, at marriage, at death, or at other points in the life-cycle. As I pointed out in trying to explain differences in matrilateral relationships, differences in the system of devolution are critical for understanding relationships between sister's son and mother's brother. But the differences in inheritance (Goody 1959), in affinal exchange (Lévi-Strauss 1949) or in structure of descent groups (Leach 1957) need to be seen in the wider context of the economy and of stratification. If one of the major functions of the family is status placement, which Goode claims 'in every society links the structures of stratification, kinship lines, and mate choices' (1964[1959]: 211), then clearly the systems of kinship and marriage must be vitally affected by the type of economy and by the type of stratification. Hence the grouping together of China with the Miwok as systems of generalized exchange, or with the Australian aborigines as elementary structures, can only be of limited analytic use. For example, the nature of cross-cousin marriage itself is likely to be influenced by the presence of diverging devolution. In Ceylon, the word translated by Yalman as 'inheritance claims' is also used to describe the right of a male cross-cousin to demand the hand of his female cross-cousin, as well as the claim of a sister's son to the clothing of his maternal uncle (1967: 133). Inheritance and marriage rules are seen as intimately related, both being linked to the mutual claims of brother and sister (p. 358).

If property is a variable and diverges in this way, one important tactic in the strategy of those engaged in marrying is to attempt to bring back the property by various forms of in-marriage, e.g. by certain types of cross-cousin marriage (FBD, FZD) or by the union of persons of the same group and equal status (the matching procedure we have spoken of above), or by preventing women from marrying outside the group when property is involved – the proto-typical case here being the restrictions placed upon the daughters of Zelophehad who demanded, and won, the rights of the (sexually) residual heir to their father's property (Num. 27: 1; 36: 1-3).

Table 4 shows that cousin marriage is likely to be forbidden in African societies and allowed in Eurasia; in this respect, the Pacific and North America resemble Africa, while South America resembles Eurasia.

Table 4. The continental distribution of prohibited and permitted marriage to cousins (percentages)

	Cousin marriage prohibited	Permitted marriage to		
		FZD	FBD	MBD
Africa	65.2 (134)	27	3.6	25
Eurasia	37.5 (60)	52.5	17.5	50.5
Pacific	70.5 (87)	22.7	6.5	20.3
N. America	82.7 (167)	13.4	2.4	13.9
S. America	37 (27)	55	11	56.4
All	62.5 (475)			

$n = 673$. The table is derived from the *Ethnographic Atlas* (1967).

There are certainly a variety of factors involved in this distribution, but one is the fact that diverging devolution in stratified systems favours close (and more especially closed) conubium, while the system of marital and inheritance transactions found in Africa tend to be found with open (and even distant) conubium.

I have shifted from talking about bridewealth and dowry to talking about forms of conubium, distant and close, open and closed. Both these contrasts are relative and with regard to the second I am more concerned with effectively open than formally open systems; in class systems, marriage may be formally open but effectively closed.

The shift is not illogical; for the distribution of bridewealth and dowry is consistent with differences in the openness of marriage. Closed systems tend to occur where property is differentiated; equally, open systems tend to be found where property is more evenly distributed. In-marriage is a policy of isolation; out-marriage involves wider exchanges, or interchanges, and it also involves a levelling off, since it is a form of redistribution. Consequently, in-marriage tends to be associated with the complex stratification of Eurasia, out-marriage with the simpler stratification of African states where marriage alliances of the ruling estate are usually diversified between the different groups in the society. This at least is the case in the majority of African societies where heterogamy has been the norm. The Imam of Bole in Western Gonja (Ghana) once put it to me in the following way: 'Here, we Muslims marry commoners, the commoners marry chiefs and the chiefs, Muslims' (Goody 1969c: 159). It would be easy to imagine that we were in the presence of a circulating system of conubium, with chiefs taking the daughters of commoners, Muslims the daughters of chiefs, and commoners the daughters of Muslims. Such a system would be consistent with marriage to the mother's brother's daughter, which ensures that women pass in a unilateral direction, at least if it is combined with a prohibition on marriage to the father's sister's daughter (Fortune 1933). But the 'model' used by this actor indicates nothing of the kind. What appears to be the expression of a circulating system of conubium is a function of the linearity of the speech form used. In fact, the Imam was emphasizing the heterogamous nature of Gonja marriage; marriage is effectively as well as formally open.

Only in a few instances does this policy of open marriage not prevail, notably where northern immigrants (often of 'white' origin) have come to dominate black agriculturalists. This was so in certain of the Interlacustrine States, such as Ruanda and Burundi, whose tragic history of recent times, the massacre of one element of the population by another, stems directly from the nature of the system of stratification which permits no intermarriage, and hence no ties of kinship, between the major social groupings. A similar situation existed in Zanzibar, leading to the expulsion of the government of the Sultan and many of the inhabitants of Arab origin, and the establishment of the Zanzibar Revolutionary Council under the late Sheikh Abeid Karume.

Karume's policies seem directly related to this situation. Shortly before his assassination, the following assessment appeared in the *Observer* (2 April 1972).

In contradiction to Nyerere, too, he is wedded to racist policies. 'Tanzania is for black Africans: if you in the mainland hide this fact from others, we in the islands do not', he said recently.

Tanzania has Europeans and Asians in its Government and Parliament, and its Constitution guarantees equality to all its citizens, irrespective of race.

But in pursuit of his own racist policies, Karume has systematically destroyed the once-flourishing Arab, Shirazi and Asian communities in the islands. He has, on occasion, bitterly attacked Amir Jamal, a prominent Asian member of Nyerere's Cabinet.

This attitude led him to adopt the policy of forcing inter-marriage between Shirazis, Asians and Africans. Six months ago he ordered several hundred Asian families to leave. He then refused to provide them with exit permits, having banned them from holding trading licences.

The racist policy ascribed to Karume plainly has historical roots. Because the Arabs tended to marry endogamously, they were separated from the mass of African, or mixed-African population. Karume's policy can be seen as a direct reversal of the pre-existing situation, a deliberate attempt to break down racial differences. Anywhere else in Africa (with the exception of Ruanda-Burundi), the population would already have been mixed. So that whatever political stratification there may have been, and political stratification inevitably meant some economic benefits, it did not lead to exclusive social groups. The notion of hypergamy hardly existed since every group was continually marrying every other.

The property situation I have described affects the wider kinship system in a number of ways. An appreciation of these helps us to understand some theoretical disputes that have arisen in the comparative study of kinship. The particular controversy that I have in mind is that between so-called alliance and descent theory. I should add that, in my opinion, to designate these as 'theories' (as do Dumont, Fortes, Schneider, Buchler and Selby) is to use that word in a very loose sense, and to overvalue and over-systematize the differences between two approaches, which are really a matter of emphasizing one set of relationships as against another.

Let us first clarify the terms of the debate. Descent is used by some to refer to eligibility to membership of a unilineal kin group; by others to any ancestor-oriented kin group (e.g. Goodenough), while others extend it to mean any kin relationship between descendants, almost the equivalent of filiation; the latter is an everyday usage in English and one into which many writers slip from time to time. Alliance is equally slippery. In recent years the role of alliance has often been narrowed to a consideration of marriage, indeed marriage of a certain repetitive type. This function of marriage as allying individuals and groups has been stressed by many writers over a long period; in everyday speech we commonly speak of the alliance created by marriage, and in French the usage is even more specific since *alliance* may also refer to the wedding ring itself. Anthropologists have used the term continuously to characterize legitimate sexual unions. Radcliffe-Brown, for example, employs it to refer to persisting interrelationships created either by intermarriage or by joking partnerships. He writes: 'The theory that is here put forward, therefore, is that both the joking relationship which constitutes an alliance between clans and tribes, and that between relatives by marriage, are modes of organising a definite and stable system of social behaviour in which conjunctive and disjunctive components, as I have called them, are maintained and combined' (1952 [1940] : 95).

Radcliffe-Brown isolates four modes of alliance or consociation:

(1) through intermarriage;
(2) by exchange of goods and services;
(3) by blood-brotherhood or exchanges of names or sacra;
(4) by the joking relationship (1952: 102).

And he distinguishes relations by alliance from true contractual relations, the latter being 'specific jural relationships entered into by two persons or two groups, in which either party has definite positive obligations towards the other and failure to carry out the obligations is subject to a legal sanction' (p. 103), the obligations in question being specific rather than general.

The sociological use of the term involves two related meanings, a union of families of the kind inevitably involved in marriage[38] and a union for political or military ends; the first is by definition affected by marriage, the second may be. But equally alliances of this more general kind may be established in a number of other ways, e.g. by joking partnership, by treaty, etc. Indeed there is a third element of meaning of a yet more general kind, the 'alliance' that is established between all the units of a society by means of cross-cutting ties, such as those created by exogamy, age sets or by informal groups. This kind of alliance was the theme of Tylor's famous paper on incest and exogamy, where he writes of Lewis Morgan 'describing how the alliance of the Iroquois tribes, made up of intermarrying clans, formed a bond of union throughout the national league...' (1889[1961]: 22). Tylor may be referring to a temporary alliance designed to 'break up the spirit of perpetual warfare, which has wasted the red race from age to age'. But elsewhere he used the same term for relationships that are a perpetual feature of society and account for its very existence: 'Among the tribes of low culture there is but one means known of keeping up permanent alliance, and that means is inter-marriage' (p. 23). Even far on in culture, the political value of intermarriage remains.

Discussing Australian societies Radcliffe-Brown developed a similar theme in a more specific context (1930: 434): 'Where there is a system of moieties one of the functions of this is that every marriage, whether by exchange of sisters or not, is an exchange between one moiety and the other. So, also in the section system all marriages are part of a continuous series of exchanges between the two sections or sub-sections of a pair'. The analysis of bilateral cross-cousin marriage systems of the main Australian kinds was extended to the asymmetrical marriage systems, especially of the Murngin type (i.e. MBD marriage) and the notion of alliance was specifically applied to these other types of system where marriage was prescribed. Needham spoke of 'asymmetric alliance' and of 'alliance cycles' where earlier Dutch scholars wrote of circulating 'cycles of marriage transactions'. Meanwhile for Dumont (1968), alliance specifically becomes 'marriage alliance' and the whole concept is tied in with 'prescriptive marriage systems', in which 'there is a rule of marriage with a prescribed category of relative'.

Dumont claims that 'the expression "marriage alliance" in which "alliance" refers to the repetition of intermarriage between larger or smaller groups, denotes what amounts to a special theory of kinship, a theory developed to deal with those types of kinship system that embody positive marriage rules, although it also affords certain general theoretical insights regarding kinship'. Earlier he wrote about cross-cousin marriage: 'the regulation causes marriage to be transmitted much as membership in the descent group is transmitted. With it marriage acquires a diachronic dimension; it becomes an institution enduring from generation to generation, which I therefore call "marriage alliance" or simply "alliance"' (1957: 24). This relationship can be between men (p. 25).

Here alliance is thought of as an affinal relationship, of a continuing, repetitive kind; hence marriage and kinship necessarily overlap and are built into one another, often by means of a Dravidian type of kinship terminology.

In the narrower sense it is easier to see how the concept is applied to prescriptive systems than to others. Such societies are relatively few in number and highly specialized in their marriage rules. But even in this limited context it hardly seems necessary to pose the question in the way Dumont has done in the title to a recent paper 'Descent or intermarriage? a relational view of Australian section systems' (1966), since these concepts are not alternatives but complementary. In any case, since few if any African societies have prescriptive forms of marriage, theories developed to explain such systems would appear to offer little help to the prospective analyst and the wider implications of 'alliance theory' become obscure.

However, there is a more general and simple-minded opposition between those who have stressed descent (or filiation) and those who have stressed alliance (in the sense of affinity). Even this opposition is somewhat obscured by the fact that alliance 'theorists' often appear to be firmly attached to an analysis in terms of descent groups, which usually emerge as the units that are 'allied'. In his useful summary of the discussion Maybury-Lewis (1965) constantly refers to the relationships between UDGs although he certainly allows for the possibility that the categories are differently defined. If, however, the argument is put in terms of categories divorced from social groups, the thesis seems (in Schneider's words) pointless. For example, Maybury-Lewis writes: 'in matrilineal, as in patrilineal societies, prescriptive matrilateral cross-cousin marriage precisely defines the relation between affinally related descent groups or categories'. But with 'categories' the sentence is surely circular, since the 'categories' are precisely what define 'prescriptive matrilateral cross-cousin marriage'. Moreover it is difficult to see in what meaningful sense categories can be allied. But this does not mean that the units involved are necessarily descent groups; as Yalman shows for Ceylon, sibling groups are often the primary elements involved in the transactions.

Another aspect of the tendency to analyse alliance largely in the context of the relationship between unilineal descent groups comes out in the attempt to treat the mother's brother as an 'affine' not only in all systems of Dravidian kin terms but in all systems of patrilineal descent. In the words of Buchler and Selby, 'Mother (in a patrilineal system) and father (in a matrilineal system) can usefully be viewed as affinals, and a fortiori, so can MB and FZ (in patrilineal and matrilineal systems respectively)' (1968: 134). Here again there seems to be some confusion between analysis that is actor-centred or observer-centred on the one hand, and that is ego-centred or socio-centred on the other. Looking at the social system purely from the standpoint of a matrilineal UDG, the father can possibly be seen as an affine. But when we shift from the framework of unilineal descent to bilateral kinship (and all societies with UDGs have both frames of reference), what is served by this violation of common sense usage? Indeed it often violates actor categories. The attempt to classify all relatives dichotomously into kin and affines on the European or Dravidian models (and both do so in different ways) certainly does not work for most societies in Africa where the basic division is often of kin in the descent group, kin outside and affines. The latter category are not difficult to isolate in the terminology and only in the Lobedu case, I believe, is the mother's brother classified as an in-law. The wholesale transfer of an analytic framework from prescriptive marriage systems seems only to confuse the issue in other types of society and arises from an over emphasis on a single fixed framework, such as the structure of unilineal descent groups. Where such a structure is absent or irrelevant, are both or neither the father and mother to be reckoned as ego's affines? The futility of the question indicates that this group-centred standpoint is only one of the factors behind kinship categorizations, one that tends to ignore the importance of generational divisions. The danger of over-determination in this field must surely be clear when we look at the terms for the second ascending and descending generations (grandparents and grandchildren) where terminology often overrides all discriminations, dichotomous or otherwise, in terms of descent or affinity, paying attention only to sex. It seems contradictory that writers who insist upon the desirability of an 'ethnoscientific' approach (e.g. to the definition of the family) and of 'etic' analysis should so easily set aside the actor's categorizations, though it is obviously a policy decision as to how far one limits oneself to an examination in these terms alone.

In terms of this simplistic opposition between alliance and descent, there is clearly room for disagreement about the relative weight to be placed upon kin groups or affinal relationships in the analysis of particular societies. However, our earlier argument suggests the differences are not simply matters of individual approach but are affected by the type of society with which one is dealing. Earlier we examined certain differences in the structure of descent groups. In the same way, marriage and affinity take on different meanings. For when the bride is a bringer of property or an heir to her father, marriage arrangements take on another hue; it then becomes more important to contract one marriage rather than another, and the profession of match-maker (primarily a Eurasian phenomenon) immediately becomes relevant.

The fact that women are heirs to significant property affects the whole nature of the conjugal relationship, leading it in a monogamous direction. With this individualizing form of marriage is associated the concept of 'love'. Gluckman has argued that 'love' serves to separate both spouses from their kin (and kin groups), uniting them into a conjugal team (1956).[39] Such separation is an aspect of love in the modern Western world; if you have to love one woman more than someone else (whether sibling, parent or partner), then a rationale is established for splitting society into spatially distinct groups based upon monogamous unions. In polygynous societies, 'love', in the sense of a preference of one above another, is often a dangerous thing. Favouritism leads to jealousy and one Ashanti folk-tale is actually entitled, 'No man should say, "This is the wife whom I love best"' (Rattray 1930: 175).[40]

A similar comment can be made about the creation of a conjugal fund (or conjugal property interest), which takes place at each new marriage when both males and females inherit or acquire interchangeable wealth. As we have seen, the establishment of such a fund weakens the corporate nature of the UDG (where these exist); at the same time, its existence clearly establishes the conjugal unit on a footing which is at once more intimate and more solid, a fact that again tends to separate the members of the unit from relationships of a lateral kind; in China the specific cause for the splitting of the property of a group of brothers often lies with their wives, the joint interest of spouses pulling the brothers apart from one another.[41] At marriage the woman is not so much incorporated in her husband's lineage as linked with him in a cross-cutting conjugal unit.

The difference bears directly upon the relationships between husband and wife. In Europe the couple are bound in some form of conjugal community. In Africa, the financial activities of husband and wife are characteristically distinct, even when there is no plural marriage. Clearly, a polygynous household can hardly operate in the same way as a monogamous one. But the matter goes deeper than this. In the coastal fishing villages of Ghana, a woman purchases fish from her husband and then goes trading on her own account. She is not endangering his capital nor is he responsible for her debts. Among the LoDagaa, the funeral ceremony includes a reckoning of what is owed between husband and wife (Goody 1962). In Accra and Kumasi, market mammies build up their own funds and may become quite independent, financially and often domestically, of their husbands. From the financial point of view, husband and wife are not of one flesh.

The position with regard to the effect of polygyny in societies with diverging devolution comes out very clearly in Yalman's study of Kandyan villages in Ceylon. Here polygyny was rare and all the men who practised this form of marriage were 'very rich' by local standards (whereas polyandry, equally uncommon, was for the poor). More importantly, from the standpoint of my present argument, the co-wives mostly lived in dwellings far removed from one another; 'the economics and social life of the two *ge* [households] were completely separate' (1967: 113). It was not only the cost that made polygyny rare and polygynous wives distant; another reason had to do with kinship obligations, or rather with 'affinity'. 'Kandyans co-operate very closely with their in-laws. This co-operation is of such an intimate and all-embracing nature that it would be difficult to share one's attentions between the two sets of in-laws. Their demands would soon come into conflict' (p. 114).

This is especially true since a man's relationship to his brother-in-law centres upon the land which his wife has to divide with her brother, either in dowry (among the rich) or by inheritance (among the poor), though in the latter case she may be unable to exercise her right if she is living outside the village. For 'the question of her land intimately involves the relations between her husband and her brother as in-laws, as well as the relations of her children with her brothers. If women do not always aggressively pursue their claims against their brothers, especially when the property is small, this must be seen in the total context of family relationships and especially in the formal claims (*urumaya*) between MB–ZS' (Yalman 1967: 135). What characterizes societies like the Sinhalese, says Yalman, is precisely this co-operation between brothers-in-law, a situation which is far indeed from the usual African picture (anyhow among agriculturalists), even though a woman remains a link between the groups and is not (as Barth claims for the Pathans) simply transferred from one group to another (Yalman 1967: 151; Barth 1959).

The kind of difference a dowry, particularly a landed dowry, can make to affinal relations is indicated in Yalman's account of the history of the black-smith of Terutenne. He had settled in the village after marrying a woman who had lands there, but to these he added much more land from his own efforts, becoming one of the richest men although of low caste. 'It is a reflection of the strength of affinal ties that when his wife died, his mother-in-law (who lived in the same house with the couple) found another woman for him' and continued to share the same household (1967: 70).

With diverging devolution, it is clearly not just the conjugal bond that is emphasized but affinal ties as well. The brother-in-law relationship, indeed all in-lawship, comes to the fore; these are the men who have established an alliance around the wife/sister/daughter. In Africa, the relationships between in-laws seems to be in general less significant, though in adjacent generations the relations with the children of siblings and with siblings of parents are perhaps given greater stress. At least this seems to be the case in terms not only of intra-group relations (where the sons of brothers usually inherit before own daughters) but especially in intergroup affairs (where, to take the same patrilineal case, complementary filiation or extra-clan kinship is of considerable importance). [42]

Among pastoral peoples of East Africa, affinity seems to play a greater part than in the agricultural societies of West Africa. That is to say, a man may join his brother-in-law for the purposes of herding livestock, as among the Turkana and the Jie (Gulliver 1955). Clearly among these pastoral peoples the question of viability of the productive enterprise involves a much more delicate balance than in the agricultural societies of Africa; herds may grow or die and the labour requirements will vary over shorter periods of time, possibly leading men to make use of their daughters to attract working sons-in-law. Rigby describes the Gogo as living in a 'marginal' economic environment where '*effective* kinship and affinal relations are primarily viewed in terms of the carrying out of certain jurally defined rights and obligations concerning the most valuable form of property, viz., livestock' (1969: 1-2). In this society 'the great majority of links binding homestead owners to each other. . .arise from affinal relationships of one kind or another' (p. 147), 34.1% being between 'brothers-in-law'. However, such relationships appear to be linked to the absence of exogamous groups and it is not clear that affines in the more usual sense of the word (Rigby includes maternal kin) form part of a domestic group or co-operate closely in primary productive activities.

In-laws and kin are never, I think, identified to the extent of being brought into the same terminological category, except among the Lobedu who practice prescriptive MBD marriage. In South India, where cross-cousin marriage is prescribed and Dravidian terms are used, such a compounding is bound to take place. However, the dichotomous distinction to which such a system gives rise is one between forbidden and potential spouses, and it seems only confusing to translate this as 'kin' and 'affines', when these terms already have prior connotations.

Where cross-cousin marriage is prohibited, the two roles are bound to be separate. Prohibited cross-cousin marriage is a feature not only of many parts of Africa but of Northern India as well. Where this prohibition occurs, as among the Tallensi of Northern Ghana, there is a clear separation between *deenam*, affines (whom you have married) and *doʸam*, kin (whom you cannot marry). In the majority of cases in Africa, even where cross-cousin marriage is permitted or, as occasionally, preferred, the categories of kin and affines still remain distinct, though it should be said that the behavioural implications of these conceptual differences are unclear. This third possibility represents the more usual situation with regard to these categories, where people may, but often do not, marry kin (especially cousins). In-law terms then refer to a quasi-contractual arrangement rather than a built-in feature of the system; marry a kinswoman and she becomes an affine. There is no inherent opposition.

The same general situation we have examined from the standpoint of conjugal relationships can also be looked at from the standpoint of the mother's brother, whose body has provided a central focus for this controversy. Descent theorists are held to interpret certain aspects of the role of the maternal uncle in patrilineal societies as related to the fact that he is the nearest male relative in the mother's group, and hence one of a person's closest kinfolk outside his own patriclan. I myself have suggested that one aspect of this relationship derives from the fact that by the rule of unilineal descent and inheritance a man is excluded from membership in, as well as the property of, the group (clan or sibling) to which his mother belonged. To generalize my earlier discussion, I would now place more emphasis on discrimination by sex within the sibling rather than the descent group, the latter being a special case of the former (Goody 1959).

In alliance theory, the role of the mother's brother has been explained in terms of the relationship of a man to his wife's brother; it follows that marriage to the MBD is regarded as an instance of 'inherited affinity' (Dumont 1957: 24ff.). In other words, whereas the 'descent' theorists see the MB–ZS relationship as an intergenerational one, the alliance theorists see it as an aspect of an intra-generational relationship, H–WB. There seems to be a certain confusion here between an ego-oriented analysis in terms of kin roles and a sociocentric one in terms of kin groups. Looking at the question in the latter highly restricted context (seeing the roles mainly in the context of the membership of patrilineal descent groups or at least 'descent lines'), we could put the matter in a simplistic way and say that descent 'theorists' stress the link through the mother's brother (complementary filiation) while the alliance 'theorists' stress the 'affinity' estab-lished between the men involved in a marriage.

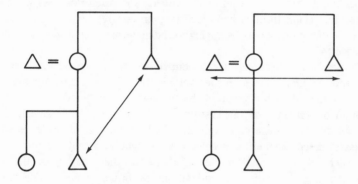

Fig. 2. The mother's brother and the wife's brother

There are several ways of explaining these different approaches.

One may point to the elements of confusion in the discussion. One can regard the 'theories' as complementary rather than opposed. That is to say, the writers concerned may be looking at similar systems from different points of view, which if taken in combination would give a better understanding. In this context a con-sideration of the developmental cycle is certainly relevant; the tie between a man and his brother-in-law may be the most important non-sexual relationship for a male at the outset of the marriage; later on it may be the relationship with his sister's children. Equally, from the other side, a man's relationship with his maternal uncle clearly precedes his acquisition of conjugal ties (and hence affinal ones, in the more specific sense); when he does get married, uncles and aunts are likely to be of less significance.

An alternative explanation is to assume that the ethnographic reports and interpretations carried out by one group of writers are wrong. As far as Africa is concerned, the material does not appear to be incorrect, not in any major sense; the ethnographical material on these relationships comes from some of the most detailed and sensitive studies made there, for example, from Evans-Pritchard's work on Nuer kinship and Fortes' study of the Tallensi.

But there is a further possibility, which is the theme of the present essay. Namely, that there are some objective differences between the societies of West Africa and those of South India (or more generally Africa and Eurasia) which are reflected in the analyses anthropologists have made. The differences have to do with the economy as well as with the whole level of complexity of the social system. We have already suggested how they would affect the structure of descent groups. But how would they affect relationships such as that between mother's brother and sister's son?

In African societies, a man in an agnatic system is prohibited from inheriting or succeeding to the property and office of his mother's descent or sibling group; the woman herself can exercise no rights, but her son often possesses what I have called a residual claim through her which is given concrete expression in customs such as the snatching of goods belonging to the maternal uncle and other members of her lineage.[43]

In societies with diverging devolution, however, a woman is entitled to property, though sometimes a smaller amount than her brother. My hypothesis would suggest that in such a situation the snatching of property would not occur. I have found no evidence of this custom in India, nor is it a characteristic mode of behaviour in Arab society. It is probably true that in all societies with an agnatic bias in descent, inheritance or succession, wherever they are found, a man has an easier relationship with the mother's brother than with the father. But with diverging devolution, considerations of property and office are dealt with by including men and women and their children, and hence we are less likely to find customs as 'ritual stealing'. Relationships with the mother's people (of which the maternal uncle is the representative actor) are always likely to be emphasized on ceremonial and ritual occasions. But as far as snatching is concerned, we would expect to see the continuing claims of the junior generation on the property of their parents' sibling group expressed in a different manner. For far from being excluded from that property, their mother has already received her share in the form of dowry, which will in turn be inherited by her offspring. However, conflict and 'ambivalence' are more likely to creep into the MB–ZS relationship when the division of the property is delayed, i.e. when a woman's claim is met by inheritance rather than dowry. On this subject Yalman makes the interesting observation that among the Kandyan Sinhalese the relationship acquires a special significance when the joint property of the mother and her brother have not been divided; here there is 'the latent possibility for unresolved conflict' (1967: 153).

The differential emphasis on matrilateral (and inter-generational ties generally) as distinct from affinal links comes out clearly when we consider the question of claims to basic productive resources in agricultural economies. In most societies, men can borrow land on a temporary or more permanent basis. In some societies the ability to control land enters into the calculation at the time of the marriage. This is clearly the case where a landed dowry prevails, but even where it does not, land may be acquired through one's wife, either because of her own potential claim on the inheritance or through affinal relationships. For example, Yalman notes that in Terutenne rice land may be borrowed from 'fathers, sons, sons-in-law, full brothers and brothers-in-law — if they are on good terms, without formal arrangements' (1967: 46).

In African societies such as the Tallensi and the LoDagaa, one borrows land not from affines but from one's matrilateral kin, specifically from the mother's brother. The generational telescoping of matrilateral and affinal relationships which is involved in much of the alliance discussion obscures this important difference, which is a matter of substance rather than interpretation.

In patrilineal societies in Africa the transfer is initially a temporary one. Some of the land returns to the original 'owner' when the use right lapses. But in other cases the land may pass imperceptibly to the new farmer, especially if it is adjacent to his existing plots. No change in personal identity is involved in this transfer. The individual retains his position as a sister's son of the donor and his lineage; it is the land that changes hands. In other societies the alternative claim to land may already be implied in the bilateral systems of affiliation (e.g. among the Lozi of Zambia); while in the Pacific the activation of such a claim may signal an immediate change in group membership. But in any case the point is that in Africa claims are generally made through the first ascending generation rather than through wives or in-laws.

Property also influences the nature of matrilateral and affinal relationships in matters of residence. Nowhere do we find every member of a lineage living in one place, even if we concentrate upon the males who normally remain on the 'family estate'. Both in Africa and Asia, members of a kin group get dispersed for a variety of reasons. In Africa, a young child may accompany the mother when she leaves her husband to return to her natal home. Or a youth may go and live with his mother's brother because he has quarrelled with his agnates. In patrilineal societies such dispersal often occurs within the framework of matrilateral relationships. For example, among the LoDagaa, the Tiv and the Tallensi of West Africa, an individual may move to another lineage or community and take up residence with his mother's people.

In many Eurasian societies with patrilineal UDGs, dispersal often occurs at a different phase of the developmental cycle, at marriage itself. Because dowry is variable, a richer woman may use it to attract a poorer man who is prepared to come and reside at her own natal home; indeed, residence of this kind may be obligatory if the conjugal pair are to exploit certain fixed economic resources, such as a farm or a shop. Such marriages are particularly likely to occur when a man has no male heirs and the daughter is used to continue a patronymic line; in this case I speak of a filiacentric union — it is Maine's 'appointed daughter'. Such an eventuality is more common than one might suppose. In societies with high fertility and high mortality, a significant proportion of couples will fail to produce a surviving male heir. However, many of these will have daughters, so that in those societies where sisters are heirs to their brothers or fathers, continuity can be preserved in an important percentage of cases by means of uxorilocal marriages. In Africa a parallel system is occasionally found where variable bridewealth payments exist, e.g. in the 'big' and 'small' marriages of the Ijaw of Eastern Nigeria, which determine residence as well as the affiliation of children. It is also found in some 'bilateral' hunting societies like the Bushmen, where the parents use their daughters to attract the services of a man. And finally, it is found as a phase in the developmental cycle of some matrilineal societies where, in the initial stages of marriage, a man has to reside with his wife's parents (e.g. among the LoWilisi and the Bemba). However, it remains true that in most patrilineal societies in Africa, bridewealth payments secure the transfer of the bride to her husband's home, as well as the attachment of her children. Whereas in Europe and Asia, the system of alternative (uxorilocal) residence and of alternative attachment of the children (in a filiacentric union) is more widespread because of the dowry system.

These residence arrangements clearly mean that varying emphases are placed on particular sets of relationships; in one case, alternative residence is influenced largely by affinal (or conjugal) ties, in the other, largely by matrilateral ones; or, in a misleading paraphrase, in one case by alliance, in the other by descent.

There is a further aspect of the filiacentric union which touches upon the situation of the maternal uncle. Where the kinship terminology distinguishes parents from uncles and cousins from siblings (a situation which is found in many societies with diverging devolution, though not of course those with a Dravidian terminology), then the offspring of such a union will have no mother's brother. This particular relational role is likely to be filled only where a virilocal marriage occurs, that is, where a woman has brothers and where she has taken her share of the parental property as dowry (or is later entitled to it as an inheritance). Once again we find a situation where the snatching of the property of the maternal uncle cannot occur, and where the lesser importance given to the MB–ZS relationship is relative to the greater importance attached to the affinal relationships.

In this section, I have suggested how we may look at some aspects of the discussion of 'alliance' and 'descent' in terms of more concrete differences in social systems. These differences are related to bridewealth and dowry, but ultimately to aspects of the economy and stratification. In so doing, I adopt a different approach to this discussion from D.M. Schneider, who sees the problem as a matter of 'muddles in the models'. Muddles there no doubt are, though some of those attributed to me are not ones I would easily recognize. Take his characterization of one supposed difference between Fortes and Goody on the one hand, and Lévi-Strauss, Leach and Dumont on the other: '(The former) do not concern themselves with the problem of whether the simplest form of organic solidarity is formed by a marriage rule and exogamy. They are concerned with segmental societies because they have a special theory of their own about how segments are formed and in what they consist, and how within segment relations are ordered and how between segment relations are structured. Marriage enters into this theory, but in a very different way' (1965: 45).

I do not myself have any special theory about the formation of segments, though nesting (i.e. segmentary) descent groups are of great importance in many societies including some I have studied (though not in others). With regard to marriage, my first published article (1956b) was on the subject of incest and exogamy, while my second was concerned with the limitations of the concept 'segmentary' (1957).[44] Fortes' second anthropological article was also on the subject of incest and exogamy (1936), followed shortly by a booklet entitled *Marriage Law among the Tallensi* (1937). However, accepting the proposition stated by Schneider that 'marriage enters into (descent) theory in a different way from alliance theory', there would seem to be something in the particular social situation the authors are examining which emphases affinity in one area as against descent in another. I therefore prefer the approach of Barnes in his article on 'African models in the New Guinea highlands' (1962) or of Leach in his discussion of bridewealth among the Kachin and Lakher (1957) where they are more concerned with differences in systems than muddles in models. Or rather I would extend these analyses and assume that since the variations had a relatively systematic character, they should be related to differences in the social systems. In the present context, I see the most critical difference as the mode of property distribution of which dowry is a part. Whatever the system of descent or kin groups, dowry systems place more emphasis on some aspects of affinal and conjugal relations. I do not claim that the explanation of all aspects of so-called alliance and descent theory lies in the fact that adherents of the former have tended to work in dowry systems, and of the latter in bridewealth systems (or rather in societies with diverging devolution and in those without). But at least some of the differences in this rather circular discussion are to be understood in this light. Moreover, this approach has the virtue of attempting to link anthropological theory more generally with developments in history, sociology, archaeology and economics, instead of attempting to develop its own explanations in an intellectual vacuum, as if the societies which these scholars study fell into quite a different category from the ones in which they live. Clearly with dowry systems this is not so.

Some supporting evidence for the implications of this approach is presented in a recent study by Boserup on *The Role of Women in Economic Development* (1970). Here she tries to sum up her argument concerning the position of women in rural communities by distinguishing two broad groups of society:

. . . the first type is found in regions where shifting cultivation predominates and the major part of agricultural work is done by women. In such communities,

45

we can expect to find a high incidence of polygamy, and bride wealth being paid by the future husband or his family. The women are hard working . . .

The second group is found where plough cultivation predominates and where women do less agricultural work than men. In such communities we may expect to find that only a tiny minority of marriages, if any, are polygamous; that a dowry is usually paid by the girl's family; that a wife is entirely dependent upon her husband for economic support; and that the husband has an obligation to support his wife and children, at least as long as the marriage is in force.

We find the first type of rural community in Africa South of the Sahara, in many parts of South East Asia and in tribal regions in many parts of the world. We also find this type among descendants of negro slaves in certain parts of America. The second type predominates in regions influenced by Arab, Hindu and Chinese culture (1970: 50).

The thesis developed by Boserup has clear similarities with the one I have tried to suggest. I myself would regard polygny and monogamy, bridewealth and dowry, as being related less directly to women's contribution to agriculture and more to the problem of 'status placement' in societies with varying degrees of socio-economic differentiation. My general argument is very similar to that pursued by Yalman on the microsociological level in the specific context of Ceylon, when he notes that 'the lack of a dowry system is associated with egalitarian and immobile villages' while 'dowry – with all that it implies in control over women and solidarity among men as a mark of status – appears to be a function of diversified communities with at least some mobility. It seems likely that the development of social hierarchies is associated with the emerging variations in marriage and inheritance behaviour' (1967: 149).

In conclusion, let me try to sum up the different implications of the two major types of marriage transaction. If one wanted a facile distinction between bridewealth and dowry, one might say that in one case the woman was paid for and in the other paid off. This is over crude; in neither case are women as such exchanged, nor do they altogether loose their ties of membership in their natal group. But dowry of the direct and indirect kind (often called brideprice in the literature) has very different implications from bridewealth, though the two do not altogether exclude one another. I have tried to sketch out some of these implications as I see them with regard to the structure of social groups, marriage systems, kin relationships, property arrangements and stratification. In my view (and I have tried to support this hypothesis elsewhere) the two latter are the major causal elements in this complex. Systems of diverging devolution, which includes dowry, have other important implications for the role compendia of the respective areas. But here I have tried to emphasize the effect that such marriage arrangements have on the kinship system in the widest sense; systems of descent take on a different colouring when women are heirs and where property is regularly channeled outside group boundaries; so too affinity is in many ways a more important matter when you have only one full spouse, when she is married with property, and when that property is placed in some kind of conjugal fund; and above all when marriage is a matter of match-making in a material sense. Dowry differentiates, just as bridewealth tends to homogenize.

I conclude with a caveat. There is danger in overpolarization. Alliance and descent are neither exclusive categories for social institutions nor exclusive approaches for the analysis of kinship; the terms of the discussion virtually eliminate the study of bilateral systems. Equally, the presence of bridewealth does not exclude dowry, nor are the two terms exhaustive of types of marriage payment. They may be present in combination; or they may not be present at all. This study has centered upon the contrast between them; but the framework does not exhaust the possibilities with which we are faced in the study of human societies. There is also some danger in over-emphasizing the difference between Africa and Eurasia, between the systems in which we find bridewealth and those where we find dowry. If I have failed at times to express the full range of variation, this is because I have wanted to understand specific societies, relationships and individuals in the context of general trends.

APPENDIX 1

The account of the endowment of Queen Medb is given at the very beginning of the *Tain* and in Kinsella's translation it goes as follows:

Once when the royal bed was laid out for Ailill and Medb in Cruachan fort in Connacht, they had this talk on the pillows:

'It is true what they say, love,' Ailill said, 'it is well for the wife of a wealthy man.'

'True enough,' the woman said. 'What put that in your mind?'

'It struck me,' Ailill said, 'how much better off you are today than the day I married you.'

'I was well enough off without you,' Medb said.

'Then your wealth was something I didn't know or hear much about,' Ailill said. 'Except for your woman's things, and the neighbouring enemies making off with loot and plunder.'

'Not at all,' Medb said, 'but with the high king of Ireland for my father — Eochaid Feidlech the steadfast, the son of Finn, the son of Finnoman, the son of Finnen, the son of Finngoll, the son of Roth, the son of Rigéon, the son of Blathacht, the son of Beothacht, the son of Enna Agnech, the son of Aengus Turbech. He had six daughters: Derbriu, Ethne, Ele, Clothru, Muguin, and myself Medb, the highest and haughtiest of them. I outdid them in grace and giving and battle and warlike combat. I had fifteen hundred soldiers in my royal pay, all exiles' sons, and the same number of freeborn native men, for every paid soldier I had ten more men, and nine more, and eight, and seven, and six, and five, and four, and three, and two, and one. And that was only our ordinary household.

'My father gave me a whole province of Ireland, this province ruled from Cruachan, which is why I am called "Medb of Cruachan." And they came from Finn the king of Leinster, Rus Ruad's son, to woo me, and from Coirpre Niafer the king of Temair, another of Rus Ruad's sons. They came from Conchobor, king of Ulster, son of Fachtna, and they came from Eochaid Bec, and I wouldn't go. For I asked a harder wedding gift than any woman ever asked before from a man in Ireland – the absence of meanness and jealousy and fear.

'If I married a mean man our union would be wrong, because I'm so full of grace and giving. It would be an insult if I were more generous than my husband, but not if the two of us were equal in this. If my husband was a timid man our union would be just as wrong because I thrive, myself, on all kinds of trouble. It is an insult for a wife to be more spirited than her husband, but not if the two are equally spirited. If I married a jealous man that would be wrong, too: I never had one man without another waiting in his shadow. So I got the kind of man I wanted: Rus Ruad's other son – yourself, Ailill, from Leinster. You aren't greedy or jealous or sluggish. When we were promised, I brought you the best wedding gift a bride can bring: apparel enough for a dozen men, a chariot worth thrice seven bondmaids, the width of your face of red gold and the weight of your left arm of light gold. So, if anyone causes you shame or upset or trouble, the right to compensation is mine,' Medb said, 'for you're a kept man.'

'By no means,' Ailill said, 'but with two kings for my brothers, Coirpre in Temair and Finn over Leinster. I let them rule because they were older, not because they are better than I am in grace or giving. I never heard, in all Ireland, of a province run by a woman except this one, which is why I came and took the kingship here, in succession to my mother Mata Muiresc, Mágach's daughter. Who better for my queen than you, a daughter of the high king of Ireland?'

'It still remains,' Medb said, 'that my fortune is greater than yours.'

'You amaze me,' Ailill said, 'No one has more property or jewels or precious things than I have, and I know it.'

Then the lowliest of their possessions were brought out, to see who had more property and jewels and precious things: their buckets and tubs and iron pots, jugs and wash-pails and vessels with handles. Then their finger-rings, bracelets, thumb-rings and gold treasures were brought out, and their cloth of purple, blue, black, green and yellow, plain grey and many-coloured, yellow-brown, checked and striped. Their herds of sheep were taken in off the fields and meadows and plains. They were measured and matched, and found to be the same in numbers and size. Even the great ram leading Medb's sheep, the worth of one bondmaid by himself, had a ram to match him leading Ailill's sheep.

From pasture and paddock their teams and herds of horses were brought in.

For the finest stallion in Medb's stud, worth one bondmaid by himself, Ailill had a stallion to match. Their vast herds of pigs were taken in from the woods and gullies and waste places. They were measured and matched and noted, and Medb had one fine boar, but Ailill had another. Then their droves and free-wandering herds of cattle were brought in from the woods and wastes of the province. These were matched and measured and noted also, and found to be the same in number and size. But there was one great bull in Ailill's herd, that had been a calf of one of Medb's cows — Finnbennach was his name, the White Horned — and Finnbennach, refusing to be led by a woman, had gone over to the king's herd. Medb couldn't find in her herd the equal of this bull, and her spirits dropped as though she hadn't a single penny. [45]

It was a result of her failure to match her husband's bull that she sent out a messenger 'to see where the match of the bull might be found, in any province of Ireland'. He reported that such a bull and better could be found in the province of Ulster, called the Brown Bull of Cuailnge, and it was the attempt to capture this 'fine jewel' that led to the subsequent adventures recounted in the epic.

APPENDIX 2

The categories used in the *Atlas* are bridewealth, dowry, bride-service, gift-exchange, token payments, sister-exchange and absence of gifts. Table 3 shows that bridewealth is the commonest form of marriage transaction in Africa (82%), the Circum-Mediterranean area (68%), East Eurasia (56%) and the Insular Pacific (53%). In Africa, bridewealth and bride-service together are found in 90% of societies. The corollary is that Africa has the lowest percentage of societies where the payments are insubstantial or merely token. 'Absence of gifts' is the most common type in North and South America; in the latter case it is closely followed by bride-service, which is connected with the prevalence of initial uxorilocal marriage in that sub-continent, the husband joining the work unit of his wife's parents for a period at the beginning of their marriage. Initial uxorilocal marriage has some association with matrilineal descent, as for example in the case of the Bemba of Zambia or the LoWilisi of the Ivory Coast (Lobi); the offspring of the union belong to the wife's matriclan. However, in South America, this practice is widely found in societies where unilineal descent groups are absent.

In North America, 'absence of gifts' is followed in frequency by bridewealth, bride-service and gift-exchange, in that order. In the Insular Pacific, bridewealth is followed by absence, and then by gift-exchange and finally by sister-exchange; this is the only area where societies with the latter form of marriage reach the 10% mark. 'Absence' is again important in the two Eurasian areas (following bridewealth). But it is also critical for the argument that Eurasia is the only area in which dowry is at all significant.

Table 5. Marriage transactions and kin groups

	Bride-wealth	Bride-service	Dowry	Gift-exchange	Sister-exchange	Transactions absent or token
Patrilineal	288 (72%)	25 (6%)	8 (2%)	12 (3%)	19 (5%)	49 (12%)
Matrilineal	44 (37%)	17 (14%)	1 (1%)	6 (5%)	2 (2%)	50 (42%)
Double	14 (52%)	1 (4%)	1 (4%)	5 (19%)	4 (15%)	2 (7%)
Bilateral	60 (19%)	52 (17%)	13 (4%)	32 (10%)	2 (1%)	150 (49%)
Total	406	95	23	55	27	251

N.B. Codes: horizontal: derived from cols. 20, 22 = Descent
vertical: col. 12 = Mode of marriage

Table 6. Marriage transactions, kin groups and continent

		Marriage Transactions						
		Bride-wealth	Bride-service	Dowry	Gift-exchange	Sister-exchange	Token or absent	Total
Africa	Patrilineal	154	10	0	1	8	3	176
	Matrilineal	22	8	0	0	0	7	37
	Double	12	0	0	0	0	0	12
	Bilateral	7	1	0	0	2	3	13
Eurasia	Patrilineal	99	3	7	2	0	14	125
	Matrilineal	7	0	1	1	0	6	15
	Double	2	0	0	0	0	1	3
	Bilateral	10	3	13	2	0	19	47
Insular Pacific	Patrilineal	25	0	1	6	9	2	43
	Matrilineal	10	1	0	3	2	12	28
	Double	0	1	1	5	4	1	12
	Bilateral	12	4	0	6	0	21	43
North* America	Patrilineal	9	6	0	3	0	24	42
	Matrilineal	3	4	0	2	0	24	33
	Bilateral	28	18	0	23	0	74	143
South* America	Patrilineal	1	6	0	0	2	6	15
	Matrilineal	2	4	0	0	0	1	7
	Bilateral	3	26	0	1	0	33	63

* Double descent systems are not recorded for the Americas

Apart from confirming generally accepted ideas of sister- and gift-exchange as a Pacific form of marriage (but not *the* Pacific form), and bride-service as the South American form, the table also shows the dominance of bridewealth in all continents except America and the absence of dowry virtually everywhere except Eurasia (and even there the figures do not suggest that it plays a very important part).

Table 5 shows the correlations between marriage transactions and kin groups. The classification is again of course crude. But it serves to bring out, or confirm, a number of points. Bridewealth is the prevailing form of transaction in societies with either patrilineal (P) or double descent groups (D), and even in those with matrilineal (M) groups it runs a close second to 'absence'. The incidence of bridewealth decreases along a scale running P———→D———→M———→B. For 'the absence of substantial transactions', the direction is more or less reversed. Of the less frequent forms of transaction, dowry and gift exchange display no strong associations with any particular kind of kin group.

In Table 6 the variables of continent, transaction and descent group are combined in order to emphasize and clarify some of the points made. In Africa bridewealth is the predominant form irrespective of the type of descent group. In Europe and Asia the same is true of patrilineal and matrilineal systems, but not of bilateral ones. In the Insular Pacific and North America it is 'absence' that predominates with all types of kin group. In South America, bride-service predominates in a similar way.

One conclusion is in a sense a negative one, that in many cases marriage transactions appear to be more closely associated with continent than with descent groups. Another possible conclusion is that we need to revaluate the role of 'diffusion' in social systems, a theme that crops up again in considering Lévi-Strauss' regional maps of folktales and myths and is the subject of a series of recent articles about 'Galton's problem'. If social structure is related to communication, and if adjacent peoples are more likely to communicate than those separated by oceans and deserts, and if interaction modifies behaviour even of the customary sort, then 'diffusion' is a proper answer to some questions about similarities in social institutions. Nevertheless, this answer takes us only a little way along the path towards an explanation and we need to look for other interconnections apart from the geographical. This is what the body of the paper tries to do, concentrating specifically upon the comparison and contrast between Europe and Asia on the one hand, and Africa on the other, attempting to relate those differences to the economic, political and status systems. If we run marriage transactions against other variables recorded in the *Ethnographic Atlas*, we find some support for this thesis, as well as suggestions of further correlations. Dowry is more commonly found with intensive agriculture, where gift-exchange, sister-exchange and bride-service rarely occur. Gift-exchange mainly appears in the simpler societies without agriculture. Both bridewealth and dowry are well represented in societies with the larger domestic animals, though in the

JACK GOODY

latter case the animals are also used to plough the land. With this difference in
economy is linked the difference in the contribution made by men and women
respectively; bridewealth is more commonly found where women make the
major contribution to agriculture, whereas dowry is restricted to those societies
where males contribute most; this is the difference between hoe agriculture and
the use of the plough, which is almost invariably in male hands. Again, dowry
is associated with societies with complex forms of stratification, whereas bride-
service and sister-exchange tend to be found with minimal stratification. Bridewealth occurs in the intermediate area. As we have remarked in the text, dowry
tends to be found with monogamy, bridewealth with general polygyny, and the
other forms of transaction with limited polygyny.

1. This difference is discussed in my paper, 'Marriage prestations, inheritance
and descent in pre-industrial societies', *J. Comp. Family Studies* (1970). 1: 37-54.
2. Systems of direct marriage exchange (or marriage exchange groups) have
been reported from several areas of West Africa, including the Tiv (East 1939;
L. and P. Bohannan 1953: 69 ff.), the Mambila (Reyfish 1960: 246) and the
Konkomba (Tait 1961). In the latter case Tait says that they occurred in about
5% of marriages.
3. I use the term reciprocity in the sense of equivalent return.
4. For the LoWiili see J. Goody, '"Normative", "recollected" and "actual"
marriage payments among the LoWiili, 1951-1966', *Africa* (1969) 39: 54-61.
For the Gonja, see E.N. Goody, *Contexts of Kinship*, Cambridge, 1973.
5. On this point see Gluckman 1950: 192 for Central and South Africa;
also Loeb 1935: 68 ff. for Sumatra.
6. A similar phenomena is found in some of the simplest societies of Africa;
e.g. among the hunters of the Kalahari such as the !Kung Bushmen (Marshall
1959). For a parallel example of high dowries and matrilocal marriage, see Yalman's
account of marriage among Hindu and Muslim communities in Ceylon (1967: 314).
7. See Gluckman for the Lozi (1950). I use the phrase 'bilateral societies'
to indicate those where named unilineal descent groups are absent; I imply
no positive characteristics (see Goodenough 1970: 54).
8. Discussing the internal differences within the Kandyan village of Terutenne,
Yalman states the low-class pattern as 'no dowry, no formal marriage' (1967:
171). In other groups a ceremony is omitted in marriages between close kin,
which is the expected marriage pattern, because 'structurally nothing happens'
(p. 172); but it is also the case that 'wealthy families prefer elaborate weddings'
(p. 168).
9. The reciprocity may or may not ignore generations. Among the LoDagaa
a man could not use a daughter's cattle to marry a bride for himself, only for
a son. This check on gerontocratic accumulation is not universal but it is
widespread.
10. Wagner 1949, quoted by Mair 1953: 52.
11. For the LoDagaa situation, see Goody 1956: 50.
12. See Gluckman 1950, 1971; Goody and Buckley 1973.
13. For the basic material on the Lobedu, see Krige 1943 and 1964; for an
analysis using the perspective of affinal exchange between unilineal descent groups

52

see Leach 1951, reprinted 1961, following the approach of Fortune (1933) and Lévi-Strauss (1949). For an approach similar to the one adopted here, see Yalman's discussion of bilateral cross-cousin marriage (1967).

14. I do not know of any specific references to preferences for an equal distribution of the sexes in Africa, even though it is implicit in the system. But M. Ruel tells me that the ideal among the Kuria of East Africa is for an alternation of this kind.

15. A Lobedu father can use his daughters' bridewealth to marry himself a wife, subject to his over-riding responsibility to provide his son with a bride (Krige 1964: 163).

16. For China, see Freedman 1966. For a general discussion, see Lorimer 1954.

17. See Ardener 1962.

18. Krige notes that migrant labour constitutes an alternative method by which a Lobedu can raise money for bridewealth payments (1964: 162).

19. Boserup also discusses the difference between 'male' towns and 'female' towns (1970: 99), the former being typical of Africa and India, the latter of Europe and the Americas.

20. Goody, *Domestic Groups*, 1973a.

21. An alternative is to import women as apparently happened among the Yakö (Charles and Forde 1938). Slave-raiding may lead to a similar imbalance (Brain 1972: 145; also Ede Dampierre on the Nzakara).

22. For the distinction, see Evans-Pritchard 1951, p. 112.

23. I mean in terms of marriage payments. Of course, she depends upon them for food and general support.

24. Writing of marriage in the New Guinea Highlands, Meggitt notes that throughout 'marriage payments are large — usually too much for an individual groom or a guardian of a bride to acquire single-handed' (1969: 6).

25. For an elaboration of this point, see my paper 'Class and marriage in Africa and Eurasia', *Am. J. Sociology* (1971) 76: 585-603.

26. See Appendix 1.

27. T. Tentori and P. Guidicini, *Borgo, Quattiere, Città*, Milan, 1972, p. 93.

28. For much of my information on African marriage, I have relied on Radcliffe-Brown's introduction (1950) and also on Mair's valuable survey (1953).

29. I have not used sampling procedures but have instead preferred to examine all the material listed in this source.

30. Table 3 is discussed more fully in Appendix 2, where there is a more extended analysis of the distribution of marriage transactions.

31. Farms were larger in the less densely populated areas inhabited by the Dagarti (Dagaba).

32. See my paper, 'Strategies of heirship', *Comparative Studies in Society and History* (1973b) 15: 3-20.

33. See for example Driver and Miles (1952) on the Babylonian codes.

34. See the material on the Ijaw (e.g. Williamson 1962, Jones 1963) and the Nyamwezi (Abrahams 1967). For a general discussion see Goodenough 1970.

35. The lineages of the Kachin also differ considerably from those reported for Africa, but in a different way. Elder sons frequently move off, leaving the younger to stay with the senior generation. As a result groups of people on the ground consist of lines of younger sons linked by a genealogy of minimal span; it is a narrow line of men, as is shown in many of the diagrams in Leach's account, *The Political Systems of Highland Burma* (e.g. p. 82).

36. Increasing differentiation is taking place even in those societies that have adopted a socialist model for development. See Thoden van Velsen 1970 and Thoden van Velsen and van Hekken 1970.

37. J. Goody, 'Sideways or downwards? Lateral and vertical succession, inheritance and descent in Africa and Eurasia', *Man* (1970), pp. 627-38.

38. Marriage is 'an alliance between two families or bodies of kin' (Radcliffe-Brown 1952: 51). For the Lobedu, the Kriges write: 'the main function of marriage is to create and perpetuate alliances between groups of people' (1943: 142).

39. M. Gluckman, *Custom and Conflict in Africa*, 1956, Oxford; also W.J. Goode, 'The theoretical importance of love', *American Sociological Review* (1959) 24: 38-47.

40. See also the Kriges' comment on the Lobedu: 'Polygyny, reinforced by the segregation of the sexes in everyday life and interests, renders the personal bond between husband and wife much less intimate than is the European ideal. Men are unwilling to spend much time in the company of women, and women prefer the company of their own sex' (1943: 71).

41. See Lin Hui-chen Wang, 1959, *The Traditional Chinese Clan Rules*. Locust Valley, New York, p. 69.

42. In their commentary on recent discussions of kinship, Buchler and Selby take up a remark by Leach and treat complementary filiation as referring only to intra-group differentiation. I find this a fundamental misunderstanding, though one perhaps implied by the use of terms like 'filiation' and 'matrilateral' which unfortunately take a unigenerational view of an inter-generational relationship. I see no alternative explanation for the sentence '*descent theory* . . . represents an internal view of society' (1968: 129). See Goody 1959: 69 for an earlier comment on this danger, which in the case of Buchler and Selby forms part of an attempt to polarize the discussion, perhaps for student consumption.

43. My use of terms for qualifying the kind of claims an individual possesses has been criticized by Schneider and, following him by Buchler and Selby. I would not defend the particular terms used; indeed I could now suggest a better analytic framework. But I believe that the latter's reference to a 'terminological morass' (1968: 133) displays a failure to understand the problem presented by these societies and a desire to find simple short cuts to the analysis of the of the world-wide range of social systems. Clearly not all claims and counter claims have the same standing, as Hohfeld (1923) for one has insisted. We cannot measure these particular differences with exact instruments nor give them numerical values. So we have to employ technical terms to avoid ambiguity, to assist explanation and to get round the barren controversies, such as that carried out by means of the counters, 'descent' and 'affinity'.

44. Schneider writes, 'On one point both alliance theory and descent theory are in agreement. If a segment is to remain discrete, conceptually or concretely, it cannot have overlapping membership with any other segment' (p. 46). But this is simply a matter of definition (see Nadel 1951). I certainly would not define segments in terms of their corporate character (p. 50): I have continually tried to reduce that vague word 'corporate' to more precise concepts, one of which turns around rights to property. If one does pursue this course, one inevitably comes up with a 'sliding scale' which Schneider sees as needing repair.

45. *The Tain*, translated from the Irish by Thomas Kinsella, Dublin, Dolmen Press, 1969, pp. 52-5.

REFERENCES

Aberle, D.F. 1961. 'Matrilineal descent in cross-cultural perspective', in D.M. Schneider and K. Gough (eds.) *Matrilineal Kinship*, University of California Press.

Abrahams, R.G. 1967. *The Peoples of Greater Unyamwezi, Tanzania*, London.

Ardener, E. 1962. *Divorce and Fertility: An African Study*, London.

Barnes, J.A. 1962. African models in the New Guinea Highlands, *Man*, 62: 5-9.

Barth, F. 1959. *Political Leadership Among the Swat Pathans*, London.

Berkner, L.K. 1972. 'The stem family and the developmental cycle of the peasant household: an eighteenth-century Austrian example', *American Historical Review*, 77: 398-418.

Bohannan, L. and P. 1953. *The Tiv of Central Nigeria*, London.

Boserup, E. 1970. *Women's Role in Economic Development*, London.

Brain, R. 1972. *Bangwa Kinship and Marriage*, Cambridge.

Brown, G.G. 1932. 'Bridewealth among the Hehe', *Africa*, 5: 145-7.

Buchler, I.R. and H.A. Selby. 1968. *Kinship and Social Organization*, New York.

Charles, E. and C.D. Forde. 1938. 'Notes on some population data from a Southern Nigerian village', *Soc. Rev.*, 30: 1-16.

Chin, Hu Hsien. 1948. *The Common Descent Group in China and its Functions*, New York.

Driver, G.R. and J.C. Miles. 1952. *The Babylonian Laws* (2 vols.), Oxford.

Dumont, L. 1957. *Hierarchy and Marriage Alliance in South Indian Kinship*, Royal Anthropological Institute Occasional Paper no. 12.

1966. 'Descent or intermarriage? A relational view of Australian section systems', *Southwestern Journal of Anthropology*, 22: 231-50.

1968. 'Marriage alliance', *Encyclopaedia of the Social Sciences*, New York.

Dunn, S.P. and E. 1967. *The Peasants of Central Russia*, New York.

East, R.M. 1939. *Akiga's Story*, London.

Ekvall, R.B. 1968. *Fields on the Hoof*, New York.

Evans-Pritchard, E.E. 1951. *Kinship and Marriage Among the Nuer*, Oxford.

Forde, D. 1951. *Marriage and the Family Among the Yakö in South-eastern Nigeria* (2nd ed.), London.

Fortes, M. 1936. 'Kinship, incest and exogamy in the Northern Territories of the Gold Coast', in L.H.D. Buxton, ed. *Custom is King: Essays Presented to R.R. Marett on his Seventieth Birthday, June 13, 1936*, London.

1937. *Marriage Law Among the Tallensi*, Accra.

1949. *The Web of Kinship among the Tallensi*, London.

Fortune, R.F. 1933. 'A note on some forms of kinship structure', *Oceania*, 4: 1-9.

Freedman, M. 1966. *Chinese Lineage and Society: Fukien and Kwangtung*, London.

Friedl, E. 1962. *Vasilika*, New York.

1963. 'Some aspects of dowry and inheritance in Boetia', in *Mediterranean Countrymen* (ed. J. Pitt-Rivers), The Hague.

Gluckman, M. 1950. 'Kinship and marriage among the Lozi of Northern Rhodesia and the Zulu of Natal', in *African Systems of Kinship and Marriage* (eds. A.R. Radcliffe-Brown and D. Forde), London.

1956. *Custom and Conflict in Africa*, Oxford.

1971. 'Postscript to marriage payments and social structure among the Lozi and Zulu', in *Kinship: Selected Readings* (ed. J. Goody), London.

Goode, W. 1959. 'The theoretical importance of love', *Am. Sociological Rev.*, 24: 38-47. Reprinted R.L. Coser (ed.), *The Family*, New York, 1964.

Goodenough, W.H. 1970. *Description and Comparison in Cultural Anthropology*, Chicago.

Goody, E.N. 1962. 'Conjugal separation and divorce among the Gonja of Northern Ghana', in *Marriage in Tribal Societies* (ed. M. Fortes), Cambridge.

1973. *Contexts of Kinship*, Cambridge.

Goody, J. 1956a. *The Social Organization of the LoWiili*, London.

1956b. 'A comparative approach to incest and adultery', *Brit. J. Soc.*, 7: 286-305.

1957. 'Fields of social control among the LoDagaba', *J.R. Anthrop. Inst.*, 87: 75-104.

1958.'The fission of domestic groups among the LoDagaba', *The Developmental Cycle in Domestic Groups*, Cambridge.

1959. 'The mother's brother and the sister's son in West Africa', *J.R. Anthrop. Inst.*, 89: 61-88. Reprinted in *Comparative Studies in Kinship*, London, 1969.

1962. *Death, Property and the Ancestors*, London.

1969a. '"Normative", "recollected" and "actual" marriage payments among the LoWiili, 1951-1968', *Africa*, 39: 54-61.

1969b. 'Inheritance, property and marriage in Africa and Eurasia', *Sociology*, 3: 55-76.

1969c. 'Marriage policy and incorporation in Northern Ghana', in *Comparative Studies in Kinship*, London.

1970a. 'Sideways or downwards? Lateral and vertical succession, inheritance and descent in Africa and Eurasia', *Man*, 5: 627-38.

1970b. 'Inheritance, social change and the boundary problem', *Échanges et Communications* (eds. J. Pouillon and P. Miranda), The Hague.

1971. 'Class and marriage in Africa and Eurasia', *Am. J. Sociol.*, 76: 585-603.

1972. *Domestic Groups*, Reading, Mass.

1973. 'Strategies of heirship', *Comparative Studies in Society and History*, 15: 3-20.

Goody, J. and E. 1966. 'Cross-cousin marriage in Northern Ghana', *Man*, 1: 343-55.

Goody, J. and J. Buckley. 1973. 'Inheritance and women's labour in Africa', *Africa*, forthcoming.

Grassby, R. 1970. 'English merchant capitalism in the late seventeenth century: the composition of business fortunes', *Past and Present*, 46: 87-107.

Gray, R.F. 1960. 'Sonjo bride-price and the question of African 'wife purchase', *American Anthrop.*, 62: 32-27.

Gulliver, P.H. 1955. *The Family Herds*, London.

Hajnal, J. 1965. 'European marriage patterns in perspective', in *Population in History* (eds. D.V. Glass and D.E.C. Eversley), London.

Harris, M. 1968. *The Rise of Anthropological Theory*, New York.

Hill, P. 1972. *Rural Hausa: A Village and a Setting*, Cambridge.

Hohfeld, W.N. 1923. *Fundamental Legal Conceptions*, New Haven.

Hsiao, Kung-Chuan. 1960. *Rural China: Imperial Control in the Nineteenth century*, Washington.

Jones, G.I. 1963. *The Trading States of the Oil Rivers*, London.

Köbben, J.F. 1967. 'Why exceptions? The logic of cross-cultural analysis', *Current Anthropology*, 8: 3-34.

Krige, E.J. 1964. 'Property, cross-cousin marriage and the family cycle among the Lobedu', in *The Family Estate in Africa* (eds. R.F. Gray and P.H. Gulliver), London.

Krige, E.J. and J.D. 1943. *The Realm of a Rain Queen*, London.

Leach, E.R. 1951. 'The structural implications of matrilateral cross-cousin marriage', *J.R. Anthrop. Inst.*, 81: 23-55.
1954. *Political Systems of Highland Burma*, London.
1957. 'Aspects of bridewealth and marriage stability among the Kachin and the nakher', *Man*, 57, 59.
1961. *Rethinking Anthropology*, London.
Lévi-Strauss, C. 1949. *Les Structures Elémentaires de la Parenté*, Paris.
Lewis, O. 1958. *Village Life in Northern India*, New York.
Loeb, E.M. 1935. *Sumatra: Its History and People*, Vienna.
Lorimer, F. 1954. *Culture and Human Fertility*, UNESCO.
Maine, H. 1891. *Ancient Law*, London.
Mair, L. 1953. *Survey of African Marriage and Family Life* (ed. A. Phillips),London.
Marshall, L. 1959. 'Marriage among the !Kung Bushmen', *Africa*, 29: 335-64.
Martinez-Alier, V. 1972. 'Elopement and seduction in nineteenth century Cuba', *Past and Present*, 55: 91-129.
Maybury-Lewis, D. 1965. 'Prescriptive marriage systems', *Southwestern J. of Anthrop.*, 21: 207-30.
Mayer, P. 1950. 'Gusii bridewealth law and custom', *Rhodes-Livingstone Papers,* no. 18.
Mayne, J.D. 1892. *A Treatise on Hindu Law and Usage* (5th ed.), Madras.
Meggitt, M.J. 1969. Introduction; in R.M. Glasse and M.J. Meggitt (eds.) *Pigs, Pearlshells and Women*, Englewood Cliffs, N.J.
Middleton, R. 1962. 'Brother-sister and father-daughter marriage in Ancient Egypt', *Am. Soc. Rev.*, 27: 603-11.
Murdock, G.P. 1967. 'The ethnographic atlas: a summary', *Ethnology*, 6: 109-236.
Nadel, S.F. 1951. *The Foundations of Social Anthropology*, London.
Peters, E.L. forthcoming. 'Sex differentiation in two Arab communities', in J. Peristiany (ed.), *Masculine and Feminine in the Mediterranean*.
Postan, M.M. 1966. 'Medieval agrarian society in its prime: England' in *Cambridge Economic History of Western Europe*, Vol. I, Cambridge.
Radcliffe-Brown, A.R. 1930. *The Social Organization of Australian Tribes*, Oceania monograph no. 1.
1952. *Structure and Function in Primitive Society*, London.
1950. Introduction to *African Systems of Kinship and Marriage*, London.
Rattray, R.S. 1927. *Religion and Art in Ashanti*, London.
1930. *Akan–Ashanti Folk-tales*, Oxford.
Rehfisch, F. 1960. 'The dynamics of multilineality on the Mambila Plateau', *Africa*, 30: 246-61.
Richards, A.I. 1939. *Land, Labour and Diet in Northern Rhodesia*, London.
Rigby, P. 1969. *Cattle and Kinship among the Gogo*, Ithaca.
Schneider, D.M. 1965. 'Some muddles in the models: or how the system really works', in *The Relevance of Models for Social Anthropology* (ed. M. Banton). A.S.A. Monographs no. 1, London.
Schneider, H.K. 1970. *The Wahi Wanyaturu: Economics in an African Society*, Viking Fund Publications in Anthropology no. 48.
Smith, T.C. 1959. *The Agrarian Origins of Modern Japan*, Stanford.
Steiner, F. 1954. 'Notes on comparative economics', *Brit. J. Sociol.*, 5: 118-29.
Tait, D. 1961. *The Konkomba of Northern Ghana*, London.
Tentori, T. and P. Guidicini. 1972. *Borgo, Quattiere, Città*, Milan.
Thoden van Velzen, H.U.E. 1970. 'Staff, kulaks and peasants', Leiden, Afrika-Studiecentrum (mimeo).

Thoden van Velzen, H.U.E. and van Hekken, P.M. 1970. 'Relative land scarcity and rural inequality', Leiden, Afrika-Studiecentrum (mimeo).

Tylor, E.B. 1889 (1961). 'On a method of investigating the development of institutions; applied to laws of marriage and descent', *J. Anthrop. Inst.*, 18: 245-72. Reprinted F.W. Moore (ed.) *Readings in Cross-cultural Methodology*, New Haven, 1960.

Wagner, G. 1949. *The Bantu of North Kavirondo*, London.

van de Walle, E. 1968. 'Marriage in African censuses and inquiries', in W. Brass et al. *The Demography of Tropical Africa*, Princeton, New Jersey.

Wang, Lin Hui-Chen. 1959. *The Traditional Chinese Clan Rules*, New York.

Williamson, K. 1962. 'Changes in the marriage system of the Okrika Ijo', *Africa*, 32: 53-60.

Wittfogel, K.A. 1957. *Oriental Despotism*, New Haven.

Yalman, N. 1963. 'On the purity of women in the castes of Ceylon and Malabar', *J.R. Anthrop. Inst.*, 93: 25-58.

1967. *Under the Bo Tree*, University of California Press.

DOWRY AND BRIDEWEALTH, AND THE PROPERTY RIGHTS OF WOMEN IN SOUTH ASIA

S.J. TAMBIAH

INTRODUCTION

The canvas on which I attempt to paint is large, for on it I must situate India, Ceylon[*] and Burma. These countries are far from constituting an arbitrarily chosen landscape. Of them India is definitely the dominant member. While India itself has been time and again inundated by the historical streams swirling through its north-western mountain passes, it in turn has fertilized South and Southeast Asia with its men and ideas. Ceylon in the South and Burma in the East are two near points on this extension, and relate to India variously as periphery to centre, as variant to dominant; sometimes as dilution, at other times as transformation of certain Indian themes.

I shall try to relate these societies and confine them to a single field in terms of a fairly delimited theme relating to the property rights of men and women, their transaction at marriage and their transmission between generations. Thus while my brushstrokes may be sweeping, broad, and not too respectful of detail, yet I hope that the few primary colours I use will introduce a compensating sharpness. My linear design is composed of five parts arranged as follows:

Part one serves the theoretical purpose of contrasting the structural patterning and social implications of bridewealth and dowry as two kinds of property transfers accompanying marriage. The ethnographic examples chosen for this exercise are wide-ranging. Then with India and Ceylon in mind as the special areas of interest, two basic features are introduced as anticipation of and orientations to the detailed substantive sections to follow: they are the double transmission of property through males and females, and the complex network of marriage prestations within which the modalities of bridewealth and dowry simultaneously occur in different combinations and weights.

Part two is an account of the traditional Indian legal concepts relating to joint-family property ownership and transmission, adoption, and female property based on the classical legal treatises (*Dharmashastras*), commentaries upon them, and subsequent modifications of the law in British and modern times. This enquiry is directed towards highlighting the continuity in Hindu concepts, and to outlining an overall scheme of ideas concerning family, marriage and inheritance which may use-

---

[*] This paper was written before the recent change of name from Ceylon to Sri Lanka.

59

fully serve as a framework for viewing and interpreting present-day norms and| practices.

Part three takes us to the ethnographic present in India and consists in documenting marriage payments in a number of contemporary Indian communities in North, Central and South India. The pattern underlying marriage payments is revealed, and variations on the basic pattern are brought out; and the degree to which payments match those enshrined in the classical legal traditions is kept in view.

In Part Four we move from India to Ceylon to survey the traditional legal customs and contemporary practices of two groups, the Jaffna Tamils and the Kandyan Sinhalese, in order to see in what manner they relate to those of the mainland.

Finally, in Part Five I delineate the Burmese pattern and try to see how Burmese society, located on the eastern periphery of India, relates dialectically to India which has historically influenced it, and to Kandyan Ceylon with which it shares certain important features.

Although this essay is focused on the theme of marriage payments, of bride-wealth and dowry, of property rights of women *vis-à-vis* men, it is hoped that it will illuminate two other issues as well:

(1)   the nature of the continuities and transformations between the historical past as enshrined in classical legal traditions and the present (of which some of those traditions are also simultaneously a part);

(2)   the proper anthropological relation between the institutions of mainland India, of the island of Ceylon, and of Burma.

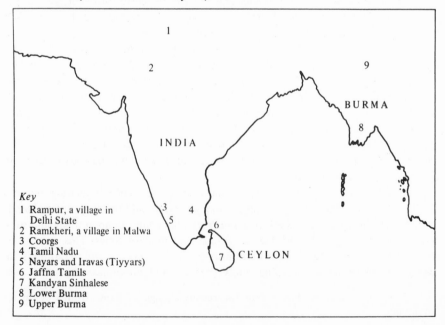

Key
1 Rampur, a village in
   Delhi State
2 Ramkheri, a village in Malwa
3 Coorgs
4 Tamil Nadu
5 Nayars and Iravas (Tiyyars)
6 Jaffna Tamils
7 Kandyan Sinhalese
8 Lower Burma
9 Upper Burma

DOWRY, BRIDEWEALTH AND WOMEN'S PROPERTY RIGHTS

PART ONE

Paradigmatic conceptions of bridewealth and dowry

First of all I do not see the phenomena of bridewealth and dowry as the direct opposite of each other. The most clear cut distinctive features of bridewealth as they appear in marriage are those we frequently encounter in Africa: the bridegroom's family (and kin) transfer to the bride's family (and kin) certain goods in return for which certain rights in the bride are transferred. The goods so transferred, usually referred to as bridewealth, are not normally given to the young couple as capital for setting up their household. In the paradigmatic case the wealth received by the bride's side by virtue of giving away a daughter or sister enables the girl's father or, better still, her brothers to use that wealth to secure wives for themselves. As a result we have the phenomena of the cattle-linked brothers and sisters found for instance among the Thonga (Junod 1927), the Lovedu (Krige 1943) and the Gusii (Mayer 1950), and in the literature on *lobola* (see Lévi-Strauss 1969: 466f.). Figure 1 below gives a simple diagrammatic representation of the passage of bridewealth in one direction and the transfer of women in the other.

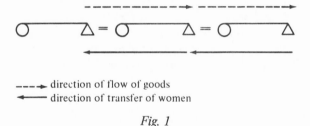

‒‒‒▶ direction of flow of goods
◀‒‒‒ direction of transfer of women

Fig. 1

The paradigm outlined also fits the 'prescriptive' or 'alliance' systems entailing asymmetrical cross-cousin marriage as for instance outlined for Upper Burma and Assam (e.g. Leach 1954, 1961a, Parry 1932, Lévi-Strauss 1969, Lehman 1963). Lévi-Strauss correctly noted that marriage by purchase (i.e. with bridewealth) is compatible with all forms of exchange. He considered that the African marriage pattern associated with *lobola* [which 'as a thread runs through a piece of fabric . . . creates an unlimited series of connections between members of the same group, and between groups' (1969: 467)] was a transformation of the prescriptive system in that the substitution of wife purchase for the right to the cousin 'thus allows generalized exchange to break away from its elementary structure, and favours the creation of a growing number of increasingly supple and extended cycles' (p. 471).

It is important to note that generally, both in Africa and elsewhere, most but not all bridewealth payments figure in the context of unilineal groups (such as lineages). It therefore makes sense to say that bridewealth payments secure the transfer of certain rights in the woman by the women's lineage to the husband's; correspondingly it also makes sense to ask to what extent the woman is incorporated in the husband's lineage and to what extent she retains rights in her natal lineage. We should however note the possibility of deviation from this mode. It is actually possible to have some kind of bridewealth paid in non-unilineal or bilateral or cognatic societies as for example among the Nyamwezi of East Africa (personal communication from R.G. Abrahams), and among the Thai peasant folk of north -east Thailand that I studied. In such instances it may be quite inappropriate to raise the question of the degree of 'incorporation' of the wife in the husband's group, and to discuss the issue of the husband's group securing rights in *genetricem,* and so on, all of which presuppose the existence of unilineal descent groups.

Now the distinctive features of dowry systems are by no means the reverse or mirror image of those of bridewealth systems. Wherever dowry is paid, wealth is not transferred in one direction and women in the other, for both wealth and women travel in the same direction. Perhaps more importantly the one cannot be held to be the reverse of the other, for the reason that men do not receive dowries from their wives' families and thereafter use them to secure husbands for their sisters. Nor do parents themselves recieve the dowry on behalf of their sons and then use it for their own purposes.

It is such vital differences that reveal the essential features of dowry. Dowry is property given to the daughter to take with her into marriage. Technically it is her property and in her own control though the husband usually has rights of management. A husband cannot transfer the dowry to his sister, partly becuase he requires his wife's consent, but more importantly because it is against the spirit of the dowry institution, which is that the dowry given a wife and in her legal possession should form part of the conjugal estate, to be enjoyed by husband and wife and to be transmitted in time to their children.

There is possibly a secondary factor that is worth investigating as a supplement to the argument that a man cannot appropriately use his wife's dowry to effect the marriage of his sister. In countries like India and Ceylon not only do sisters marry at an earlier age than their brothers but also brothers usually cannot marry until their sisters are married unless a large age gap separates them.

There are of course deviations from this norm in both India and Ceylon whereby a daughter-in-law's dowry may in full or part be used by her husband's parents to dowry their own daughters. That these occurances are a violation of the spirit of the system is evidenced by the fact that they are done *sub-rosa*, are not publicized and considered somewhat contemptible.

Perhaps a good demonstration of my paradigmatic notion of dowry is provided by the example of a near violation in modern India. Among contemporary Brahman families in many parts of India a payment which is actually a sort of 'bridegroom price' but euphemistically called *vara-dakshina* (ceremonial payment to the bridegroom) is paid to the bridegroom's family in order to secure their consent to their son's marriage. But of this institution Derrett has given the legal interpretation that 'the presumed intension is not that the father of the bridegroom should keep it and use it for his own purposes (e.g. the dowry for his unmarried daughters), still less that he should profit from the "sale" of his son but that the money should serve as a nucleus of the married couple's estate. Consequently such monies are held by the father as an express trustee for the bridegroom himself.' (1963: 146)

It cannot be denied that the normative and sterotype notion of dowry may in the face of contemporary developments in India and Ceylon show a further shift whereby it may amount to a 'sale' of the son in marriage. For example, J. Stirrat (personal communication) reports that the dowry transactions made by a segment of a fishing community located on the west coast of Ceylon (near Chilaw) resemble 'bridegroom price' in that the dowries are given the bridegrooms who enjoy their sole possession. Furthermore it is the case that, under conditions of modernization and urbanization, parents invest large sums in their sons' education so that they can secure professional or administrative jobs. Parents may therefore feel that these 'investments' on their sons should be 'recouped' at their marriage. Such developments can be expected to manifest themselves fully among the urban middle classes rather than their poorer brethren. This is an instance where modernization may accentuate and distort a traditional arrangement rather than eradicate it!

But let us return to our conception of dowry, which is that it is wealth given with the duaghter at her marriage for the couple to use as the nucleus of their conjugal estate. It is necessary to take note that the concept 'conjugal estate' does not necessarily mean that husband and wife merge their property in a common pool, though income is usually enjoyed in common. Typically each partner retains control over his or her own property; the wife however is usually obliged to secure her husband's consent before she can alienate or dispose of her property; also the husband may enjoy the right to manage his wife's property. Evidence to support the essential separateness of the properties can be found in ethnographic description and legal treatises. Among the Kandyan Sinhalese: on the death of one partner the other did not usually inherit the deceased's property but (enjoying the usufruct) held it in trust for transmission to the common children of the deceased and the surviving spouse. And traditionally in Indian treatises a woman's share in her deceased husband's property was equal to that of each son yet she held her share in the capacity of a trustee with the children's interests in mind. The modalities of the conjugal estate as regards the rights of husband and wife over each other's property may range from the Brahmanical conception (with great emphasis on marriage stability and no divorce possible) at one end to the Kandyan Sinhalèse of Ceylon at the other end (with easy divorce).

Ideally the objective of conjugal estate is best achieved if not only the bride brings to marriage property endowed to her by her parents (and kin) but also the bridegroom himself receives from his parents (and kin) all or part of his inheritance at the same time. This however does not customarily happen in India or Ceylon, though the prospective inheritance of the bridegroom is importantly taken into account when the amount of the dowry is decided (just as today in the towns the occupation of the groom is a decisive criterion in the determination of the size of the dowry).

Thus by and large we can say dowry in India and Ceylon stresses the notion of female property (*stridhanam*) and female rights to property in a way that is not true of bridewealth situations. I want to argue that the institution of dowry can best be understood by keeping in the very forefront of our attention the twin principles that support it: dowry connotes female property or female right to property which is transferred at a woman's marriage as a sort of pre-mortem inheritance; dowry also connotes, in complementary fashion, that property is transferred together with a daughter so that she is enabled to enter into marriage. In other words, and this is the second principle, a daughter and her dowry become vehicles for setting up a relation of affinity between the bride's family and the husband's family – between the bride's parents and her husband's, between the husband and his wife's brothers, and so on. This relationship of affinity is accompanied by gift-giving which persists long after the marriage rite as we shall see in the ethnographic examples thta will be cited later.

A critical difference between bridewealth and dowry shows itself in divorce or at the dissolution of marriage. If the marriage breaks up, the bridewealth paid in whole or part (the actual amount depending on circumstances of which the critical factors are the number of children born the length of marriage in African unilineal societies) is in theory returnable by the wife's family to the husband's family. Even in an extreme case the principle is there in a transformed state; thus the notorious Sonjo (Gray 1960) practise the custom by which the husband can claim compensation equivalent to the returnable bridewealth from his estranged wife's new husband (rather than from her parents). In contrast, in societies where dowry prevails, the wife takes away with her on the dissolution of marriage the dowry property (or that portion which remains) which has always remained legally and formally in her possession.

Bridewealth and dowry have different potentialities in the way they can link up with the politico-economic institutions of the society where they are found. Bridewealth can neatly tie in with polygyny, with concubinage, with men of high status or great wealth 'acquiring' women of low status or in poor circumstances. When such propensities are carried to extremes there is a distinct flavour of 'purchasing' women, of maintaining 'harems' and the like. Dowry on the other hand lends itself to being dressed up as a 'gift' that accompanies the 'gift of the virgin' (*kanya dana*). The conception which is ideologically central in India eminently lends itself to hypergamy whereby a family of lower status but not necessarily of inferior wealth attempts to raise its position and its prestige by contracting a superior marriage for its daughters and sisters.[1] Here there is an exchange of status for wealth, and no doubt the dowry-givers can themselves get their return by demanding higher dowries from their own wife-givers. This last point enables us to modify a previous comparison: in dowry systems while men do not transfer their wives' dowries to their sisters' husbands, men do give away their sisters (or their daughters) with dowry in the full knowledge that they themselves in turn can recoup at their own marriages by receiving dowries from their wives' (or their daughter-in-laws') families.

In India the 'gift of a virgin' accompanied by a dowry appears to be associated with the ideal of monogamy, an ideal that is symbolized in the notion of husband and wife being a united and inseparable pair which reached its ultimate elaboration in the institution of *suttee* (the widow burning herself on her husband's pyre). Blunt (1931: 67) noted that 'In theory polygamy is legal for all Hindus, but in practise it is uncommon: in 1911 there were only 1,009 married women to 1,000 married men.' While Blunt felt that poverty was an impediment to polygamy, he nevertheless noted the interesting fact that 'Hindus of the better class rarely contract a second union in the lifetime of the first wife save in exceptional circumstances, such as the wife's barrenness or her failure to bear a son.' However, it would be incorrect to argue that the dowry system cannot coexist with polygyny. It is simply that where polygyny occurs it will lead to stratification of the women according to the economic assets they bring, and the ranking of their social status into 'primary' and 'secondary' wives and still lower concubines, their issue similarly having differential property and succession rights and degrees of legitimation. Dramatic instances of this stratification were to be found for example in the royal palaces of Southeast Asian monarchs. Thus it is said that the Kings of Burma were by traditional law expected to have eight Queens (*mibuya*) who were differentiated into the Chief Queen, who was 'always a sister, usually a half-sister' and who alone sat with the King on the throne, three other principal queens of the north, west and centre, and four queens of second rank. The king added indefinitely to their number several 'minor ladies' (*myosa*) or concubines who were often received for reasons of state policy as political gifts from the Shan States, from China, etc. (George Scott 1900: 89). Dowries and material presentations came with these queens and concubines. The royal children themselves were correspondingly ranked. Thus in the Siamese courts royal children were ranked into different classes: Chao Fa who were children of the principal queens and therefore eligible to succeed to the throne, Phra Ong Chao (children of minor queens), and other children of lesser princely rank. Father Sangermano reported thus on the inheritance customs in Burma no doubt among the polygynous upper strata: 'The son of the first wife has four parts; the children of the inferior wives or concubines one part; the children had by slaves only half a share. . . ' (Jardine 1893: 227). And one of the versions of the Dhammathat (Burmese traditional collections of customary laws), the Manugye, composed in the mid-eighteenth century, makes the following distinctions between classes of children who have the right to inherit: *orasa*, child born of a legitimate union; *keittima*, a child adopted publicly with a view to inherit; *hethima*, a child by a concubine who does not 'eat out of the same dish' with the husband; and *khettaja*, a child by a female slave of husband or wife, or by a female slave bought from joint property of husband and wife (Maung 1963: 84, 85). This is not a full list, but I have cited four of the six classes of heirs to show their ranking in status, especially the *orasa, hethima* and the *khettaja*.

The Kallars of South India (Dumont 1957a) provide an example at a less elevated, more pedestrian level:[2] they rank their multiple marriages into first and second marriages and concubines. The important distinction for them is that between the principle marriage which is the 'elder' or 'senior' and others which are 'younger' or 'junior', thus indicating that a distinction of age is not separable from a distinction of status.

This kind of ranking and its consequences are quite different from the gradation of wives that operates in polygyny accompanied by bridewealth, in that a ranking into senior and junior wives in this latter situation does not usually carry decisive jural distinctions of status and rights to inheritance and succession as far as the children are concerned. Take for instance the Hausa of Zaria who we are told (M.G. Smith 1965) are allowed under Islamic law four wives and an unlimited number of concubines. The status of concubines approximates that of a wife in many respects and their unions enjoy legal sanction. It is remarkable that – no doubt prompted by Islamic principles – the offspring of concubines are defined as lawful children of their father with rights of inheritance and succession similar to those of his children by marriage. Thus at least one King of Zaria in the last century was the son of a concubine. Furthermore, the child of a slave concubine by her master was free, of the same status as the father, and a member of the latter's descent group. Thus here we see how a configuration of Islamic principles, patriliny and bridewealth transfer, under conditions of polygyny tends to produce siblings who are undifferentiated and equal in relation to their father in spite of the unequal status of wives. I am not advancing the Zaria as a typical case but as a case which illustrates the direction in which polygyny combined with dowry (or strong female property rights) cannot lead.

India developed an unusual and notorious form of polygyny, dubbed 'Kulinism', which we must place in its proper context. Rather than considering it a 'normal' occurrence resulting from collective rules, we should judge it as an 'aberration' that was the inevitable result of hypergamy being practised by the member subcastes of the highest Rarhi Braham caste of Bengal. I refer to the danger of an accumulation of unmarried girls at the very top level or stratum unless some solution was found. Hutton's account (1951: 5, 56) shows the logic of polygyny among the Rarhi Brahmans, who divided into two ranked sub-castes: the Kulins and the Srotriya (and the latter again into three ranked sections). The women of their own Kulin subcaste and of the two superior sections of the Srotriya were available to Kulin men.

The consequences of this situation were clearly seen by Hutton[2] (1951: 53):

> The Rarhi Brahman pattern of hypergamy is clearly liable to lead to an excess of
> unmarried girls in the Kulin subcaste, since their choice of bridegrooms in that
> subcaste is much more limited than is the choice of brides, who may be taken
> from three sub-castes. This superfluity perhaps, together with the duty incum-
> bent on respectable Brahmans of getting their daughters married before puberty,

has led to the practise known as 'Kulinism' by which a man of a Kulin subcaste would often marry a large number of brides, whom he never intended to support, in order to remove from their parents the risk of failure to get their daughters married.

The girls stayed with their families and were visited by their roving husband, and the children were brought up by the mothers – a situation which reminds us of the Nayars. Hutton might also have speculated that while the martial Rajputs who practised hypergamy resorted to female infanticide in the topmost clan to avoid the accumulation of unmarried girls, this violent solution was not open to Brahmans devoted to the practise of non-violence and vegetarianism.

It is very unlikely that marriage with dowry can be associated with hypogamy whereas marriage with bridewealth clearly can. There is no social logic in superior status women who are endowed with property marrying men of both lower socio-political status and inferior economic endownment. But on the contrary, superior status families in societies whose women are not themselves invested with strong property rights can use them as pawns and make them available to men of inferior status (hypogamy), provided these men are prepared to recompense in terms of material wealth (bridewealth) and political support. The prototypes of this are of course the Lakher-and Kachin-type societies (Parry 1932; Leach 1961(a), 1961(c). As a result of this discussion we are able to add this more mundane reason to supplement and add another dimension to the Indian theory of caste marriage which allows *anuloma* (with the hair) hypogamy but not *pratiloma* (against the hair) hypogamy on the grounds of protecting the purity of women and so forth. It would further appear that my conclusions do not contradict those arrived at by Leach after considering the structural implications of cross-cousin marriage:

> If the status between wife givers and wife receivers is equal one cannot predict from first principles which of the two groups will be the senior. . . It seems plausible that a costly brideprice in terms of consumer goods and labour implies that wife givers rank higher than wife receivers. Conversely a dowry expressed in consumer goods implies that wife givers rank lower than wife receivers. . . (1961(c): 102).

Male and female property in India and Ceylon

A major point of orientation in this study is that the Dharmashastras and other classical legal treatises of India distinctly portray the notion of female property (*stridhanam*) as complementary to the more heavily accented notion of male property rights. Scholars have usually stressed the provisions for male co-parcenership in Indian joint-family property, and how this property devolves agnatically. What is lost sight of is that the same texts have a fine regard for female property, some of which, if not all, being transmitted exclusively through females. In Ceylon the equal rights of males and females to *the same categories of property* was traditionally granted and accepted as for example among the Jaffna Tamils and the Kandyan Sinhalese. Thus it would appear that in this part of the world the notion of dowry is *intimately connected with the double transmission of property through both males and females.* In this respect India and Ceylon stand very much in contrast to the majority of unilineal societies in Africa — where although there may exist sex-linked property (e.g. things like baskets, pots, female clothes which pass from mother to daughter) there is no firm or decisive notion of female rights to property corresponding to the agnatically transmitted property.

Ceylon carries the conception of female property rights further than most groups in India. In the classical Hindu pattern which holds for most of India (except some parts of the South) female property is largely confined to movables whereas in Ceylon among the groups mentioned it can include land as well. There is a further possible association here which I shall probe in greater detail later: the dowry in movables in the classical Indian pattern relates logically to virilocal residence and the right of wife-removal (as is usually the case with bridewealth marriage) with deviation to uxorilocal residence allowed only in somewhat extreme circumstances, but in Ceylon the fact that women can themselves inherit *land* or receive it as dowry opens the possibility of a wider and freer occurrence of uxorilocal residence together with virilocal (and neolocal) residence. In my view these circumstances provide the shift and transition to bilateral kinship and ambilocal residence, a view which will be substantiated in the fourth part of this essay.

The Burmese shift is similar to Ceylon's, in that women inherit equally and without prejudice with their brothers all categories of patrimonial property. Although dowry as such is not a developed institution in Burma, the concept of separate properties which spouses may bring to marriage and may inherit subsequent to marriage is, as we shall see, clearly formulated. Together with the property rights go bilateral kinship, ambilocal residence, and a general flexibility in the patterning of kinship.

The configuration of marriage prestations in India

The next major point of orientation may appear at first sight to be not so much a matter of structure as of culture. I have in mind certain preferences associated with dowry and brideprice which in the Indian context are stressed on religious and moral grounds. (However, since possibly the same resonances are found in some parts of China, it could be argued that at a deeper level these ideological features may be seen to be of a structural order associated with female property rights, scale of family, etc.)

Let us begin with the Code of Manu which asserts: 'No father who knows (the law) must take even the smallest gratuity for his daughter; for a man who, through avarice, takes a gratuity, is a seller of his offspring' (III, 51).

Manu's pronouncement is the severe but prestigious Brahmanical formulation which whether they in fact follow it or not, represents the standard of excellence to all Hindus. The Brahmanical evaluation of 'bridewealth' payment is clear: it is tantamount to sale of a daughter for profit and is therefore reprehensible. The recommended act is the 'gift of the virgin daughter' (*kanya dana*).

Now, despite this clear injunction it is well known that Manu recognized 'eight marriage rites used by the four castes [varna] which partly secure benefits and partly produce evil both in this life and after death', namely Brahma, Daiva, Arsha, Pragapatya, Asura, Gandharva, Rakshasa, and Paisaca (Manu III, 21; 34). These eight forms[4] which are ranked cover in our terms marriage with dowry, marriage with bridewealth, free romantic union, forcible abduction, and seduction.

The first four forms – the Brahma, Daiva, Arsha and Pragapatya – are all grouped together as comprising 'gift of a daughter' but with certain differences as regards associated prestations. The Brahma and Daiva forms specify the gift of a daughter after decking her with costly garments and ornaments and jewels (i.e. dowry in valuables). The Arsha form does not include material gifts accompanying the bride but states that the father of the bride receives 'a cow and a bull or two pairs' from the bridegroom and that this is not accounted as sale of the daughter. The Pragapatya form is a gift of a girl without any mention of material transfer either way.

The marriage rite that is clearly posed as the opposite of the gift of the virgin is the Asura form: 'When (the bridegroom) receives a maiden, after having given as much wealth as he can afford, to the kinsmen and to the bride herself, according to his own will, that is the Asura rite' (Manu, III, 31).

It should be further noted that Manu allowed, among others, both the gift and brideprice type of marriage to Brahmans in that order, and declared only the brideprice type (and other inferior forms) as lawful for the other status orders – the Kshatriyas (warriors and rulers), Vaisyas (merchants and husbandmen) and Shudras (unfree servants) – while denying them the superior gift type. Thus one may say that the classical literature is cognizant of both dowry and brideprice within the same society, but evaluates marriage with dowry (connoting the gift par excellence) as the more acceptable and prestigious form for the high born. One traditional *shastric* authority – Baudhayana – having declared that 'he who gives his daughter by sale sells his merit', recommended Asura (and Paisaca) marriage to Vaisyas and Shudras for they 'do not keep their wives under restraints, they having to do the work of ploughing and waiting upon other varnas' (Kane 1941: 505, 522). One may note here the acuteness of the economic observation in the religio-juridical literature!

What relevance has all this for contemporary India? Two features need to be stressed. Firstly although marriage with dowry is the prestigious form in India today, marriage with brideprice is also found to co-exist in many parts. But their incidence tends to correlate with hierarchical status. As Karve (1953: 132) puts it: All over India there is the custom of giving brideprice among the poorer castes and of receiving dowry among the higher castes.' Earlier still Blunt (1931: 70-1) remarked on this distribution of brideprice and dowry and gave us an enumeration of castes practising one or the other.[5] But India can provide startling exceptions even among the highest. Such an example is provided by the Kashmir Brahmans among whom three differentially evaluated marriage types co-exist. In microcosm they illustrate the essence of the Indian situation both classical and contemporary.

The Kashmiri Pandit (Bhatta) caste, described by Madan (1965), is as may be expected patrilineal, and is divided into two sub-castes (*gor* or *karkun*) which are roughly priestly versus secular. Madan portrays the marriage customs as follows:

> There are three types of marriage among the Pandits. The ideal is represented by marriage with a 'dowry' (ornaments and clothes for the bride, domestic utensils and other gifts in cash and kind for her relatives-in-law). The Pandits say that such a marriage is unsullied by any elements of bargining on either side. But the incidence of reciprocal marriages, involving the exchange of women and gifts, gives them considerable importance for they are the commonest type of marriage. [The author means here the simultaneous exchange of women (e.g. exchange marriage between two pairs of brothers and sisters) and gifts so that equivalence and symmetry are achieved.] The third type of marriage involves payments in cash and/or kind by the girl-receiving *chulah* to the girl-giving *chulah*. These payments may be intended to provide for the marriage expenses or part thereof, or may be a bride price in the literal sense of the term (p. 114).

The incidence of the three types of marriage in a sample of 148 marriages was 38% for the prestigious dowry type, 45% for the symmetrical exchange type, and only 17% for the brideprice type.

Let us exclude from further discussions the reciprocal form which like brideprice marriage goes counter to Brahmanical values. 'The Pandits agree' says Madan, 'that reciprocal marriages offend against the basic notion of marriage being the ritual gift of a daughter to her chosen husband'. Let us rather contrast the social significance of the dowry and brideprice forms of marriage for the Pandits. We are told that marriages involving payments (in cash or kind) to the girl's household by her future husband are not only frequent but *concealed*, for they are deemed to be immoral and to connote sale of the child. There are apparently special factors that account for brideprice marriage: 'A man who buys himself a wife is generally a widower, or a bachelor of advanced age, who has given up all hopes of marriage by the usual means.' On the other side 'It is extreme poverty and the presence of several nubile daughters in the household which compel it to resort to this kind of marriage.' (p. 118).

As compared with the *sub rosa* nature of brideprice marriage, the giving of dowry (with the associated female rights to property) is publicly attested. A women married patrivirilocally retains the right periodically to visit and receive gifts from her natal household. More importantly, she receives a marriage portion known as *stridhan* ('woman's wealth') which she takes with her to her new home. It consists of movable and personal possessions such as clothes, ornaments, domestic utensils, bedding, etc. Exceptionally, the rich parents of a girl may even give her cattle and land. The *stridhan* is, jurally speaking, a woman's exclusive property, and may be regarded as a substitute for the right of inheritance. Her husband and relatives-in-law acquire no interest therein, and her daughters are expected to inherit it after her death.[6] This contemporary 'legal' position concerning the dowry which a woman takes with her into marriage is perfectly consonant with the tenets stated in the classical legal treatises. It is therefore time to look back into the past to investigate to what degree the present situation can be understood in terms of the classical doctrine.

But before we do so one last point has to be made. It is not only that in India the spectrum of marriage from dowry to brideprice is found, but also that every marriage involves multiple transactions and payments, some unilateral and others reciprocal, so that it would be said that the modalities of bridewealth and dowry coexist in the same series with one or the other type of transaction gaining dominance and outshining the other in specific situations. Or to put it differently: marriage in Hindu India typically involves prestations that go back and forth; in this array we might see in relief the outlines of transactions which we call brideprice and dowry, with one or the other coming to the fore in particular contexts. But by and large in India it is dowry that is publicly and ideologically and morally validated, and brideprice that is considered the 'degraded' and immoral form, and is therefore always under pressure to be converted back into dowry. I mean that wherever brideprice is given there is pressure on the bride's parents to redirect it in part or full as dowry accompanying the bride to form the nucleus of her conjugal estate. We shall observe this process at work both in the classical legal texts and in contemporary transactions.

It is convenient here to introduce a comparative issue concerning the similarities between India and China. I previously hinted that what looked like Indian cultural values concerning the 'gift' of a woman in marriage, female rights to property etc., may find their resonances in China, thereby rendering them not unique to India. The following structural similarities between the Fukien and Kwantung areas of China (as discussed by Freedman 1966) and India in respect of the joint family and marriage customs certainly provide food for thought, especially as they present a marked contrast to most of Africa.

(1) Every Chinese male is a coparcener to the joint-family property at birth (as in the Indian Mitakshara system), but comes into his inheritance only with his father's death (as in the Indian Dayabhaga system).

(2) Despite the emphasis on patrivirilocal marriage, a fair number of uxorilocal marriages resulting in resident sons-in-law occur for the same reasons as in India.

(3) In China both brideprice and dowry occur together: a brideprice is received for a woman who also takes a dowry (of movables) with her, a pattern reminiscent of India. Freedman says that a poor woman may be equipped with a few items of personal property (her trousseau), *some or*

71

all of which may have been paid for out of the brideprice received for her.
'The daughter of a rich family can expect to be sent off with a substantial
dowry in the form of jewellery and cash, in addition to the bedroom fur-
nishings that form a standard part of the bride's trousseau' (Freedman
1966: 55).

(4)   A Chinese woman's property is pooled with her husband's to form a
conjugal estate within the larger joint family – an arrangement similar to
much of Indian practice.

(5)   Divorce with primary marriage is not sanctioned and is practically non-
existent in Fukien and Kwantung; this again conforms with Brahmanical
and high caste ideas.

There is, however, one difference of stress between my view of the Indian system and Freedman's view of the Chinese. I have previously stated that the dowry
system in India rests on two complementary principles – on the one hand dowry
reflects female rights to (movable and not patrimonial) property as enshrined in the
concept of *stridhanam*, and on the other it is a superb pawn to use in the formation
of marriage alliance and in pursuing the status game of hypergamy. Freedman puts
a unilateral stress on the significance of dowry. He says that while the endowment
of the bride by her rich family represents for the men in it 'a considerable economic sacrifice' yet 'They make it not because the girl has any specific economic
claims on them (she is not a member of the property-owning unit) but because
their own status is at stake; a bride-giving family must, in order to assert itself
against the family to which it has lost a woman, send her off in the greatest manner
they can afford. And it is no accident, therefore, that dowry and trousseau are put
on open display; they are not private benefactions to the girl but a public demonstration of the means and standing of her natal family' (1966: 55). In India as we
have seen the use of dowry to express a status relation between wife-giver and taker
does not contradict but meshes with the notion of female property rights.

PART TWO

The traditional Indian legal concepts

My prime interest in the traditional Indian legal literature is to sort out the rights of males and females to property. I have already made the point that most students concentrate on the rules of male co-parcenership in the Hindu joint family property and the transmission of this property through agnates, without bringing to our attention the complementary, though perhaps less stressed, conceptions of female succession to property and of female property as a distinct category. In the ensuing examination the searchlight will be focused particularly on female rights because they are directly linked to the presence or absence of dowry, at least in India and Ceylon.

Since specialist treatises exist on the sources and complex diverse details of Hindu Law (e.g. Mayne 1883, Kane 1930-62, Derrett 1963), I shall only attempt an elucidation of the general features relevant to the interests of this essay. The classical Indian legal treatises are called Dharmashastras meaning 'science of righteousness'. Derrett (1963: 2) describes this literature as 'no less character- istically jurisprudential than their coevals, the Roman and the Jewish law'. Hindu law was already some two thousand years old when the British undertook to ad- minister it to the Indians in the mid-eighteenth century. The *Dharmashastras* are said to be based on the *Smritis*, that which the sages 'remembered' after the 'self-existent' had explained the science of righteousness to them (although their gen- ealogy is claimed to extend still further to the antecedent Vedas, that which was 'heard' from the 'self-existent'). All *smritis* are attributed to sages, many of whom appear as the mythical ancestors of the Brahmanical *gotras*; the principal *smritis* written either in verse or in mixed verse and prose are attributed to famous sages such as Manu, Narada, Brihaspati, Katyayana, and Yajnavalkya. It would appear that most of these works did not attain their present shape earlier than about 200 B.C. or later than A.D. 200 (Derrett *ibid*).

But Hindu legal literature has been continuous, cumulative and expanding. Fresh additions were made and commentaries composed from the fourth to the ninth centuries and even later. Faced with conflicting viewpoints in the *smritis* them- selves or wishing to eliminate and alter or edit portions inconsistent with the taste or morality of subsequent times, later jurists composed digests and fathered them upon the acient sages or the deities themselves. However, this rich proliferation naturally also led to diversity and to the formation of rival schools of traditional law. As Derrett puts it: 'The view that everything could be right, and yet that some ways were more right than others, led to the proliferation of compositions on the subject of righteousness; and the comparison, explanation, and digesting of such texts, which were at first oral, became a science.' Thus variant schools of law, differing on particulars, came to hold sway in different parts of India.

The British Judges in India began to have access to this traditional law around the 1770s and translations were progressively made, but until 1864 the Hindu law was administered by the courts with the help of Brahman pandits; Derrett (1961) discusses the implications of this practice. The British applied traditional law in all suits regarding inheritance, marriage, joint family, caste, and other religious institutions and usages. In doing so, modifications and amendments were made over time to suit contemporary conditions and needs, and a body of law (in some respects influenced by the rules of English law) developed in the nineteenth century which we may recognize as Anglo-Hindu law.

In more recent times, since the gaining of Independence, the period of modern Hindu law has been ushered in. This law, while organically connected with the past has experienced still more changes in matters regarding marriage and succession (e.g. The Hindu Marriage Act of 1955, The Hindu Succession Act of 1956, The Hindu Adoptions and Maintenance Act of 1956, The Dowry Prohibition Act of 1961). These new statutes, intended to have countrywide application, allow in limited ways for the claims of deviant 'custom' (as for example the rules relating to the *taravad* ot *illatom* adoption in the South).

In this essay I am not concerned with these recent changes in modern Hindu law. Although on paper some of the recent codes seem to have initiated dramatic changes in matters concerning dowry, inheritance to joint-family property etc., judged by contemporary rural ethnography, traditional custom by and large appears to prevail — and so does the legal maxim that 'what ought not to have been done may well be legally binding when done'. I am thus more concerned to disentangle the strong thread of continuity that runs from the past to the present. Despite the growth of modifications over time and dialectal regional variations over space, the main architectural principles of the Indian edifice of family and marriage appear to have remained remarkably intact. The proof of this is offered later by contemporary ethnography itself.

I should like to remind the reader that there was and is no single body of traditional Hindu law. The following are the main variant schools holding sway over Hindu society in different parts of India. The major bifurcation is between the dominant Mitakshara law (which was written about A.D. 1125 in the Deccan and is attributed to Vijnaneshvara) and the Dayabhaga founded by Jimutvahana and his followers whose provenance is Bengal and Assam. The main stream and the supreme authority, the Mitakshara School, itself branches into some four sub-schools (which supplement or modify some of its doctrines), namely the Benares School (confined to Maharashtra), the Mithila School, the Bombay School, and the Dravida or Madras School which developed between the 13th to 16th centuries.[7] It is sufficient for my purpose, which consists in mapping the main principles, to concentrate primarily on the Mitakshara system and to indicate differences whereever necessary or appropriate.

DOWRY, BRIDEWEALTH AND WOMEN'S PROPERTY RIGHTS

The joint family and the property rights of the coparcener

There is some confusion in the discussions on the Indian joint family which stems from the fact that the social demarcation of the joint family as a collection of kin or families maintaining a 'common household' (e.g. residence and common cooking) is not congruent with the legal definition of the Indian joint family as a collection or group of coparceners in landed property. (See Shah 1964; also Kolenda 1968).

The two conceptions cannot dovetail because the anthropologist or sociologist wishes to place the joint family in a series which includes. nuclear family, stem family, and kinds of extended or grand families (to which the Indian form is sought to be assimilated), whereas the notion of joint family in a classical *emic* sense (formulated for example in traditional Mitakshara law) as a group of coparceners can minimally include two persons (father and son or two brothers, who need not compose a 'family') and maximally some four generations of males who have joint rights to corporate property but need not be co-resident. Thus the 'legal' concept of 'joint family' need not coincide with the sociological conception in terms of a collection of co-resident families enjoying some sort of common household economy.[8]

I shall be unorthodox and insist — against modern social/sociological definitions of the joint family — that the core of the Indian conception of joint family, as first embedded in the classical Dharmashastric law texts, then later interpreted by modern Hindu law, focuses on *relations between persons in terms of their interests in property*, and that this should also be in the forefront of our sociological discussion. (Incidentally Sir Henry Maine keenly appreciated this fact.) Let us see how the other illustrious Mayne defines the joint family (Mayne 1883: 230):

> When we speak of a Hindu joint family as constituting a coparcenary, we refer not to the entire number of persons who can trace from a common ancestor, and among whom no partition has ever taken place; we include only those persons who, by virtue of relationship, have the right to enjoy and hold the joint property, to restrain the acts of each other in respect of it, to burden it with their debts, and at their pleasure to enforce its partition. Outside this body there is a fringe of persons who possess inferior rights such as that of maintenance, or who may, under certain contingencies, hope to enter the coparcenary.

Now it is important for our purposes to realize that in effect the Hindu joint family consists of a collection of persons who have interests in a common estate, but that the membership is highly differentiated in terms of the rights enjoyed. Although the backbone consists of the co-parceners, there are other subordinate or fringe members who have rights of ownership in the estate. As Mayne puts it the whole body of an undivided Hindu family 'consisting of males and females, constitutes a sort of corporation, some of the members of which are co-parceners, this is, persons who on partition will be entitled to a share, while others are only entitled to maintenance'. (p. 230):[9] We should note that the notion of

75

maintenance is wider than we are accustomed to think.

Thus the following persons are normally considered to be the members of a joint family (whose co-parceners have not yet partitioned): (i) the male co-parceners, (ii) their mothers and step-mothers, (iii) their wives, (iv) their unmarried daughters, (v) the widows and unmarried daughters of co-parceners who died in a state of jointness, (vi) married daughters whose husbands by custom take up permanent residence in the home of their parents-in-law (e.g. *gharjamai* son-in-law and other uxorilocal forms of marriage).

Now the above listing makes a division between co-parceners (who in this instance are taken to consist of male agnates who own the joint property) and other members of the joint family who have other rights in the property. The latter category of persons is primarily female in their capacity either as *incoming wives* or as *daughters* of the joint family. As such these female members are *entitled* to maintenance which includes residence, food, clothing, medical attention, education, etc. The incoming wives have rights of maintenance even when reduced to widowhood, and co-parceners cannot defeat this right; furthermore this right cannot be denied on the grounds that a woman may possess her separate *stridhanam* property.

It is the daughters of the joint family that particularly interest us, for in addition to the right of maintenance until their marriage, they are entitled to their marriage expenses and to dowries (where these are customary) which they take away with them.

Now we can briefly discuss the notion of *co-parcenary*. We have already seen that the ownership rights of the co-parceners are circumscribed by the maintenance rights and other rights of incoming wives and daughters. The distinctive features of co-parcenership are that it is only co-parceners who can alienate and partition the property, and it is they who are the principal sharers at partition. Membership of the co-parcenary is confined to the male descendants in the male line from a common living ancestor up to four degrees inclusive. Membership in the co-parcenary is acquired by legitimate birth or by valid adoption. A co-parcener loses his membership in the joint family by partitioning or by being given away in adoption to a non-member. Co-parceners enjoy the benefit of survivorship (i.e. inherit the property of deceased co-parceners); this is often advanced as a reason why co-parceners prolong their membership and postpone partition. Because of the right of survivorship a co-parcener's share is *not* fixed but shifts with births and deaths in the joint family.[10]

There are of course regional variations within India as regards the rights of co-parceners, e.g. while normally a co-parcener cannot alienate his undivided interest he can do so in South India; in Maharashtra and Gujarat a son may not sever from his father against the father's will when the father himself is joint with his own ascendant or collaterals. But, rather than go into intricacies, I shall now summarize what I consider to be the major rules under the Mitakshara system.

Rule 1. In an undivided joint family each member transmits to his male issue his own share in the joint property; such issue take *per capita inter se*, but *per stirpes* regards the issue of other members (Kane Vol. III, 1946: 569).

Rule 2. Who are the members who become co-parceners and take an interest in the property by birth? They are the three generations next to the owner in unbroken male descent, i.e. a man, his living sons, grandsons and great-grandsons constitute a single co-parcenary with himself.[11] (Note: more junior descendants are excluded unless the apical ancestor dies). As each fresh member takes a share, his descendants to the third generation below him take an interest in that share.

Thus while the four generation group is theoretically the *maximum* group, the rule also ensures that when a fifth generation is born partition must inevitably take place if its rights to property are to be ensured. This inevitability of partition because the corporation has only a four generation depth has not usually been recognized as an important structural principle built into the constitution of the joint family.

Rule 3. Self-acquisition, such as gains accuring from learning and valour, constitutes joint property if the learning had been imparted at the expense of the joint family or if the warrior had used his father's sword. But whatever is acquired by a co-parcener without obligation to his father's estate (e.g. as a gift from a friend or a gift received at his nuptials) is immune to the claims of other co-parceners.

Rule 4. Any co-parcener may sue for partition, and every co-parcener is entitled to a share upon partition. But some persons are entitled to a share upon partition who cannot sue for it themselves. While in Bengal under the Dayabhaga system a son has no right to demand partition during the lifetime of the father, the Mitakshara explicitly asserts the son's right to partition even against the father's wish. (Kane Vol. III, 1946: 569-70). (Public opinion has always been opposed to the son's exercising this right but, by the late 19th century, it was settled in the courts that the son had the right to partition even against the wishes of the father.)

This Mitakshara rule that 'the son has an absolute right of partition of ancestral property during the father's lifetime even against the father's wish' (Kane) is open to doubts as regards its interpretation. One such doubt for instance is whether the grandson can or cannot demand a share in the grandfather's wealth if the father is himself joint with his own father; or if the grandson has partition rights, can he exercise them only if the father consents.

According to Kane (1946: 570) the Mitakshara emphatically combats these doubts and upholds the grandson's right to partition since it is axiomatic that father and son have ownership rights in the grandfather's property. It would thus seem that Mayne was in error when he propounded that a succeeding generation cannot usually demand partition from their father, when this father himself has not divided from his own father.[12]

Female inheritance, adoption and the uxorilocal son-in-law
The following quotation from Devala and Parsara (also confirmed by the Mitakshara) could be taken as the text of this section: 'To unmarried daughters a nuptial portion must be given out of the estate of the father; and his own daughter, lawfully

begotten, shall take, like a son, the estate of him who leaves no male issue'. Another ancient legal writer, Parsara, enlarges the above rule as follows: 'The unmarried daughter shall take the inheritance of the deceased, who left no male issue, and on failure of her, the married daughter.' (Mayne 1883: 501.)

I have already referred in the previous section to a woman's right to a nuptial portion: this will be more fully discussed in the succeeding section which is devoted to *stridhanam* (female property).

Here we are concerned with a woman's right under certain circumstances to be a direct heir or indirectly through her issue to produce heirs to property that is traditionally considered joint-family property. This issue arises in relation to the question: who succeeds to property when a man has no male issue to be his heirs?

Before answering this question, let me first summarize the implications of our previous examination of Mitakshara law concerning rights over joint property.

The joint family consists of a core of male co-parceners and a fringe of female members composed of incoming wives and daughters of the house. Both kinds of women have rights of maintenance, the incoming wives even as widows and the daughters until marriage. A daughter enjoys under the aspect of maintenance also the right to marriage expenses and a dowry of movable property. This is part of the notion of *stridhanam*.

Ideally the Mitakshara envisages a four generation agnatic male exclusive corporation of co-parceners in a joint estate; while they remain a co-parcenary the property devolves on other mlaes by survivorship and reversion, and females, both widows and daughters are rigorously exclued.

But we also saw that the four generation rule of co-parcenary rights and the right of partition granted members did produce the fission of the ideal corporation. When partition takes place the co-parceners become independent owners and cannot any more exercise survivorship rights in respect of one another. The property must descend according to ordinary rules of inheritance – to the issue of these separate owners.

Although sons infrequently demanded partition from their living fathers, the partition of property was frequent when the co-parceners were siblings alone. With such partitions, independent nuclear families were established and the cycle began again.

My thesis is that in India this frequent separation of and partition between siblings displaced the emphasis, when a co-parcener had no male issue, away from survivorship and reversion (i.e. from inheritance by colleterals) and on to inheritance by lineal descendants, even by females directly or indirectly. It is this tendency that culminates in the institutions of the appointed daughter, the uxorilocal son-in-law and adoption, which guard against property developing on collaterals in preference to lineals. Thus we may say that where India in fact emphasizes the lineal before the collateral heir, and stresses partition, adoption, inheritance through the appointed daughter or daughter's son, etc., West Africa (the non-Islamic part) emphasizes the rules of male survivorship and reversion to male collaterals, women being rigorously excluded as heirs.

Consider as an example the following order of distribution under traditional *Mitakshara Law* as modified by the *Mayukha* sub-school (*Vyavaharamayukha*) (see Derrett 388-90). I present only the first few classes in the list:

Son, predeceased son's son, predeceased son's predeceased
    son's son, widow: all sharing equally
Daughter
Daughter's son
Mother
Father
Full brother
Half-brother
Brother's son of the full blood
Brother's son of the half blood
Father's mother
Son's son's son's son
Son's son's son's son's son
Son's son's son's son's son's son, etc.

Now this list clearly shows – if we ignore the widow for the moment – that a male descendant down to the great-grandson always had first preference (the four generational rule), but thereafter a daughter and failing her a daughter's son were preferred before parents, and siblings and other collaterals. It is this system of preference that I call the rule of *lineal before collateral heir*.

We see that the widow has a special position in traditional law – her right stems from the fact of membership in the deceased husband's family. The widow's right however is limited and temporary; while she inherits as an heir she could not at her death transmit to her heirs, only to the heirs of her deceased husband. She had only a limited estate and kept the property until the true heir was able to take control of it.

The daughter's right; the 'appointed daughter'; the daughter's son. The *putrika-putra*, 'the daughter treated as a son' or to give another construction 'the son of an appointed daughter', is a justly famous concept in traditional Hindu law, which highlights the fact that in the absence of male issue the daughter becomes the link in the chain of continuity.

In the case of the appointed daughter the classical formulation was that she was appointed in order that she might raise a son for her sonless father. The daughter so appointed resided uxorilocally with her father's family, and her son was considered the son of her father (and not her husband's). Thus an heir was produced to continue the line. The logic of the operation was something like this according to some commentators. The appointed daughter herself was considered equivalent to a son, and therefore her son was equivalent to a grandson. As the merits of a son and grandson are equal (e.g. in offerings made to ancestors) the latter ranked as a son.

(See Manu IX: 127-36; Vasishta XVII: 12; Mayne 1883: 543).

This practice of the appointment of a daughter to raise up an heir for her father in time became obsolete, but concurrently the daughter's own claims as a consanguine were asserted (and through her, as a later heir, her son who ranked next to her). *The Mitakshara* formulated the legitimacy of a daughter as an heir on the basis of filiation alone thus: 'As a son, so does the daughter of a man proceed from his several limbs. How then should any other person take her father's wealth?'

These developments in the inheritance customs under the Mitakshara system are summed up thus by Derrett: '*Sapindas* were originally exclusively agnates, but the daughter's son was intruded as, first, a substitute son and later an heir in his own right but after all daughters, and the daughter herself gradually won a right to succession after the widow.' Derrett then spells out the further changes during British times: 'The widow's right to compete on an equal footing with sons or other male issue was introduced in British India by the Hindu Women's Rights to Property Act 1937. . . The widowed daughter-in-law, and the widow of a predeceased son of a predeceased son, likewise benefited along with the widow, sharing as if they had been their respective husbands in case the latter left no male issue, but as the latter's son if male issue were left.' (1963: 381-2).

Adoption

Mayne, who had an antipathy to the religious explanation of adoption (which said that in the absence of male issue a man needed to adopt a son who would make the necessary funeral and other offerings to the dead), made the remark – which has a great deal of truth in it – 'Paupers have souls to be saved, but they are not in the habit of adopting . . . ' (p. 88). It is not necessary to consider the religious and property arguments as being mutually exclusive for they are both expressions of a deeper underlying feature of the Hindu family: the accent on the independent and separate existence of each brother, although brothers form the core of the lineage.

The 'adopted son' appeared low on the list of sons recognized in the early literature: of the fourteen authorities cited by Mayne only five (including Manu) place the *adopted* son, *dattaka*, who is differentiated from the natural son *aurasa* (born of the body), among the first six. Kane too remarks that it is not in the *sutras* or *smrtis* (or even the medieval Mitakshara) but in works of the seventeenth century and later that the *dattaka* receives an elaborate treatment.

The reasons for this were three. A man who had a son, grandson or great-grandson actually alive was precluded from adopting because any of these persons was his immediate heir and was capable of performing his funeral rites with full efficacy.

Secondly, even if there were no such male issue, yet for religious purposes the son of the appointed daughter was equal in efficacy to the natural son.

Thirdly, where any of several brothers had a son he was considered to be the son of all the brothers. As one commentator (Kulluka Bhatta) put it: 'So that if such nephew would be the heir, the uncles have no power to adopt a son.' This reminds one of the typical situations in the patrilineal societies of West Africa, where reversion of property is to other male collaterals.

If these were the earlier circumstances, then how and why did adoption become subsequently an important institution? Although a brother's son might procure for his uncle the required spiritual blessings, still only an adopted son can make possible the celebration of name and the due perpetuation of the deceased's line. Furthermore, it would appear that as partition of property and self-acquired wealth became more common, adoption also came to the fore to take care of transmission of property where a man had no male issue.

There is no doubt that the Sanskritic writers[13] emphasized the religious motives in adoption. For instance Baudhayana says that the adopter receives the child with the words: 'I take thee for the fulfilment of religious duties. I take thee to continue the line of my ancestors.' In commenting upon this, Mayne (1883) argued that 'the spititual theory is not the sole object of an adoption, even upon Brahmanical principles' and that 'it can only be applied with the greatest possible caution in the case of non-Aryan tribes, or such as dissent from Orthodox Hinduism' (p. 93).

Because adoption was so closely meshed with the performance of religious duties to ancestors and with the transmission of joint-family property rights, it had in India everything to do with male children and little to do with female children Adoption was of two types: the *dattaka* form, which is the true form that applies to the adoption of a child, and the less frequent *kritima* form which relates to the adoption of adults. 'Adoption is the taking by an adult of a child into a relationship with himself or herself like that of legitimate parent and child' (Derrett 1963: 92).[14]

One rule concerning adoption has an interesting judicial history. It is the rule that requires the adopted boy to be a *putracchayavaha* — one who bears a resemblance to or is a 'reflection of a natural (*aurasa*) son'. Some interpreters invoked the obsolete *niyoga*[15] custom that a brother's son or a *sapinda's* son or a *sagotra's* son could be adopted because the adopter could have fathered the boy in question by the practice of *niyoga* on the wives of the men in question. Others said that the same rule prevented the adoption of a daughter's son and a sister's son because the adopter could not marry the daughter or the sister or procreate through them.

By a curious misunderstanding of the text the Anglo-Indian courts manned by British judges evolved the interpretation that no one could be adopted whose mother the adopter could not have married in her maiden state. This became the law in all the Presidencies except Bombay (Kane 1946: 682-3).

Mayne's formulation of the formula 'the reflection of the son' is based on this misreading, which became law. The criteria of the adopted son's eligibility and the consequences for him of adoption are enumerated by him as follows:

He was to be a person whose mother might have been married by the adopter; he was to be of the same class; he was to be so young that his ceremonies might all be performed in the adoptive family; he was to be absolutely severed from his natural family, and to become so completely a part of his new family as to be unable to marry within its limits. His introduction into the family must appear to be a matter of love and free will, unsullied by every mercenary element. All these restrictions had the effect of eliminating the other forms of adotpion, and leaving the *dattaka* alone in force.' (1883: 90-1).

The British judges apparently made the rules more inflexible than they really were in the traditional writers. Most of Mayne's assertions could be qualified (see Kane 1946: ch. XXVII). Though most *smrti* writers hold that the boy must be of the same caste, one at least allowed a Brahman to adopt a Kshatriya boy. It was preferred that the boy to be adopted was not five or more years old; but older boys for whom some of the ceremonies including the *upanayana* had already been performed could be adopted. The alleged severance of the adopted son from his natural family means no more than exclusion from inheritance and *pinda* rites to ancestors; the severance is not total since he must continue to observe the marriage prohibitions applying to his natural kin. True to form, India even had the *dvayamusyayana*, the only son who was simultaneously the son of the natural father and the adoptive father!

The same qualifications should apply to the alleged rules concerning the unsuitability of only sons and eldest sons for adoption. It is for instance reported that authorities like Vasishta and Baudhayana laid down that an only son cannot be adopted:' Let no man give or accept an only son, since he must remain for the obsequies of his ancestor.' Some authorities it is said extended the prohibition to the eldest son as well on the ground that this father has the right to appropriate his virtues. But Kane points out, on the basis of a survey of all the writers, that such rules concerning the only and eldest sons were recommendatory and not absolute.

Despite all the qualifications and allowances for flexibility which we should graft on to Mayne's elucidation there seem to be two major points about adoption worthy of our general attention.

(1) The adopted son is subject to the marriage (and incest) prohibitions as regards both his 'natural' kin and his new 'adoptive' kin (i.e. both categories are his *sapinda*).

(2) But for this above restriction, an adopted child is deemed to be the child of his adoptive parent for all purposes from the date of adoption; from this date all his ties with the family of his bitrh are deemed severed for religious, civil, and secular purposes.

(3) (a) There are property implications deriving from this notion. According to the Mitakshara system (but not the Dayabhaga) any interest which he had in his natal joint-family property (together with any liabilities attached thereto) ceased on his adoption as if he had then died. (In actual fact, as discussed by Derrett (p. 117) Manu's precept (IX, 142) that 'the adopted son shall never take the . . . estate of his natural father' has been interpreted differently in different Courts: whereas the Bombay High

Court in 1916 divested him of all property in his natal joint family, the Madras Court (1906) declarded that the adopted son was prohibited from taking with him or subsequently inheriting only what was not vested in him at the time of adoption. Both views thus agree that the adopted son forgoes rights to future inheritance not held at the time of adoption: they differ in respect of whether an adopted boy can have rights in the property of two separate joint families.

(b) Corresponding to the loss of his rights in his natal joint family, the adopted boy acquires (under Mitakshara) interest in the property of his adoptive father from the moment of adoption as if he had been born as a legitimate son. However, if after adoption a natural son is born, the Dharmashastras appear to think that the natural son inherits a larger proportion of the patrimony than the adopted son (who, it is said, gets only a fourth' share', the interpretation of which phrase is contentious) (Kane 1946: 698).

In India although a stranger or non-kinsman of the right status category can be validly adopted, the fiction of sonship dictated that the adopted person was indeed a close *sapinda* kinsman. A brother's son was considered eminently acceptable since already he was a son to his uncle. In many parts of India the sister's son, the daughter's son (or the mother's sister's son) have also been acceptable. This preference is understandable in terms of our previous discussion of the 'appointed daughter'.

Two related questions are: Who can give away a child into adoption, and who can take a child in adoption? Only the father and mother — no other relation — can give away a child.[16] This power vested solely in parents cannot be delegated to other kin. (Today the guardian of a child can give a child in adoption with the court's permission.) Thus traditionally an orphan cannot be adopted, because he can neither give himself away, nor be given by any one else with authority to do so.[17]

With respect to powers to adopt, while any male Hindu (of sound mind and right age) who has no living son, grandson or greatgrandson can adopt a son,[18] the rights of the wife or widow are not the same as the husband's. In fact the extent to which a woman is allowed to adopt independently or in the absence of her husband is a test case of the powers and rights vested in the Hindu wife. The basic rule is that a wife cannot adopt during her husband's life time without his consent. And after a man's death the only person who can adopt on his behalf is his widow. But authorities are greatly divided on this question of the power of the widow to adopt: does the basic rule allow, for instance, adoption by a widow without the prior consent of her deceased husband? The matter is important because it has implications for the devolution of joint-family property if the husband had been a co-parcener.[19] The views of the *shastric* sub-schools and later interpretations up to the present time are too tortuous and complex to report here (see Kane, 1946: 670-4).

There remains the *kritima* adoption to describe. This form of adoption pertains to the adoption of an *adult*, and therefore requires the consent of the adoptee. Unlike the *dattaka* the fiction of a new birth into the adoptive family does not and cannot exist. A *kritima* son (as for example according to the Mithila school) though related to the adoptive parent for all other purposes (e.g. performance of obsequies) does not however lose his property rights in his natal family. Nor does he assume the surname of the adoptive father. While he takes the inheritance of his adoptive parent this right does not extend to the property of his adoptive parents' kinsmen.

The uxorilocal son-in-law

The uxorilocal son-in-law in a patrilineal and normally patrilocal society is an established and customary occurance in India. The *illatam* practised in Madras and Andhra Pradesh, the *sarvasvadanam* by the Nambudiri of Kerala, and the *gharjamai* of Western India and Punjab are arrangements which 'while they serve to give the man concerned a certain status in the house of his bride and a *contractual* right of succession to some or all of his father-in-law's property even after an *aurasa* (natural) son is born, are mainly concerned with the conversion of what would otherwise be a virilocal into a uxorilocal marriage'. (Derrett 1963: 132-3). Each of these customary institutions was intended to enable a sonless father to keep a married daughter with him; or to do the same if his only child was a daughter, thereby obtaining through her an heir to the estate. Furthermore the uxorilocal son-in-law would contribute the labour and services equivalent to those of a resident son. The uxorilocal son-in-law is invested with important rights in some parts of India. The *sarvasvadanam* form of the Nambudiri is the strongest – the incoming son-in-law may himself be instituted as heir of the sonless father. Customarily the *illatam* and *gharjamai* sons-in-law enjoyed the right to succeed to the father-in-law's property on the same footing as statutory heirs – but not to the estate of other relatives. Neither enjoys the right of survivorship as this is enjoyed by co-parceners in a joint family.

It is clear from this account that the uxorilocal son-in-law institution is similar to the now obsolete appointed daughter arrangement, in that the logic of both lies in the production of an heir (grandson) who will inherit the estate. Such arrangements became necessary when male issue were lacking, and were not infrequent in incidence.

To sum up our discussion. In India two institutions are relied upon today when a family finds itself lacking a male son to inherit, to perform religious rites, and to carry on the line. One is adoption: we should note that the adopted sons are usually close kin such as a brother's son or a daughter's son. The second is the uxorilocal son-in-law who in time produces a legal heir through a man's daughter. But this institution, if it is to be attractive to a man in the context of patrilineal groups and patrilocal residence, must concede to the incoming son-in-law important rights. The institution of uxorilocal son-in-law is therefore only a stop gap and a temporary discontinuity in the patrilineal-patrilocal fabric. We should remember this when we come to compare this institution with residence arrangements prevalent in Ceylon among the Jaffna Tamils and the Kandyan Sinhalese.

In this section we have discussed institutional arrangements whereby, either directly or indirectly through a daughter, breaches in an otherwise patrilineal-patrilocal edifice are repaired. We now turn to the property rights of a woman in her own own right as daughter and wife expressed in the concept of *stridhanam* and the rules of succession to it.

Stridhanam: [20] *female property*

It would appear that in the earliest texts properties held to be owned by women were presents made at the time of their marriage such as ornaments and clothes and household articles under the control of women (Kane 1946: 771). They also give evidence that *stridhanam* as woman's property excluded immovable property.

The oldest extant statement on *stridhanam* in Dharmashastric work is that of Manu:

> What (was) given before (nuptial fire (*adhyagni*), what (was given) on the bridal procession, what was given in token of love (*dattam priti – karmani*), and what was received from a brother, a mother, or a father, are considered as the sixfold (separate) property of a (married) woman (Manu IX, 194).
>
> (Such property), as well as a gift subsequent and what was given (to her) by her affectionate husband, shall go to her offspring, (even) if she dies in the lifetime of her husband (*Ibid.* IX, 195).

The succeeding verses (196 and 197) go on to declare that property given a woman according to Asura marriage (i.e. with brideprice) reverts to a woman's parents and not her husband, while the property she received through the Brahma and Daiva, etc. rites (i.e. 'gift of a virgin' with dowry), goes to her husband if she has no issue.

Katyayana, who is a late *smrti* writer sums up the ideas of his predecessors and provides an enumeration of the components of stridhanam which is continually repeated in the later medieval works. He wrote that what is given to women at the time of marriage before nuptial fire is declared to be *adhyagni*; that which she receives when she is taken in procession from her father's house is *adhyavahanika*; whatever is given to her through affection by the father-in-law and mother-in-law (and from elders) is *pritidatta* (gift through affection); finally that is declared to be *sulka* (bride's fee) which is obtained as the price of household utensils, of beasts of burden, of milch cattle, ornaments and slaves (Kane 1946: 774; Banerjee 1879: 227).

By the time of the later *smrti* writers *stridhanam* had become a more inclusive term standing for property which was 'obtained by a woman either as a maiden or at marriage or after marriage, from her parents or the family or relatives of the parents or from the husband and his family (except immovable property given by the husband), [but] what was obtained by a woman after her marriage by her own labour or from strangers did not become stridhana' (Kane 1946: 779-80).

It would appear that this 'technical' notion of *stridhanam* was expanded still further under Mitakshara to include property of any description belonging to a woman even if it was inherited by her from a male as a widow or mother, or through partition as a wife or mother. On the other hand the Dayabhaga appears to have a more restricted definition: 'that alone is stridhana which a woman has authority to donate, sell or enjoy independently of her husband's control'. Dayabhaga law made an explicit distinction which is implicit in most systems of traditional law and important to stress: a distinction between *stridhanam* property which a woman received from her parents and relatives before and at marriage and from her husband (*except* immovable property) on the one hand, and on the other property she may have inherited or obtained by partition (in the capacity of wife, widow, etc.) and property acquired by her through the exercise of her labour.[21] This bifurcation, which corresponds to that which distinguishes between the 'technical' or restrictive notion and the expanded 'non-technical' notion of *stridhana*, is important because in traditional law it is over the first category that a woman exercised dominion independently of her husband. Kane sums up the view of the *smrti* texts thus: 'that a Hindu woman during her maidenhood could dispose of her stridhana property of every description at her pleasure, that during widowhood she' could dispose of every kind of stridhana including movable property given by the husband but not immovable property given by him and that a married woman could dispose at her pleasure only of that kind of property called *saudayika* (i.e. gifts from relatives other than those made by the husband)' (p. 784). The later *smrtis* also emphasized the separate rights of husband and wife in respect of debts. They held that the husband and wife were separate as regards their properties. The wife's separate debts were not binding on the husband and *vice versa*; however under conditions of distress (disease, family debts) the wife's property could be liable for the debts incurred by the husband.

It is the first kind of *stridhanam*, which we would identify as dowry. It was (and is) the commonest form of female property in India, and therefore the entity that interests us at this stage. We have already seen that even the shorthand concept of dowry for gifts associated with marriage encompasses numerous prestations given by diverse agents. It is composed of clothes and jewellery received by the bride from her parents before marriage, betrothal presents from the bridegroom, presents received by her at marriage from her parents and kin, and gifts received after marriage from her husband.

Of these various components of *stridhanam* one figures importantly in the classical literature − *sulkam* (*sulka*).[22] The intriguing feature about *sulkam* is that its features are not so much vague as multi-dimensional. It is particularly intriguing for us because it seems to comprise 'brideprice' in the classical sense, but brideprice which, however, the receiving parents in turn endow their marrying daughter with as a part of the dowry![23] It is as if, given the Indian value placed on the 'gift of a virgin' and the opprobrium aimed at 'selling the daughter', the 'brideprice' received is transformed into 'dowry' and the property of the woman marrying. We shall see later how this picture and interpretation holds good for contemporary marriage payments as well.

First, let us see how the *sulkam* was glossed by classical writers. Mayne interpreting these classical views writes: 'The *sulka* or fee is variously described as being a special present to the bride to induce her to go cheerfully to the mansion of her lord (Vyasa), or as the gratuity for the receipt of which a girl is given in marriage.'[24] This statement seems to be saying that the *sulka* may be interpreted either as a *dower* given to the girl by her bridegroom or as a brideprice. The second implication is unambiguously asserted by Varadraja who refers to 'what is given to the possessors of a maiden by way of price for the sale of a maiden' (Mayne: 1883 p. 629).

Kane's citations on *sulka* (which he translates as 'bride's fee', 'bride's gratuity') contain both connotations of brideprice and dower: the Smritichandrika (a South Indian authority) is said to explain *sulka* as 'the price of the articles which the bride groom was in the habit of presenting to the bride at the time of marriage or when he started a house'. Varadaraja is said to have stated that *sulka* had two senses: what is given as the price of the girl to her guardians (which goes on her death to her brother and mother), and what is given by the bridegroom as ornaments to the girl and as household gear. (Kane 1946: 775-6).

Over time the *sulkam* seems to have undergone a shift which is clearly glossed by Derrett as follows. After pointing out that in the Mitakshara *sulkam* is referred to when *stridhanam* is discussed, Derrett explains: 'There is some doubt as to what the term originally meant, but it is now understood that it meant property paid to the parents of the bride to induce them to give in marriage, and afterwards given by them to the bride herself.' (1963: 398). It thus seems to me that Mayne may have hit upon the right interpretation when he said in historical terms 'These various meanings [of *sulka*] probably mark the different steps, by which that which was originally received by the parents for the sale of their daughter, was converted into dowry for herself.' (Mayne 1883: 629). Indeed today *sulkam* is virtually unknown as a concept of marriage proceedings (although there seem to exist its unacknowledged analogues, which will be pointed out later).

Now this thesis that the *sulkam* historically constitutes the brideprice transformed into dowry gets additional confirmation from the Mitakshara rule concerning the transmission of *sulkam*: 'It seems to have been believed that it belonged morally to her family and *not to her husband or his heirs, nor even her children, and therefore if passed to her full brothers,* in their default to her mother and (it appears) after her to her father and in his default to the father's heirs' (Derrett 1963: 398-9; see also Banerjee 1879: 378). An anthropologist immediately recognizes that the logic of this peculiar rule of transmission whereby a girl's brothers have preference over her heirs or her husband can plausibly lie in the fact that as in the classical African situation the 'brideprice' of the sister is meant to go to her brother (who uses it to acquire his own wife). In the Indian situation, it appears as if the brothers temporarily renounced this right, transferring the brideprice to the bride as (part of) her dowry, but retaining the right to resume ownership when the sister died.[25]

This interpretation gains greater plausibility when we discover that the Mitakshara law proposes two lines of succession, one for *sulka* (which we have stated above devolves firstly on the full brothers and then on the mother) and another for all the remaining categories of *stridhana*. The order of succession for the latter kinds of *stridhana* is: (1) unmarried daughter (2) married daughter who is indigent (3) married daughter who is well provided for (4) daughter's daughter (5) daughter's son (6) sons (7) son's sons according to the *per stirpes* rule (8) husband, etc. It is immediately apparent that the line of passage of these categories of female property (which exclude *sulka*) is the exact opposite of the passage of male property, thereby signifying that the Indian legal systems emphasized the concept of female property (owned by and transmitted first and foremost through females) to complement the idea of male property transmitted primarily through males.

We have now arrived at the point where we would benefit by viewing more closely the devolution of *stridhanam* in particular legal systems which differentiate the various categories of property, recognized by the various classical law schools as comprising *stridhanam*, according to their source of origin. By way of illustration I shall confine myself here to briefly describing the provisions contained in two sub-schools of the Mitakshara system and in the Dayabhaga system (the Bengal school).

The Mayukha school (Bombay school) made careful distinctions between the following categories (see Derrett 1963) of *stridhanam* and their devolution:

(1) *Sulkam* which was transmitted in the manner described earlier for Mitakshara in general (*to full brothers*, then mother, then father and his heirs).

(2) Gifts and bequests from husband (*bhartidatta-stridhanam*) and gifts from relations *subsequent to marriage* (*anvadheya*): these passed in the following order: (a) *sons and unmarried daughters equally*, (b) sons and married daughters, (c) daughter's daughter and daughter's son (d) son's son, (e) husband or his heirs, the father or his heirs, etc.

(3) Gifts made to the bride at the time *of marriage* (*yautaka*) were destined first for *unmarried daughters*, then unprovided married daughters, then provided married daughters, daughters and daughter's sons, son's son's son etc., in that order.

(4) The remaining property (i.e. 'non-technical' *stridhanam*), e.g. what she has earned or acquired by her labour, investment, etc., passes to: (a) *sons*, daughter's son, (c) son's son's son, (d) daughters, (e) daughter's sons, (f) daughter's daughter, (g) residual heirs, in that order.

In the above listing I have italicized the first category of heirs to emphasize the differential emphasis in the transmission of the different components of the *stridhanam*: *sulkam* goes to a woman's brothers and not her decendants (I am tempted to say that here the 'brideprice' returns to the rightful owners); gifts given at marriage go primarily to (unmarried) daughters, gifts received after marriage devolve bilaterally on sons and (unmarried) daughters, and personally acquired wealth goes to sons first.

Kane provides an example pertaining to the same area which makes clear the distinction between 'technical' and 'non-technical' *stridhanam*. He reports that the *Vyaraharamayukha* which is the paramount authority in Gujarat, Bombay island and North Konkan proposes the following lines of categorization of property and its devolution (1946: 795-96). It first divides *stridhana* into technical (*paribhasika*) and non-technical (*aparibhasika*) categories.

The first is subdivided into four classes which are transmitted in the following order:

(1) *sulka* which passes as in the Mitakshara system;

(2) *yautaka*: (i) unmarried daughters, (ii) (probably) married daughters;

(3) *anvadheya* and *bhatrpriti-datta* (husband's gift through affection): (i) sons and unmarried daughters, (ii) sons and married daughters, (iii) daughter's issue, (iv) son's sons;

(4) *other kinds*: devolve as under Mitakshara.

The non-technical *stridhana* is inherited by: son, son's sons, son's son's sons, daughters, daughter's sons, daughter's daughters, in that order.

Let us now see how *stridhanam* is categorized and transmitted in Dayabhaga law (see Derrett 1963: 403ff). The categories of property are:

(1) *sulkam*: present to induce the bride to go to her husband's house (now practically obsolete);

(2) *yautaka*: presents from kin and guests, etc. *during the wedding festivities*;

(3) *pitridatta*: gifts and bequests given to a woman *after her marriage by the father*;

(4) *ayautaka*: gifts and bequests from relatives *before or after the marriage*.

Table 1 summarizes the lines of transmission in the order of priority of heirs to of various categories of property comprising *stridhanam*.

Leaving aside the *sulkam* which devolves in the same manner in both systems (first heirs are blood brothers), the Dayabhaga puts a greater emphasis on transmission through females than does the Bombay School. It is to be noted that under both systems *yautaka* (property given at the nuptials) alwasy passes to a woman's daughters (unmarried being preferred to married) and then to other issue. Thus Vasishta said 'Let the daughters share the nuptial gifts of their mother' (Vasishta XVII, 24.) Manu confirms that 'Property given to the mother on her marriage (*yautaka*) is inherited by her (unmarried) daughters' (IX, 131).[26] The idea enshrined here being that this property is eminently a woman's separate property and thus appropriately devolves on her daughters. By and large we see that in the transmission of *stridhanam* property given a woman by her parents and relatives during the marriage festivities tends to be treated as something that passes first and foremost in the female line. Perhaps this represents the core of 'dowry'

Table 1   Devolution of stridhanam (female property) according to the Dayabhaga
system

	Categories of property			
	Sulkam	Yautaka	Pitridatta	Ayautaka
	(given by bridegroom's family to induce the bride to marry)	(gifts given by kin and friends *during* wedding festtitivites)	(gifts given by woman's father *subsequent* to marriage)	(gifts from relatives *before* and *after* marriage)
Heirs in order of priority — Lines of transmission	full brothers mother father father's heirs	unbetrothed daughters betrothed daughters married daughters having or capable of having son barren or childless married daughter sons daughter's sons, etc.	unbetrothed daughters betrothed daughters sons married or widowed daughter barren married daughter daughters' sons, etc.	sons and unbetrothed daughters betrothed daughters married daughters having or capable of having son son's sons daughter's sons barren married daughters, etc.

though,it does not exhaust it.

One final problem remains as regards *stridhanam*. Many writers are accustomed to take the Aryan/non-Aryan distinction (roughly also corresponding to North and South India) as critical for many institutional features and customs. Thus Derrett (1962), despite the traditional common sharing of the concept of *stridhanam* (I include its linguistic variants such as the Tamil *citanam* or *chidenam*) in both the North and the South, appears to think that the South Indian conception actually represents a non-Aryan form. For instance, the South Indian inscriptions show that *stridhanam* implied that a man acquires impartible property by way of his wife's dowry and that this property is subject to the husband's control and is not a species of female's separate property as is normally implied by *stridhanam* in the Dharmasatras and in Anglo-Hindu and modern Hindu law. Correspondingly the non-Aryan wife is said to have had greater rights in the property of the marriage, e.g. half share of the corpus on divorce or her husband's death. Derrett cites two legal systems from Ceylon, the Thesavalamai and Kandyan law, as evidence for these assertions. In my view Derrett is mistaken about a North — South distinction in the conception of *stridhanam*; in any case there are no distinctive signs of differences as regards this matter between the contemporary *patrilineal* societies of the North and South; furthermore, in my view the Ceylonese systems show a shift from the *classical* pan-Indian form with concomitant transformations in kinship structure. They therefore should be treated separately — as I do in a subsequent section.

PART THREE

The ethnography: marriage payments in contemporary rural India

Having distilled some of the major principles of traditional Indian law, I shall now examine some samples of contemporary ethnography in order to establish the patterning of marriage payments and how it relates to the former. Before so doing, let me map the major points of orientation for viewing the payments.

(1)   Firstly, marriage payments in India usually comprise an elaborate series of payments back and forth between the marrying families.

Secondly, this series extends over a long period of time and persists after marriage, e.g. in the form of the mother's brother's obligations to his sister's children.

Given these two circumstances, is it possible to separate out particular transactions as standing for 'brideprice' or 'dowry'? I think that it is useful to retain these concepts and that we can isolate them provided we make some distinctions.

Marriage and post-marriage prestations could be classified into two groups:

(a)   the series of payments begining with engagement and concluding with the bride actually going to reside in the groom's house, which can be separated from

(b)   the series that persists after marriage and matures in the form of the gift-giving by the mother's brother to the sister's children, usually concluding with the marriage of these children.

In this essay we are concentrating on the larger and more important first category. Within the series of marriage prestations, I believe both on the basis of classical texts and contemporary practice that two major payments can be separated out: (a) an analogue of a 'brideprice' which in the Indian context is redirected and transformed (because brideprice as such is devalued) into a gift of jewellery to the bride which she takes to her new home and (b) dowry proper which is given to the bride by her parents and consists of jewellery, household effects, clothes and cash. The net effect is that both sets of parents virtually contribute to a conjugal estate.

We should also note in the Indian context that although there is a two-way exchange of gifts and prestations, over time it is the wife's kin who pay out more in North, Central and South India (among the groups considered). Now it is remarkable that whether it is in North or South India the role and gift-giving obligations of the mother's brother and other close affines are remarkably similar, whereas marriage prohibitions and preferences are quite different. North India is not only famous for its hypergamous practices but also for its marriage rules which disallow marriage with close cognates (*sapinda*) and into the lineages/clans of one's mother, father's mother, mother's mother and so on (the so-called 'three clan'. 'five clan' exogamy rules), thereby legislating against cross-cousin marriage and repeated

92

marriage (which has been dubbed as 'alliance' by Dumont). South India by contrast places emphasis on alliance and on marriage of status equals in respect of the primary marriage, which features have the overtones of restricted exchange. In the light of the North (and Central Indian) pattern, how are we to regard Dumont's assertion with regard to South India that the obligations of the maternal uncle are best considered as a particular case of the alliance pattern and that indeed it is the ceremonial gift-giving which constitutes 'the most conspicuous feature of alliance as an enduring marriage institution?' (Dumont 1957).

This is not the place to solve the riddle of the North Indian versus South Indian marriage and kinship patterns [see Dumont's attempted but still unsatisfactory solution in *Contributions* Vols. V (1961), VII (1964), IX (1966)]. Two statements seem to be in order and may aid solution.

Firstly, whatever the particularities and variations of kinship and marriage structure, there is a striking similarity on a pan-Indian Hindu-society scale (with some exceptions) concerning the overall pattern of marriage payments, the gifts to the woman at marriage in movables, cash, and jewellery which constitute *stridhanam* (female property) and their concomitant exclusion from a formal share in the patrimony, especially land.

Secondly, North India in contrast to South India appears to assert that a marriage once made and affinity once established should give rise to enduring ties — at least over two or three generations — without the repetition of marriage. Indeed North India insists that immediate repetitions of marriage with affines are an anathema. It seems to me that the continuance of affinal gifts and the mother's brother's generosity are consistent with both the North Indian rejection of repeated marriage and the South Indian preference for repeated alliance with affines.

The consequence of the North Indian notion of affinity is seemingly to drive marriage outwards towards the formation of newer and newer affinal links. This meshes in beautifully with the ideals of hypergamy, which demands a constant search for more and more prestigious wife-takers on the one hand and richer and richer wife-givers to exploit on the other. Correspondingly, since repeated marriage would fix and solidify status inequalities between takers and givers, it is antithetical to the spirit of the hypergamous system which constantly seeks an elevation of status, or less ambitiously at least a validation and maintenance of status. At the same time the North Indian marriage prohibitions, while denying repeated and successive marriage into the same affinal families by members of the same family or to the same set of siblings, however permit one's more distant male collaterals (patrilateral first and more remote cousins) to establish marriages with one's own affines without violating the rules of prohibition, as long as the same direction of marriage and hypergamous advantage is maintained. It is in this fashion, by repeating marriage links not at the level of lineal kin (up to a restricted number of generations) or blood siblingship, but at a different level of the lineage and clan, that affinity in hypergamous North India seems to be renewed. But another contrapuntal dynamism comes into play: fission and differentiation in status within localized lineage groups inevitably result in this climate of competition for status, thereby ensuring that enduring asymmetrical relations are not built up between lineages at the group level. Furthermore, since the marriage prohibitions last only a certain number of finite generations there is no enduring set of affines either, and the tantalizing prospect presents itself that the lineage/family of ego's antecedent wife-giver may hope to take a wife from the lineage/family of ego's more recent wife-giver, or that an antecedent wife-giver may attempt to reverse the direction of exchange by becoming one's own superior wife-taker. [27]

All this is the very stuff of status preoccupation. The hypergamy rule which Blunt propounded (1931: 62) was that 'no man may take a bride from any family to which his own family has given a bride within the memory of man'. Mercifully man's memory is often short and genealogical amnesia a convenient source of flexibility.

In the course of his study of some South Indian groups Dumont related inherit-*ance* to *gifts* in the following way: 'The most conspicious feature of alliance as an enduring marriage institution that defines and links the two kinds of relatives consists in ceremonial gifts and functions . . . If ceremonial gifts are essentially affinal and if they are important, it should follow that, *in societies with male predominance, property is transmitted from one generation to the next under two forms: by inheritance in the male line, and also by gifts to in-laws, namely from father-in-law* . . . In the groups with which we are immediately concerned, apart from the Nangudi Vellalar among whom female property is important, *daughters have no formal share in their father's property, but they are entitled to maintenance and to the expenses necessary for their marriage and establishment.*' (1957a: 29; my italics)

The same argument is elucidated again at another place in the essay thus: '. . . normally a man inherits his father's property with the charge of establishing his sister, that is, in fact, with the charge not only of the marriage gifts but also of the subsequent oriented gifts, including the presents to be given to the sister's children. These are provided or compensated for by the fact that the sister had no formal share in the inheritage, her share consisting precisely in such presents.' The women are thus dissociated from land in the final instance.

The transmission of property is regulated in fact in two ways: a part of it is inherited by the sons, while another part is disposed of under the form of gifts (and ceremonial expenses), namely as affinal gifts to the daughters' households and children (p. 44).

Now this double transmission of property confirmed for Dumont the opposistion between kin and alliance in South India. It did not escape Dumont that from this conclusion a generalization for (most of) India might be attempted: 'The same rule, if it is not absolute and universal, has a widespread validity in Indian customary law, where it makes itself felt even when it is contradicted' (p. 29) and cites Jolly and Mayne as his authorities. The reader should note that what is here being referred to is the tenet of the *Dharmashastras – that it is essentially males who inherit the patrimony while women are entitled to maintenance, marriage expenses and gifts.*

In the context of our wider survey both in time depth and space, we can confirm the correctness of Dumont's remarks about the transmission of landed property in the male line and the complementary transmission of gifts at marriage and other oriented gifts to the females which we have labelled dowry. But we should also note that this is a virtually pan-Indian classical pattern. In so far as it applies to the North and elsewhere, this pattern of property transmission cannot be accounted for as gaining its *raison d'être* only from alliance as an enduring marriage institution in the Southern style. It is just that the double transmission fits into the marriage institutions of all parts of Hindu India (with certain exceptions).

Now let us inspect actual ethnographic accounts of marriage payments in different parts of India in order to substantiate these assertions.

Marriage payments in North India

In North India we confront groups in the Delhi region (Lewis 1958) with hypergamous values which are achieved to a variable degree in actual practice. It is the bride's parents who first of all seek and 'solicit' the groom, and at the engagement ceremony (*sagai*) held at the groom's house, the groom is honoured and receives a gift of money from his prospective father-in-law.

The pattern of prestations between the marrying families shows the following features (see Table 2).

Whatever is given by the groom's side in the way of clothes ornaments are exclusively for the bride's use, thus signifying that this is not 'bridewealth' in the paradigmatic sense, since it is accepted by and diverted from the bride's parents to the bride herself. In comparison the payments on the bride's family's side are not only larger but also more varied. First of all they endow the bride with a dowry consisting of cash, jewellery, household effects, etc. which goes to form part of the conjugal fund of the couple. Furthermore the bride's family give gifts to other kin of the groom particularly his mother.

We may thus note the co-existence of gifts by the groom's side, which in the Indian context are channelled back to the wife, and of dowry given by the bride's side which is the larger contribution. In the North Indian context, where hypergamous tendencies prevail, this asymmetry in payments serves to buttress the status superiority of the wife-takers over the wife-givers. This asymmetry is supported by further evidence which shows that relations between affines are restricted after marriage and could be described as avoidance. The groom's household and agnatic group in the village, and hence the whole village, tend to be regarded as out of bounds for the bride's family. After the bride has gone to live with her husband 'only her brother may visit her there, except when she is ill, at which times others may call' (Lewis 1958: 188). Ibbetson (1882: *Census Report for the Punjab for 1881*) is quoted as having written: 'The village into which his daughter is married is utterly tabooed for the father and her elder brothers, and all near elder relations.

95

Table 2 Marriage payments in Rampur Village in North India

Payments by bride's family	Payments by bridegroom's family
Sagai (engagement held in groom's parental house): bride's father makes a money gift to bridegroom — might also give money to his nearest kin and to girls of his clan married in the groom's village.	No reciprocal gift made.
Lagan (ceremony before wedding held separately at house of bride and groom): bride's family send gifts of dress, cloth, shoes, etc. primarily to *groom's mother*.	The groom's family send back gifts (mainly clothing) for the bride.
Wedding ceremony (held at bride's house): *Kanyan dan* — when ceremonially presenting daughter to the groom, the bride's father gives *groom* the *dowry* consisting of *money* (usually 51-100 rupees) and *utensils*; and dresses for bridegroom's mother (which she in turn distributes among her daughters and her husband's sisters).	*Chunri*: Groom's father gives to bride's parents ornaments, ribbons, etc. *for the bride*, which she wears for the rite. Ornaments are the largest item of expense.
Gona (consummation of marriage): bride's parents provide bride with trousseau, jewellery and household articles before she leaves for bridegroom's house. Bride's mother also sends clothes for bridegroom's family.	When bridegroom comes to take bride, he brings her a set of clothes (indicative of his future support of her).
Other: bride's father feasts the groom's party at wedding.	Groom's father pays expenses for groom's procession to bridal house.

Source: Oscar Lewis, *Village Life in Northern India: studies in a Delhi Village*, 1958.

They may not go to it, even drink water from a well in that village for it is shameful to take anything from one's daughter or her belongings. On the other hand, the father is continually giving things to his daughter and her husband as long as he lives. Even the more distant elder relatives will not eat or drink from the house into which the girl is married, though they do not taboo the whole village . . . ' One infers from Ibbetson's statement that a woman's younger brother could visit her more freely; Lewis himself incidentally reports that when the bride is finally taken to her husband's home, none of her kin accompanies her except her younger brother.

Even during the marriage proceedings and festivities the groom's and bride's kin eat separately. After the *sagai* (engagement) ceremony at the groom's house while the groom's kin feast, the bride's kin leave without food 'for they may not eat while in the boy's village, and hence leave as soon as the *sagai* ceremony is over' (Lewis 1958: 169). Again at the wedding, after the presentation of *chunri*, the bride's parents feast the groom's kin, but the kin on the bride's side do not participate. While the groom's kin can be feasted by the bride's kin, return hospitality is neither sought nor given.

Thus North India presents us with the paradoxical situation that the wife-givers are persistent gift-givers and lavish hosts, while they are at the same time excluded from intimate social contact with the receivers, as that would smack of equality. The paradox is consistent with hypergamy. In conformity with the pattern of the gift, the bride's father makes it a point of honour not to receive anything in exchange other than the reflected glory of his son-in-law's family, which will be higher than his own. Karve confirms this when she says that 'One who gives the daughter should not receive anything.' (1953: 130).

Lewis reports that at the wedding, the father of the bride in addition to the payments he has to make to the groom's family and the dowry he gives the bride, also gives presents of dresses to his other married daughters, his sisters, and his father's sisters. Furthermore the husbands of these women also receive small cash gifts. Thus these superior affines, although they themselves are obliged to give presents (internal prestations), in turn take away gifts.

The persisting gift-giving of the affines is best expressed in the North Indian context (as it is in the rest of India) by the obligations of the mother's brother.

At the wedding the mother's brother gives the bride or groom, as the case may be, the *bhat* gift which consists of the wedding clothes (that will be worn at the rite), money, a crown for the boy and a ring for the girl. Sometimes he may also give small money gifts to his sisters' husbands' brothers.

It is important and significant that the father's mother's brother (i.e. the mother's brother of the previous ascending generation) also sometimes contributes a *barabhat* gift of clothes to the person getting married (i.e. to his sister's son's son or daughter). This signifies the possible persistence of affinal obligations over two generations.

The ritual role of the mother's brother in Rampur at the wedding has a direct parallel in many other parts of India, including South India. It is the mother's brother who carries the bride in and places her in front of the groom; after the rite is over he again carries and places the bride in a palanquin (or cart or car) in which she is taken to the groom's village.

It is also at the wedding of his sister's child that the mother's brother's social inferiority to his sister's husband and avoidance with her household comes to an end. We are told that in Rampur, before he makes his *bhat* gift, his sister (the mother of the bride or groom) does him honour by performing *arati*, then presents him with uncooked rice (and other articles). Then after he has given his gift,he is given food to eat for the first time in the house of his sister's husband because 'before this he was not permitted to eat at his sister's house'. It is as if the relationship of affinity, first with his sister's husband and then shifted a generation down to his sister's child in some way 'concludes' with the latter's marriage. After this event, he is no more an inferior affine and his obligations come to an end so to say (a man as we have seen may still give gifts at the marriage of his sister's son's children, but this appears not to be obligatory). A new cycle of affinal relationships can begin at this point.

Marriage payments in Central India

Exchange between bride's and groom's families (see Table 3). According to Mayer 1960) the marriage expenses in Ramkheri incurred by both sides are fairly equal, with the boy's if anything the heavier. We should note two features: the payments made by the groom's side of jewellery and clothes (tha analogue of 'brideprice') are entirely for the bride's use and she takes them with her upon marriage; similarly the major payment by the bride's family consists of the *dowry* which again goes to form the conjugal fund of the couple. Secondly, the gifts and payments should be seen as a long series: Mayer points out that after marriage, the flow of prestations is increasingly one way with the bride's family giving more to the couple, especially the mother's brother who is expected to give clothes at all the major ceremonies at his sister's house. This aspect of gift obligations after marriage reflects a general Indian pattern.

The Central Indian pattern documented here does in certain other ways stand in contrast to North Indian and South Indian patterns. In the North Indian case it appears that the payments at marriage by the bride's side exceed those made by the groom's; this may be associated with the hypergamous trends there as opposed to marriage between status equals in Ramkheri. And in South India the fact that there are a larger number of reversible gifts exchanged between the parental families indicates that 'alliance' there is stronger than in Central India.

Marriage gifts made by kin of parents of bride and groom. Whereas in the previous section we looked at the payments exchanged by the bride's and groom's families, here let us examine the contributions of the kin of each set of parents when their child marries. The patterning of the prestations indicate the nature of agnatic as opposed to affinal obligations — the latter may be taken to be a continuation of exchanges discussed in the previous section.

The basic distinction in the Central Indian case (Ramkheri) from the point of view of the marrying person is between the father's agnatic kin, on the one side, and on the other the mother's kin (uterine kin) and the affines of ego's married siblings who are all collectively called *mausal*.

At the marriage the agnates of the father and his village brothers give *ban* — these are cash gifts given to help defray expenses. They are strictly reversible gifts which the receiver will pay back at an appropriate occasion.

In contrast the *mausal* kin give *manere* which consist invariably of clothes and

98

Table 3   Marriage payments in Ramkheri in Central India

Payments by groom's family	Payments by bride's family
Engagement Groom's family give *ornaments to the bride.* Groom's family give annual gifts of clothes to bride during engagement period.	
Wedding Groom's family present clothes to *bride* and give cash payment to bride's family to help defray expenses.	Bride's parents provide dowry (*dahej*) to bride consisting of furniture, vessels, jewellery and cash. Bride's close agnates give *paharavani* — gifts of clothes to groom and his agnates. Bride's family feast groom's retinue and kin.

Source: Adrian Mayer, *Caste and Kinship in Central India: a Village and its Region*, 1960.

are given to the parents and siblings of the person marrying. The *mausal* kin can be subdivided into the following categories:
(a)   Mother's agnates: mother's brother, mother's father and mother's father's brothers who give gifts to ego's parents.
(b)   Affines (wife's brothers and wife's father) of married siblings: these affines give chiefly to the married siblings themselves (i.e. their brothers-in-law and sons--n-law respectively).

Mayer makes the significant point that by including both uterine and affinal kin under the collective term *mausal*, and by designating the gifts made by them as *manere*, the people of Ramkheri see kin through marriage as a single category. Mayer also indicates the affinal content in these relations. But he also stresses that unlike in South India there is in Ramkheri no positive marriage regulation linking the two sets of patrikin of mother and father, and that the composition of the *mausal* changes after two or three generations (i.e. it is not an enduring affinal grouping of the kind produced by repeated marriage).

Amongst all *mausal* it is the mother's brother who is singled out for special prestations at marriage. The mother's brother must give the largest number of *manere* presents. He also gives *sivacauni* which consists of ornaments and cows and becomes the personal property (*stridhan*) of the bride. He also makes other gifts and feasts the groom's retinue (*barat*).

Subsequent to the wedding, of course, the wife's brother becomes the mother's brother with the birth of a child and he continues to give gifts which parallel those given in North and South India. It is said in Ramkheri 'One hundred Brahmans, one sister's son' meaning a man should give liberally to his sister's son without thought of return. Unlike the father's agnates, a mother's brother lives in another village 'and usually appears only as a gift giver or as a helper in time of financial trouble. If he is not willing to fill this place, he does not come at all . . . ' (Mayer 1960: 224).

Unlike Rampur (North India) the relationship between affines in Ramkheri (Central India) is more like that of equals. The relation between affines begins with the engagement, the relationship between the prospective fathers-in-law being prone to some tension because of haggling over marriage payments. But after the wedding is concluded the fathers-in-law have an informal joking relationship. Unlike in North India, here a father often arrives to fetch his daughter from her conjugal home. A man jokes with his son's wife's mother, and mothers-in-law joke broadly among themselves. Relations with the more distant affines are freest of all.

Although in the early years of marriage a girl frequently goes to visit and stay with her parents, in time she is fully incorporated into her conjugal household and visits her parents only occasionally. From this time onwards the relationship between affines can take a variable course. Mayer says that the relations will depend on the degree to which the mother's brother fulfils his duties towards his sister's children. If such obligations are fulfilled a man has an easy relationship with his wife's brother and may act as a go-between in the marriages of his children. Thus in Ramkheri in so far as a mother's brother is active in arranging the marriages of his sister's children, he may be instrumental in the continuation of matrilateral links through repeated marriages (within the defined rules of marriage prohibition) and of marriage links between villages.

We may sum up the Ramkheri situation as follows: Since marriage is between status equals, there is also possibility of bilateral marriage exchange between villages. There is no wife-giving/wife-taking village distinction, hence the affines are not graded and their relative equality allows for their equal mixing,[28] We also saw that marriage payments are nearly equal. This very expression of equality does not make a persisting relation between affines obligatory, and the mother's brother's role is therefore variable, though by and large Central India confirms the crucial all-Indian pattern.

Marriage prestations and inheritance in South India

Marriage prestations among the Coorgs. Srinivas's classic monograph on the Coorgs (1952), though not particularly concerned with the details of marriage prestations is nevertheless a useful point of entry into South India, coming as we have done from the North. Although the Coorg evidence is fragmentary and dispersed, yet when brought together it suggests an unmistakable continuity with the principles already uncovered.

The Coorg *okka* requires no elaborate elucidation. In Coorg the agnatically related males form a corporate body enjoying the bulk of the rights in the *okka*.
Srinivas described the *okka* as the patrilineal *localized* lineage (or joint family)
associated with an ancestral estate, The patrilineal *okka* is highly reminiscent in
mirror image fashion of the Nayar matrilineal *taravad*. The resemblance increases
when we note that unlike the theory of co-parcenership under the Mitakshara system, which gave sons shares at birth and a right to claim partition from their
fathers, the Coorg estate was considered impartible much as the Nayar *taravad* was.
In practice partition, which took place when all members were agreed, was a fission
into subsidiary lines or subsidiary joint families rather than into individual owner-
ships. Again, as with the *taravad*, it was the eldest male member of the most senior
agnatic branch (matrilineal in the case of the Nayar) who was the head of the
okka.

It is no surprise then that this strongly patrilineal-patrilocal society, with a stress
on male inheritance of land,[29] should stage its marriage ceremony as a transfer
of rights in the girl (expressed in the transfer of eleven pebbles to the husband's
okka and the retention of one). But a woman has certain rights: to the dowry
and movables given her at marriage, and to return to her natal *okka* on divorce
and to marry from there. The marriage ceremony itself enacts the granting to the
bride rights of membership in her husband's *okka* − referred to as the giving of
sammanda.

Cross-cousin marriage is 'preferred and frequent' while marriage prohibitions extend to the parallel third cousin range on the patrilateral side. Bilateral cross-cousin
marriage is practised but there is said to be a slight preference for the patrilateral
form, which of course creates equal exchange in the form of return of a bride and
dowry in the following generation. That the Coorgs are likely to be preoccupied
with equality of exchange and reciprocity is to be inferred from other features.
There exists among the Coorg − once again reminiscent of the *enangar* relationship between Nayar lineages − the institution of *aruvame* (hereditary friendship)
between neighbouring *okka*. Affinal relations between such friendly *okka* are common, and they perform for each other the ritual duties that are usually assigned to
affines in South India: the headman of the friendly *okka* acts as master of ceremonies at weddings and divorces (i.e. plays the role of a mother's brother), the
womenfolk of a friendly *okka* cook and serve food to the mourners (just as affines
and non-agnates do).

Although the dowry transfer of movables − clothes, jewellery, etc. − is not
described by Srinivas, that such transfer is a significant part of the proceedings is
clear from the Kodagi texts relating to marriage and divorce which he cites: 'Bride's
Family Friend: On the marriage of our child into your *okka* our servants will carry
on their heads goods worth a thousand birans in a box worth five hundred
birans . . .' (p. 132). At divorce proceedings the same functionary repeats that,
when the girl in question married, the goods mentioned above were carried by

servants to her husband's house; he therefore now asks for the return of goods that remain. (p. 136-7).

An attempt will be made to enumerate as far as is possible from the available facts the pattern of other gifts made at marriage and at funeral rites.

The mother's brother, father's sister and married sister (we should really take into account the husbands of the latter two) are required to bring marriage gifts called *ketame* consisting of provisions, food, and sheets of cloth; the bringers of *ketame* are given in return token gifts of cooked pork and sweet dishes. The composition of the *ketame* givers shows the symmetry and equality in the obligations of both kinds of affines — wife-takers (*kondavanu*, literally 'he who took') (i.e. father's sister's husband, sister's husband) and wife-givers (*kodtavanu*, literally 'he who gave' i.e. mother's brother). We shall see later that this symmetry does not prevail among the Pramalai Kallaʀ who practise asymmetrical-matrilateral cross-cousin marriage.

Srinivas gives slightly more information regarding prestations at funeral rites, but the account is neither systematic nor coherent. The givers of *ketame* at marriage contribute at funerals roughly the same items (provisions and cloth) now called *adatale*. They also bring *kellati* consisting of the band and rifle and more cloth.

The agnatic kin, in contrast, contribute *muri* (white cloth). Affines such as the natal *okkas* of mother and wives (i.e. wife-givers) are also said to contribute *sameya* which is composed of coconuts, rice, cooked meat, sweet dishes, etc. Finally in funeral song the closest *kondavanu* (wife-taker) and *kodtavanu* (wife-giver), namely the sister's husband and the wife's brother, but in actual fact the sister's son in the case of a male ego and the brother's daughter in the case of a female ego, are called upon to present *kendanolli* (which consists of red silk); this custom again underlines in theory the symmetry of the obligations of affines, with possibly a slighter emphasis laid on the obligation of wife takers rather than receivers, since it is the deceased's sister's sons (i.e. the sons of takers) who bring the red silk. Srinivas reports that the givers of red cloth are considered among the closest of kin who together with the deceased's eldest son and widow perform the important pot breaking rite which severs the dead man's connection with his living relatives (Srinivas 1952: 87).

The Coorg information suggests that prestations are classified into those made by own patrilineal kin and those by affines, and that the affines are divided into wife-takers and -givers, though it is their equality and symmetry of obligations that is emphasized, thereby corresponding to the social relations of equal marriage exchange between *okka*, of bilateral cross-cousin marriages with a patrilateral preference, and of friendship/affinity *aruvame* relationship between whole *okka*. On the whole it is the gift obligations of the affines that is stressed, over and above those of agnates.

What we learn from the Coorg dowry is that, true to the classical Indian form, it consists of movables (and not land). We also learn that dowry is compatible with cross-cousin marriage, even when there is return of dowry over time, and with marriage between equals, and therefore not necessarily or only linked with hypergamy. The Coorg example also confirms the principles established already that in the Indian context, it is the affines on the wife's side who give most; they give the wife the goods that go with her, and after marriage persist with prestations. But in the Coorg context the dowry and other oriented (i.e. unilateral) prestations seem to by made in an overall context of symmetrical and reciprocal reversible exchanges.

This general pattern of long-term symmetrical exchange between wife-takers and -givers, with in fact the oriented dowry often returning by virtue of preferred marriage with the patrilateral cross-cousin within the context of bilateral cross-cousin exchange, presents as we shall see shortly a discernible contrast to the Pramalai Kallar amongst whom an asymmetry results between the prestations of wife-givers and -takers by virtue of the preferred matrilateral cross-cousin marriage. In a way the Coorg–Kallar contrast seems to echo the Central India–North India contrast between an egalitarian bilateral marriage exchange between status equals and hypergamous exchange between unequals.

Marriage gifts among some Tamil Nadu groups. According to Dumont the most salient feature of the marriage ceremonies of the South Indian groups in question was not sacramental acts and the *tali* tying, nor the common meeting of the relatives on both sides, but 'the long series of alternate shiftings of the couple from one place to the other and back again, which takes place from the marriage onwards *and* is accompanied by gifts in one direction and increased *gifts in return*. This chain of gifts, or 'prestations' and 'counter prestations', symbolizes the alliance tie and is the most important feature of marriage ceremonies from the point of view of the relation between the two families' (1957a: 29-30).

Dumont makes a distinction between *external prestations* which are made between the families of the bride and bridegroom and the *internal prestations* which are money contributions given by the kin of each family to help it defray its wedding expenses. The *internal* prestations are called *moy* (a multitude or crowd) and are usually reciprocal and reversible. The *external* prestations are called *cir* (if made in kind) and *curul* (if made in money); significantly *curul* means a 'rolling up' or circular movement', connoting the cumulative return.

If we confine ourselves to the marriage prestations alone and say that they conclude with the final 'gift which accompanies the gift of the girl' i.e. when the young couple finally set up as an independent household after a shifting residence in the house of their parents, then the liabilities of the groom's side and the bride's side may be set out as shown in Table 4. It is clear from this listing that on the whole the contributions from the bride's side − both to the groom's parents and to the new couple − are larger than the contributions of the groom's family. The direction and relative quantities of the prestations are summed up in the Pramalai Kallar's statement that 'gifts sent to the bride's house return increased twofold or threefold'.

103

Table 4   Marriage prestations in South India

External prestations

(a)   *Reversible gifts* – these are gifts in kind (food, clothes, etc.), which are initiated by groom's side and usually returned 'multiplied' by the bride's side; the series is continued as the young couple visit their parents in turn back and forth, but always *the bride's side returns the gifts more lavishly*; in the case of some gifts there is exact reciprocity or equivalent value.

(b)   *Gifts from groom's side to bride's side*
1. Initial gift of money (*paricam*; *curul*), which may be utilized by bride's parents for making jewellery for the bride. (This payment is lacking among Arupangu). This money payment may be looked upon as *'bride price'* channelled back as 'dowry', but see Dumont's reservations.

2. Tali is provided by the groom's family.

(c)   *Gifts from the bride's family to the married couple*
All these gifts may be viewed as constituting 'dowry' (*cidanam*):
(a) Jewellery provided for bride amongst all groups (except perhaps among Mudukullattur for whom it is insignificant). Among Pramalai Kallar jewellery given bride is equivalent to twice the *paricam* payment.

(b) Pots, pans and household equipment when couple set up separate establishment.

(c) Among two groups – the Paganeri and Ambalakkarar land may also be given to bride.

Interal prestations

(d)   *Moy*
Kin on both sides make gifts to parents of bride and groom. Parents reciprocate with symbolic gifts. (This is absent among Mudukullatur and Ambulukkarar.) The mother's brother's gifts are the most important and they are 'oriented', while *moy* among other kin is usually reversible.

Source: L. Dumont, *Hierarchy and Marriage Alliance in South Indian Kinship, 1957.*

In terms of the interests of this essay, what can we say are comparable to bride-price and/or dowry in this array of prestations? Dumont emphasized the chain-like character of the prestations and therefore the inappropriateness of isolating certain payments as 'brideprice' and 'dowry'. In the list of payments above, perhaps item (b) containing the *paricam* appears to correspond to 'brideprice' that is re-chanelled to the bride, and item (c) enumerating the gifts from the bride's family appears to correspond to *cidanam*.

But Dumont says 'It is clearly impossible to single out one of the marriage "payments", the *paricam* and to call it "bride-price", because it represents in the examples cited "the contribution of the husband's family" to the buying of jewels which will be worn by the wife but normally become the property of the household, as can be ascertained from their treatment in case of divorce' (1957a: 31). Echoing but not acknowledging Aiyappan's earlier gloss (1945) that the Irava *achcharam* can be interpreted as 'earnest money', Dumont continues: 'The *paricam* appears rather as a kind of earnest-money which is destined to come back increased' (1957a: 31). But our examination of the classical ideas shows that we can regard it as a transformed brideprice. The Dharmashastras were instructive about the fate of the *sulkam* given by the groom's parents. It appeared that sometimes it was given to the bride by the bride's parents and constituted a conjugal estate, but that sometimes it reverted to her brothers when she died, reminding us of its true 'brideprice' origin.

It is apposite to mention here that Srinivas in a work on Mysore written in his salad days (*Marriage and Family in Mysore*, Bombay 1942), described the *tera* (a payment of money) customarily given by various Mysore groups as 'brideprice'. But he gives the valuable information that, among the Morasu Okkaligas for instance, 'the *tera* goes to the virgin's father, but he generally uses it for some jewel to be presented to the girl' (1942: 17). At another point although he translated *tera* as 'wife purchase', Srinivas documented the Indian penchant for converting brideprice into dowry. He says that some parents who think that *tera* is degrading add some money to the *tera* contributed by the bridegroom's family and 'either lent at usurious rates of interest in the girl's name, or converted into a gold ornament, which the bride will wear' (p. 18). This ploy, we have already noted, has classical precedent!

According to Dumont, the Pramalai Kallar call *cidanam* (*stridhana*, 'wife's or woman's property) *all gifts due from the wife's family including the future gifts of her brother to his sister's children*. The net result of the protracted exchange of gifts is 'a gift which accompanies the gift of the girl'. Regarding the cycle of gifts which over time increase as they are reciprocated by the wife's side, Dumont points out the now familiar pattern: . . . masculine [i.e. from the bridegroom's side] gifts will decrease as time goes on, while feminine gifts will increase; the latter are substantial, the former initiatory and provocative. Generosity lies on the girl's side, but it has to be set in motion . . .' (1957a: 32). It is possible and sensible to argue that 'dowry' is not one isolated payment but an array of gifts given over time; once again I wish to point out that these are the characteristics of female property (*stridhana*) discussed in the classical texts. But it is also clear that amongst the array of payments that constitute dowry, that given at the time of marriage is the *most important and conspicuous*.

We can thus sum up the above discussion by saying that Dumont's display of the marriage prestations among some South Indian groups (especially the Pramalai Kallar) shows a remarkable correspondance with the transactions in the other groups examined and with those discussed in the classical texts.

The problem of the matrilineal variant in South India. South India is of course famous for its variant kinship institutions, which appear to present a remarkable exception to the classical pan-Indian form which I have hitherto outlined.

The matrilineal Malabar groups of the past are of course the most dramatic variant, and of these the Nayars (of present day Central Kerala) with their *taravad* property cum residential group (composed of brothers and sisters, and sisters' children, and children of sisters' daughters and so on), and with their lack of stable marriage and lack of marriage prestations such as dowry as these are known in orthodox India – have been the ethnographer's wonder (see e.g. Logan 1887, Iyer 1909-12, Gough 1961). I shall deal only briefly with the Malabar groups in this essay: firstly because the Nayars, both the northern and central groups are clearly in some ways a deviation from the classical norm, though they can partly be understood in terms of a dialectical relationship to that norm (see Dumont's interpretation of Nayar marriage 1961), and secondly because some of the problems presented by other matrilineal groups can be more conveniently treated by reference to those that figure in Dumont's discussion of Tamil Nadu.

Let me however point out a lesson that the matrilineal Tiyyar of North Kerala and their brethren called Iravas in Central Kerala can teach us. It is clear from Gough's account that:

(1) The matrilineal Tiyyar (who traditionally had virilocal-avunculocal residence but today have mixed residence which includes virilocal-patrilocality but not matrilocality as such) not only practice the preferred matrilateral cross-cousin marriage but have firmly delineated marriage prestations which are already familiar to us (the coexistence of 'earnest money', 'bridewealth' and 'dowry', the latter being more stressed and consisting of movable wealth).

The marriage ceremony itself consisted of the bridegroom's presenting one loin cloth to his wife and another to her mother. The marriage feast in the bride's house was jointly supplied by the couple's matrilineal groups. After the feast the bridegroom's *karanavan* paid a small bride-wealth in *panams* (traditional Malabari coins) to the *karanavan* of the bride. The bride's party in turn supplied a dowry of jewellery and cooking vessels. After the marriage had been consummated the couple were blessed by the girl's elders and departed to the bridegroom's house' (Gough 1961: 411).

(2) Gough has described the Iravas of Central Kerala as having 'a double unilineal kinship system with localized lineages'. We are interested in the fact that they are patrilocal, that land passes from father to son and that women bring a dowry of movables, particularly jewellery and cooking vessels, with them (Aiyappan 1945, Gough 1955).

Aiyappan asserts that both the northern and southern Iravas (Tiyyars) traditionally had the same pattern of marriage transactions despite their descent rules. The bridegroom's side first paid 'earnest money' (achcharam) which he also glosses as 'bridewealth' (1945: 158): the amounts paid were from 8-29 panams which though not large were not insignificant in the past either. We are told that 'In North Malabar this earnest money is called "kanam", which is used in the terminology of land tenure for the amount advanced by a cultivator to the landlord as an interest-bearing premium, to be returned when the property is surrendered on demand . . .' (p. 91). This gloss throws light on the function of the payment from the groom's side. In turn the girl brings a dowry, the amount of which is determined previously during the negotiations. 'The dowry consists of gold and silver ornaments, plates, spouted pots, spittoons, lamps, etc., of bell metal, and in the case of richer people, cows, buffalos, copper vessels, servant maid and boy. About half a century ago, slaves were also given as part of the dowry. Apart from these, it is customary for the girl to present her ornaments. Among the patrilineal Iravas the payments of the stipulated dowry is insisted upon, since the girl has no right of inheriting her paternal property' (p. 92).[30]

What I wish tentatively to suggest from the Irava example is that matrilineality *per se* need not affect the pan-Indian picture of orthodox marriage prestations (particularly the giving in movables) so long as residence remains dominantly patri-local or avunculocal (or neolocal), and not (or only exceptionally) matrilocal or ambilocal (either patri-or matrilocal).

The Nayars can be summarily dealt with apropos this hypothesis in the following way. The Central Nayar of the past with their lack of 'marriage' (in the sense of enduring co-residence of the couple) and with their residence of brothers and sisters simultaneously matrilocally and avunculocally, so to say, do not contradict the hypothesis. The Northern Nayar who, like their central brethren, do not pay either 'brideprice' or 'dowry' are more problematic, though they do not altogether contradict it. For one thing they combine virilocal-avunculocal residence with some measure of uxorilocal-matrilocal residence; secondly in Trobriand fashion sons return to their matrilineal *taravad*, and wives also return when their husbands die. Finally, as among the Trobriands, the wife's natal *taravad* is charged with (partially) maintaining the married sister with gifts of rice, grain, food and clothing, which is tantamount to enduring affinal gifts on the wider Indian pattern (Gough 1961: 411).

Let us now return to Dumont's account of the Tamil Nadu groups (1957a) and attempt to establish the implications of the Nangudi Vellalar's startling deviation form the normative pattern of marriage payments and affinal prestations which Dumont outlines (and which is well represented by the Kallar who will therefore act as a comparative foil).

The Nangudi Vellalar (located near Srivaikuntham in Tinnevelly District in the South Eastern tip) are a startling deviation from Dumont's generalization because they do not make the usual reciprocal gifts at marriage. The bridegroom's side give no *paricam*, *tali* or *sari*; nor do kin on both sides contribute *moy*. The dominant transaction is the provision by the bride's parents of the bride's dowry composed of jewellery, land and household effects. The bridegroom's parents are merely charged with providing foodstuffs regularly once the couple have set up house. Two features need to be noted: there seems to be a clear cut *cidanam* (dowry-cum-female-property) which unlike the dominant Indian pattern includes *strong rights in land*.

What are the institutional features that accompany this marriage pattern? The Nangudi Vellalar are matrilineal; their inheritance customs are such that there is a double transmission of property *including land* from father to son and from mother to daughter. In a village, part of the property is held by men and transmitted from father to son and the other part (nearly half in their main village) is held by women and transmitted from mother to daughter. Houses are female property while the offices of chieftain descends patrilineally from father to son. Residence is matrilocal, the young couple being given a separate house; in the case of chiefs there may be a pattern of dual residence. The contradiction between male avuncular authority and matrilocal residence is sometimes resolved by a man returning to his parental house in old age. A small local settelment contains representives of three matrilines, who in fact belong to two intermarrying mitrilineages. *Patrilateral cross-cousin marriage is the preferred type*, manifested strongly among chiefly families.

A direct contrast to these Vellalar are the Pramalai Kallar, who conform to the general pattern of marriage prestations depicted by Dumont (1957a, 1957b). These Kallar are patrilineal and patrilocal. Inheritance again is patrilineal; and although the patrilineage is not directly indentified with locality, the residence pattern results in quite solid patrilineages of a permanent character. Sons inherit the property of their fathers equally; if there are no sons then the property passes to brothers or parallel cousins, and *never to girls*; in this the Kallars of South India resemble the Jats of the North in their strong patrilineal ideals. The preferred marriage is with the matrilateral cross-cousin. Such marriage is an obligation for the eldest son which, if not fulfilled, results in a compensation payment.

Now to deal with Kallar marriage payments which Dumont divides into: (1) 'external' prestations between the marrying families; and (2) 'internal' prestations within the respective kin groups of bride and bridegroom.

(1)   The bridegroom's father gives *paricam* usually in the form of cash to the bride's father before marriage. In return the bride's father has usually to spend twice the value of *paricam* towards the bride's jewellery. In effect the *paricam* itself is thus transferred into a part of the bride's jewellery and dowry.

There are other prestations such as the *madi cire* consisting of baskets of bananas, betel nuts, etc. given by the groom's family which is returned by the bride's family in a different composition of bananas, rice, etc.

The couple regularly visit and stay with the wife's parents during the first three years of marriage, and return to the husband's father's home with gifts of *cire*; only the final gift of *cire* and of jewellery to the wife actually goes to the young couple as dowry (and conjugal estate).

(2)   Of the internal prestations, called *moy*, made within the kin group, it is the mother's brother's gift that is important. His gifts are 'oriented' (and given at the brith of a child, at its circumcision or puberty, as its marriage, etc.) while other prestations are 'reversible' as in the case of funeral gifts.

Thus two contrasting patterns — in close physical proximity — are in evidence in Tamil Nadu. The Kallar pattern has the following components: strongly patrilineal descent, patrilocal residence, matrilateral cross-cousin marriage which results in asymmetrical exchange whereby the side that continuously gives the bride also on balance gives more material oriented prestations (including the dowry). The Nangudi Vellalar pattern is an almost precise reversal: matrilineal, matrilocal (or less frequently duolocal) with the junior couple living in households 'independent' of parents-in-law, patrilateral cross cousin marriage, unilateral transfer of dowry unaccompanied by any noteworthy reciprocal affinal prestations from the bridegroom's family, though the patrilateral marriage formula ensures equal exchange over time. But the Vellalar features seem to be associated with a marked notion of female property rights (as compared with the weaker Kallar form which is also the general Indian pattern), which includes land. They also seem to signify that, since symmetrical reciprocity over time is a built-in feature, and female inheritance is sanctioned, there is no need to mark ceremonially, and through prestations to create and emphasize and maintain, bonds of affinity. The chain of prestations diminishes correspondingly as the notion of female property becomes sharpened and independently established.

I wish to suggest that the uniqueness of the Nangudi Vellalar rests not on their preference for patrilateral cross cousin marriage (which preference is shared with certain other groups), but stems from their matrilocal and duolocal) residence. It is this which allows the concept of female property to include strong rights in land. Once this pattern is established the patrilateral cross cousin marriage wherever systematically practised between 'lines' sets up symmetrical exchange.

Let us be clear as to what I am proposing. My argument is that the most general Indian pattern of dowry in movable wealth and of an intricate pattern of affinal prestations etc. is associated with and occurs in conjunction with the norm of patrilocality (or avunculocality). In contrast the definition that a woman's dowry rights includes inheritance of land (and other patrimonial immovable wealth) which she shares equally with her brother can only occur in conjunction with matrilocality or duolocality (moving from patrilocality to matrilocality or vice versa) or ambilocality (open choice to live with the husband's parents or the wife's parents) as the main form of residence. It can also plausibly be argued that shifts toward egalitarian property rights between male and female siblings and toward an open residence pattern of virilocality or uxorilocality or of living with the husband's or wife's parents can create (if pushed far enough) a shift from unilineal descent to bilateral kinship.

This is precisely what happens on the island of Ceylon at the south eastern tip of India. Ceylon comes into focus at this point becuase there are groups there such as the Vellalars* of North Ceylon who render the Nangudi Vellalar of South India not so unique, and more importantly, manifest a systematic structural shift towards the bilaterality mentioned above. Another group, the Kandyan Sinhalese, also approach the paradigm of bilaterality by a shift represented in the form of a 'weakening' and 'softening' of the dominant Indian classical pattern. Thus these two Ceylonese groups I shall examine – the Vellalahs of North Ceylon (Jaffna peninsula) and the Kandyan Sinhalese (central Ceylon) – have arrived at the pattern of bilaterality by somewhat similar, though not identical, routes.

* Following the spelling adopted by certain writers (e.g. H.W. Tambiah and M. Banks) I render this North Ceylon caste group as Vellah.

DOWRY, BRIDEWEALTH AND WOMEN'S PROPERTY RIGHTS

PART FOUR

Two Ceylonese groups

The two Ceylonese groups I have chosen will not receive equal treatment in respect of space devoted to them for a simple reason. The Tamils of North Ceylon are virtually unknown in the ethnographic literature (but for a single essay by Banks (1960); their traditional laws are somewhat better known (H.W. Tambiah n.d.). But there is much ethnographic information buried in Banks' unpublished doctoral dissertation (1957) which deserves to be made known. And the traditional laws of the Jaffna Tamils deserve an interpretation from an anthropological perspective. On both counts the Jaffna Tamils are given more space here than the Kandyan Sinhalese whose traditional laws have been codified and commented upon in several texts by several writers (e.g. D'Oyly 1929, Sawers [several versions], Armour 1860, Le Mesurier and Panabokke 1880, Modder 1914, Hayley 1923, H.W. Tambiah 1968), and whose contemporary ethnography have again received full and excellent documentation (Leach 1961d, Yalman 1967, S.J. Tambiah 1958, 1966, 1965; Robinson 1968).[31] In the light of this prolific literature I shall limit myself to arranging the main principles of the Kandyan system according to, and in confirmation of, the theoretical scheme I have in mind.

As I have done previously for India, I shall deal with aspects of both traditional law and of contemporary ethnography. The written codified versions of the Ceylonese legal systems are of relatively recent origin compared with the classical Indian *shastric* literature. The traditional legal customs of the Jaffna Tamils were for the first time committed to writing and codified under Dutch colonial inspiration in the early eighteenth century. The legal customs of the Kandyan Sinhalese were similarly codified by the British in the first few decades of the nineteenth century.[32] One cannot but note in this respect the 'provinciality' of the Ceylonese legal traditions compared with those of the Indian high culture.

These codified traditional laws were themselves modified or changed in part during the period of British administration. I shall not be concerned so much with this aspect as with demonstrating the *continuity* between these stated traditional laws and current contemporary patterns of life.

The Tamils of North Ceylon

My method of exposition is first to elucidate the main features concerning marriage, residence, dowry and inheritance as stated in the *Thesawalamai* (Customs of the Land) and then to expound the kinship system as described in Banks' study (1957).[33]

The Thesawalamai Code

The Thesawalamai, literally meaning 'Customs of the Land', is a collection of the customs of the Tamil inhabitants of Jaffna in North Ceylon made under the orders

111

of the Dutch Governor of Maritime Ceylon, Governor Simons, in 1706-7. The actual codification accomplished under the surveillance of Claus Isaaksz, was submitted to and approved by twelve Mudaliyars (native chiefs) and thereafter promulgated as an authoritative exposition of the usages of the Jaffna Tamils. The British who succeeded the Dutch as colonial rulers declared that the Thesawalamai (as collected by the Order of Governor Simons in 1706) should be considered to be in full force by the Regulation of 1806; this was confirmed again by Ordinance No. 5 of 1869. I shall first set out the main features of the Thesawalamai which pertain to our enquiry about marriage payments.

The Thesawalamai, in its beginning part, says that several changes had taken place in the traditional laws particularly during the times of the Portuguese (who controlled the Ceylonese littoral, the low country and the north during the sixteenth and first half of the seventeenth centuries).

Although it is impossible to validate this statement, it is interesting to gather an impression of what the traditional features were imagined to have been and, wherever relevant, to speculate about their possible implications by comparison with the codified system.

The alleged pre-Portuguese system. From ancient times three categories of property were said to have been recognized:

(1) *Modesium (mudisam)*: hereditary property brought by the husband.
(2) *Chidenam*: hereditary property brought by the wife (also referred to as *dowry*). Note that etymologically *chidenam* is derived from, and is similar to, the Sanskrit concept *stridhanam*, meaning 'female property'.
(3) *Tediatetam (thediathetam)*: the profits during marriage or 'acquisition' (I shall hereafter transliterate these Tamil categories as *mudisam, chidenam* and *thediathetam*).

The traditional inheritance system is imagined as a sex-determined bifurcating devolution whereby (1) the mother's property which she brought into marriage as her dowry (*chidenam*) is transferred to her daughters alone *at marriage* as their dowries; (2) the father's *mudisam* property (i.e. goods and land brought by him to the marriage) is inherited only *on his death* by the sons; (3) and the property acquired during the marriage (*thediathetam*) is divided among the sons and daughters alike. As the code puts it, the result of these rules is that 'invariably the husband's property always remains with the male heirs, and the wife's property with the female heirs'.

But the Thesawalamai goes on to state that owing to the changes undergone particularly during Portuguese times, 'at present, whenever a husband and wife give a daughter or daughters in marriage the *dowry* is taken indiscriminately from the property of husband and wife, both inherited and acquired'. As we shall see in a moment, what this states then is that the *property transferred to daughters at marriage* is taken from the conjugal estate and has usually priority in time over the subsequent succession or inheritance of the sons. The three categories of property themselves remained valid at the time of codification.[34] Let us take the *chidenam* and *mudisam*, female and male property respectively, in turn.

The Chidenam (dowry). From the sections in the Code concerning *dowry* the following features can be abstracted:

(1) It is clearly stated or implied that women can receive as dowry all categories of property, namely, immovable property such as fields and gardens (land), and movables such as cash, jewellery and household effects. Slaves are also included. This alone makes it clear that the Thesawalamai (as was the practice among the Nangudi Vellalar) has a much stronger notion of female property rights than is contained in the classical Indian formulation in the Dharmashastras.

(2) The Code also makes it clear that the dowry is a kind of pre-mortem inheritance of the daughter given at the time of her marriage, with the understanding that she has no further claims on the parents.[35] This idea is further strengthened by the fact (a) that the property is to be transferred by *doty ola* (i.e. a legal documentary transaction) and (b) that the daughter and her husband forfeit the claim to the property (gardens, slaves, etc.) given at marriage if they do not take possession of it within ten years. What is interesting about this stipulation is that the daughter's property is in customary law considered to have been actually given away at the time of or soon after her marriage and not retained by the donor until his or her death.

The Code, however makes certain concessions to the claims of daughters to additional property after the dowry has been given: should it happen that after the marriage of the daughters the parents prosper considerably, 'the daughters are at liberty to induce their parents to increase the *doty*, which the parents have an undoubted right to do so'. We may note that the daughters are at 'liberty to induce' and do not have a right to claim under the circumstances stated.

(3) The Code also asserts the complementary idea to that of pre-mortem inheritance, namely that the dowry is more than simply pre-mortem inheritance, or rather that it is pre-mortem inheritance precisely because it can be used to effect a marriage and to find a husband who himself looks forward to managing and enjoying its proceeds. In the Code's own words, the *doty ola* should be properly drawn up and executed 'because it is by this means that most of the girls obtain husbands, and it is not for the girls but for the property that most of the men marry . . .' A further fact to be taken into account is that there is no notion that all daughters should get dowries of identical value; as we shall see later, they vary according to the 'market value' of the husband.

(4) The rules of reversion of a woman's *chidenam* property once again emphasize the strength of the female claim. If a dowried married daughter dies without issue her property devolved in the following order of priority:

(a)   her other sisters, their daughters and their granddaughters (in that order);

113

(b)   if none in (a) above, then on her brothers, their sons, and their grand-sons (in that order);

(c)   if none in (b) above, then on her parents if they are alive;

(d)   if her parents are not alive, then that part of the property which is her father's hereditary property (*mudisam*) and half of the *thediathetam* devolved first on the father's brothers, their sons and grandsons, and that part of the property which is her mother's *chidenam* and the other half of the acquired property devolves on her sisters, their daughters or granddaughters.

These rules of reversion concerning the property of married women contain important principles which are best elucidated after the discussion of the inheritance portions of sons and the transmission of that property.

Concerning the marriage of sons and their inheritance portion

(1) Whereas daughters are given their *chidenam* property at marriage, the sons cannot claim anything whatsoever so long as the parents live. On the contrary they are bound to bring into the common estate all they they have earned or gained during the whole time of their bachelorhood (except personal jewellery acquired by themselves or given them by their parents), and this they are bound to do 'until the parents die, even if the sons have married and quitted the paternal roof'.

(2) The sons 'then *first* inherit the property left by their parents, which is called *modesium*, or hereditary property' when the parents die. While this is the legal position, the Code however makes the following provision for informal division of parental *acquired* property during the lifetime of the parents: should age render the parents incapable of administering their own acquired property, the sons may divide it in order that they may maintain their parents with it, but if sons, having induced their parents to so divide with the promise to support them during the rest of their life fail to fulfil this promise, then the parents are at liberty to resume the property.

The obligation of sons toward their parents receives its maximum emphasis in their subjection to a condition from which daughters are exempt: even if parents do not leave anything for the sons to inherit when they die, the sons are nevertheless bound to pay the debts contracted by their parents; they are held so accountable even if they do not have the means for paying such debts.

The rules of devolution and reversion if a son dies without issue are the symmetrical opposite of the rules pertaining to daughters: it first devolves on other men in the order of brothers, brother's sons and brothers' grandsons; if there are none in these categories, it devolves on his sisters, their daughters and their granddaughters. Thereafter the rules are the same as for their sisters: it reverts to parents, and thereafter to their siblings of the same sex etc.

Widow's and widower's rights. If a man with infant children dies, the whole property remains with his wife, but she must dowry her daughters as they get married, while her sons await her death to inherit.

If the wife dies first the father remains in full possession of the estate and administers it in the same manner.

It is noteworthy that the Thesawalamai legitimated the remarriage of widows, but saw to it that in such an event the property rights of the children, especially the sons by different fathers, were kept separate. Thus when a widow remarries and bears children, the daughters of both marriages get their dowries from their mother's *chidenam* and acquired property and from the property of their respective fathers; the sons of the first marriage and the second marriage get what remains of their respective fathers' properties (*mudisam* and acquired). There are even finer rules about the rights of sons to the remainder of the mother's acquired property, but this need not concern us here. What we note in the above provision is that in widow remarriage, while daughters by different husbands but by the same mother are classed as one category as far as their dowry rights are concerned, the sons by different fathers are differentiated in respect of their inheritances; the first essentially because their mother's *chidenam* is common to the daughters, the second because the source of their respective *mudisam* is different.

What happens when a widower with children remarries?

The Code says that generally the care of children who are minors is entrusted to the mother-in-law (the deceased wife's mother) or nearest relation, and the father must ensure that the dowry and acquired property of the deceased mother is used first to dowry the daughters by that marriage and that the remainder goes to the sons by the same marriage; the father could of course contribute from his own property as well to the dowries in question. The daughters by the second marriage are dowried in the normal way. The sons of both marriages divide equally their common father's *mudisam* and share of acquired property. Thus in this instance the essential principle being emphasized is that daughters by different mothers but the same father derive the major part of their dowries from separate sources (i.e. their own mothers), whereas sons by different mothers inherit their major portions from the property of their common father.

All these provisions once again emphasize the bifurcation between male and female property on the basis of equality; hence descendants take their inheritance according to their relation to the source of the property in question.

Adoption. In the case of adoption another facet of the equal claims of males and females is portrayed. An adoption is said to require the consent of the brothers and sisters of the adopter (or in their absence, the next closest relatives) in their capacity as prospective heirs who now forgo their rights. Thus the preferred child for adoption as heir is the child of a sibling; if siblings are unwilling to provide a child or none is available then a stranger-child can be adopted conditional to the consent of siblings. A non-kin can be adopted against the wishes of siblings but in such a case the child has inferior inheritance rights (to about a tenth of the property of the adopter). A fully adopted child loses all claims to inheritance in his own family; if other children are born after adoption, the adopted child has the same rights as the natural children of the adopting family. But full inheritance rights are ensured only if the parents of the child and the brothers and sisters of the adopters dip their hands in saffron water which is then drunk by the adopters and the adopted.

The separate property rights of a man and his wife reappear even in adoption. A husband, but not his wife, may adopt by himself alone drinking the saffron water, and the child adopted becomes heir only to his property, but the child however retains claims to his own natural mother's property (though not his natural father's). Correspondingly a married woman may adopt, with symmetrically reversed implications.

Discussion. Now we can pull together the implication of the property rights of daughters and sons, and of married women and married men.

I have already commented on the strength of female property rights as signified by the fact that daughters are entitled to receive all categories of property including land. The provisions concerning the rights of widows and widowers and their children and the rights of adoption of husband and wife carry the same message of duality. It is also remarkable that not only has a husband no control (outside of management) of the property of his wife but he has no right in the traditional code to inherit the property of his wife dying without issue. This further strengthens the idea that in theory the properties of husband and wife were meant to be kept separate although they could be enjoyed together as a merged conjugal estate. Under the traditional code a woman's dowry property, being considered her separate property, was not liable for her husband's debts, nor were the rents and profits of that property liable to seizure for the husband's debts.

While the bachelor sons are expected to contribute their earnings until the parents' death, and cannot claim any part of them at their marriage, the daughters in contrast take away their property at marriage without any further obligations to their parents such as supporting them in their old age and paying their debts which the sons are obliged to undertake. What we have here is the contrast between pre-mortem inheritance of daughters and the post-mortem inheritance of sons, a contrast that is linked to different points of time in the family cycle. It looks as if married sons are supposed either to stay in a dependent position with their parents or live more independently on the wife's dowry, until such time as they themselves inherit and succeed to the parents' property. If this was the true consequence or implication of the Thesawalamai, then in theory we should expect a tendency among married sons toward uxorilocal residence soon after marriage and either persistence therein or a change to virilocal residence later in life when men succeed to the property of their parents.

However, it is very difficult to conclude firmly that this was actually the

116

case, for the Code itself as we have seen provides for sons to divide at least a part of parental property in the lifetime of their parents. The possibility is there then that sons could succeed to their parents in the latters' old age and simply await their death for final *de jure* control. Thus one could predict on the basis of these facts that residence would show a wide dispersion of uxorilocal and virilocal cases, and instances of shifts from one to the other.

It is also difficult from the Code to decide on the relative weights of another matter. It is quite clear that, in effect, daughters have first call on their parents' property, for they take it at their marriage. What is not clear is whether the dowries of daughters in general exceeded the delayed inheritances of sons. Clearly the alleged pre-Portuguese customs which asserted that sons inherited their father's *mudisam* and daughters their mother's *chidenam* (*plus* equal division of acquired property) guaranteed the patrimony of sons, as much as it did the property rights of daughters. For the subsequent period, the best bet would be to predicate a situation of bilateral inheritance, with the possibility of skewing in the female or male direction according to particular social circumstances and the material wealth of the parents.

There is another remarkable feature about the Code which stems from the rules of reversion we have examined. A cardinal rule is that, in the absence of descendants, collaterals succeed before descendants, siblings before parents, siblings of same sex before siblings of opposite sex, etc. It is difficult to see what sociological feature is implied by the fact that property reverts to siblings before parents (the source whence property came): perhaps it indicates that according to the traditional view transmission of property from parents to children, from ascendants to descendants, was considered preferably not reversed once transmission had taken place.

We can conclude this discussion of the *Thesawalamai* by comparing its provisions with those enshrined in the Dharmashastras which comprise the basis for the classical Hindu pattern. In my view it is misguided and off-course to trace the origins and affinities of Thesawalamai to the Malabar *marumakkatayam* matrilineal succession and the matrilineal *taravad.* [36]

On the contrary, we can learn something by comparing the main features of the Thesawalamai with those in the Indian classical legal systems, particularly the Mitakshara.

It is clear that the Thesawalamai invests women with stronger property rights that the Indian *shastric* systems. Whereas in North Ceylon women inherited land, Indian systems restricted them to movables, and only exceptionally to land.

Although both *shastric* law and Thesawalamai distinguish between male hereditary property and female property, yet the incidents attaching to each of these are not the same. In Thesawalamai the woman's *chidenam* passes first to the daughters (and the remainder to the sons), whereas under Indian classical law, as we have seen, the *stridhanam* is composed of different categories which are transmitted in different directions: the *sulkam* to a woman's brothers, while the *yautaka* (given by the bride's parents and kin) alone passes to her daughters, and other categories are shared out between sons and daughters.

Furthermore while in Thesawalamai, the *chidenam* is given entirely by the girl's parents, the corresponding *stridhanam* of Hindu law is composed of female property derived from diverse sources.

But in a more general comparative sense the classical Indian *shastric* and the Thesawalamai systems can be seen as members of the same family. The former has as we have seen a strong notion of male property — but under certain circumstances transmittable through sons of females — complemented by a weaker notion of female property limited to movables. The Thesawalamai credits males and females with equal rights to the same kinds of properties — it thus produces a symmetrical system of dual devolution. In fact the strength of a woman's position in Thesewalamai is to be seen in the fact that sons should not claim anything from the property of parents until the last daughter is dowried.[37] Ultimately in both systems, female property is transmitted to the woman at her marriage and therefore it serves an effective role as dowry in the making of marriages and the setting up of relatively enduring relations with affines.

The system of marriage and property rights among contemporary Jaffna Tamils
Having documented the salient points of the Thesawalamai (as collated in 1706-7) concerning categories of property and their mode of transmission with special reference to the rights of females, I shall now proceed to state briefly some of the dominant social features of a contemporary Jaffna village studied between 1952-4 by Banks (1957).

The Thesawalamai provisions themselves, to which the British gave legal force in 1806, were changed in some respects during British rule, particularly by Ordinance No. 1 of 1911, and Ordinance No. 58 of 1947. I shall not deal with these changes here (see H.W. Tambiah, n.d.). What we shall see is the remarkable continuity in the customs documented in the early eighteenth century and those of today; furthermore some of the social patterns of today will no doubt help us to clarify some of the indeterminacies about the implications of the traditional Code.

Banks's study, especially those features pertaining to marriage, kinship and property, is practically limited to the dominant Vellalah caste — traditionally the agricultural, landowning caste around whom were articulated the services of 'slave' agricultural labouring castes, and of the ritually pure (but immigrant) priestly Brahman caste. What is thus described here are Vellalah customs and institutions.

Kinship relationships and behaviour. The *brother–sister* relationship is one of mutual support (whereas the brother–brother relation is one of competition and tension). *Brothers in Chiruppiddi cannot get married before their sisters* (unless there is a great age disparity between an older brother and a younger

118

sister). As opposed to the relationship between male siblings, the relationship between *machan* (male cross-cousins, brothers-in-law) is one of friendship, loyalty and mutual reciprocity.

Cross-cousin marriage is the ideologically preferred form among the Jaffna Tamils, at least traditionally; the advantages of such marriage are usually spelled out in terms of the ensuring of purity of caste or, within caste or status, of ensuring a stable marriage between persons whose backgrounds and character are known and predictable, and as enabling the recombination of the properties of a man and his sister through their children (an argument that can only apply to the patrilateral form). We shall return again to the question of the actual incidence of cross-cousin marriage and its implication for property.

Chidenam (*dowry*) *among the Jaffna Tamils.* Traditional categories of property such as *mudisam* and *chidenam* are still in vogue among the Jaffnese. Significantly it is the latter that enjoys the limelight for several reasons, the most important of which is that it is intimately connected with the contracting of marriage.

The *chidenam* in the role of dowry is separated out from the parental property and in theory given to the daughter at her marriage; sons on the other hand do not fully inherit until their parents' death. Brothers are on the whole willing to adopt a generous attitude as regards their sisters' dowries, for it is only after the sisters are married off that brothers can themselves marry in turn and recoup through the dowries their own wives bring. Thus we can say that dowry given away with the sister is compensated for by the dowry received when the brother marries, but as I have argued before, this sort of linked series is quite different from the notion of 'cattle-linked sisters' in the brideprice marriage systems of say the Lovedu or the Gusii in Africa. The mirror image is impossible for two reasons which have already been elucidated. A man generally cannot use his wife's dowry to finance his sister's marriage because brothers can marry only after their sisters are married, and secondly, more importantly, the dowry of a man's wife is her property under her control and her husband cannot alienate it without her express consent.

The components of the dowry. The dowry called *chidenam* is an essential part of every marriage negotiation and of nearly every Vellalah caste marriage. The dowry consists in Jaffna of three main components – land, jewels, and cash, *of which by far the most valuable part is land.* Land is thus the major and most important component of the dowry, while jewels and cash are of secondary significance. Land is usually classified into the following types: (1) garden land (*thotum*) which is sub-classified into palmyrah garden (*panethotum*), coconut garden (*thenemarram thotum*), and thirdly land on which vegetables, tobacco, bananas, etc. are grown); (2) paddy land (*vayal*); (3) house compound land (*nilum*) and (4) waste. It is noteworthy that all these kinds of land figure in the dowries given.[38]

119

All types of wealth composing the *chidenam* are legally transferred by her parents to the daughter marrying and *not to the husband.* But of course, as is the usual Indian pattern, the dowry forms part of the conjugal estate whose proceeds are enjoyed in common. The husband usually has the rights of management, and the wife though owner cannot dispose of her property without her husband's consent so long as they live together. Banks reports – and I can confirm this – that in most rich or propertied families the dowry is transferred in a written legal deed and the marriage rites as such do not occur until such a deed has been drawn up (and I may add scrutinized by the bridegroom's father or some such near kinsman). No written or attested deeds are insisted upon in poorer families, but an oral promise is made in front of two witnesses. This procedure is legally binding.

The major difference between the Jaffna Tamil notion of *chidenam* and the usual South Indian forms occurring not only in many of the groups reported by Dumont, but also among the Tanjore Brahman and Vellalar groups (as reported by Gough) and the Coorgs (as reported by Srinivas) is that whereas in Jaffna (as is the case with the matrilineal matrilocal Nangudi Vellalar) land is the major component of dowry supplemented by jewellery and cash, in the South Indian groups listed above as examples, it is jewellery, cash and household effects which constitute the major share, land being rarely if ever transferred to women.

A note on marriage payments. It is clear that among the Jaffna Tamils the *chidenam* contributed by the bride's family looms as the most conspicuous item in the marriage payments. And what I had previously deduced and confirmed as regards the Nangudi Vellalar must also hold for the Vellalahs of Jaffna: in the context of strong female property rights, other marriage prestations will be highly abbreviated and much smaller in value, particularly the counter prestations from the bridegroom's side.

Arumugam wrote an account in 1892 (published in the *Ceylon Antiquary* Vol. II, Part IV, 1916) of a Vellalah wedding (in which Brahman priests are described as officiating) from which we can abstract the following facts:

Given to the bride from the bridegroom's side is the *parisam* (contents not listed) on the day of the wedding. The bridegroom's procession carries the *tali* (the gold necklace with pendant which the groom ties on the bride as a sign of marriage) and the *kurai* (the *sari* which the bride will wear at the rites).

The bride's parents and family transfer to the bridegroom together with the bride herself (*kannikathanam* [Skt. = *kanya dana*] i.e. the gift of the virgin), betel leaves, areca nut and gold coins. The largest material item transferred is the dowry (which includes jewellery, land etc. and is transferred by deed).

From Michael Banks' account I derive the following transactions:

Banks refers to the gifts from the bridegroom's side as *parisam* and interestingly construes *parisam* as presents from the bridegroom to the bride at the time of marriage and lists them as made up of the following:

(a) *Tali*: the marriage necklace with pendant which is carried in the bridegroom's procession by a woman of the servant Koviyar caste (it can cost up to 10 gold sovereigns for the well-to-do).

(b) *Kurai*: wedding sari — which among the rich is a silk cloth with gold embroidery — costing in 1953 from Rs 200-300 to Rs 1,000. The bride wears this sari for the marriage rites and her wearing of the cloth provided by the bridegroom connotes her transfer and his corresponding material support of her.

(c) Toilet articles such as scent, comb, mirror, soap, powder, which are presented with the *kurai*; these articles can be interpreted as symbols of sexual rights and intimacy.

From the side of the bride we suppose what is transferred is the dowry, or rather the dowry deed (or promise of dowry) to be realized soon after marriage.

Now Banks fails to comment on the gifts given by the bride's kin and the bridegroom's kin either as internal or external prestations. I am inclined to think that he fails to do so because perhaps they are essentially unimportant.

When these transactions are contrasted with those enumerated by Dumont, particularly for the Kallar and Maravar groups, we see how in Jaffna the whole complex of give and take is not ceremonially emphasized: it is as if among the Jaffna Vellalahs (and among the Nangudi Vellalar in South India) the bride's marriage portion which she takes with her as her right is guaranteed *ab initio*, while in the other cases the gifts back and forth one might say actually 'forgo' and establish the marriage alliance. Furthermore we saw in the latter instances that although the gifts from the bride's family exceed those from the groom's, they are still restricted to movables only. Taking our cue from the Jaffna Tamils and the Nangudi we can say that as female property rights, especially to land and other immovables, loom larger and are guaranteed in a woman's dowry, so correspondingly do the counter prestations from the groom's side fade away into relative insignificance.

Michael Banks, having remarked on the difference in the constituents of dowry among the Jaffna Vellalahs on the one hand and the Tanjore Brahmans and Tanjore Vellalar on the other, the former concentrating on land and the latter on jewellery and cash, suggests the following hypothesis which I myself had quite independently evolved in a more complex form. He writes 'This [difference in dowry] is clearly connected with the fact that Tanjore villages had or have an agnatic core of landowners, organized in a defined genealogical framework and in no sense bilateral groupings' as are the Jaffna Tamil groupings. He has in mind here *residentially* bilateral groupings. We should perhaps consider a more complex form of this hypothesis: wherever there are strong *patrilocal* or *avunculocal* groupings (whether the descent system is patrilineal, or matrilineal, or bilineal), there women's property, where it prevails, will be in movables only;

where there are matrilocal-uxorilocal groupings, women will be invested with land not necessarily to the exclusion of males (as among the Nangudi Vellalar). Where there are bilateral *ambilocal* local groupings and a free mixture of virilocal and uxorilocal residence, there both men and women can plausibly be endowed with equal property rights in both movables and immovables. It is my thesis that the Jaffna Tamils are of this sort; so are the Kandyan Sinhalese (and most Sinhalese groups) a variant of this pattern. We can now take up the question of residence among the Jaffna Vellalahs.

Household composition and residential pattern. When I expounded the rules of the Thesawalamai I conjectured that if daughters are given their dowries when they marry and if sons must await their parents' death in order to inherit, then marriages may tend to be uxorilocal at the start of marriages and may or may not show a shift to virilocal residence later on. Of the contemporary Jaffna Tamils Banks writes:

> The preferred pattern, at least at the beginning of a marriage, is for the wife to have a house in her dowry land and for the newly married couple to live there, that is U-locally; but this is not necessarily a life-long pattern.

But although this is the preferred verbalized pattern the Jaffna residence pattern from the very beginning of marriage shows a free and equal distribution between uxorilocality and virilocality.

Banks makes a distinction in his presentation between virilocal and uxorilocal residence on the one hand signifying living together as part of the same household (a commensal unit) as the husband's or wife's parents, and on the other U-local and V-local residence by which he means living in the same ward (or neighbourhood) as the parents but not as part of their household.

At whatever level we look at the facts the Jaffna village shows a marked ambilocal bilateral pattern. For instance Banks classifies household types in his sample as follows:

Elementary family	42
Complex family	42
Single person family	4
	88

If we look only at the complex families (i.e. two or more families forming a single household) it is remarkable that paternal and maternal grandparents of husband and wife, parents of husband and of wife (and other ascendant relatives) are likely to be equally present. The household of co-resident married siblings is rare.

Now the 42 elementary families themselves were not, in, the main, living neolocally but in the wards of either set of parents — that is V-locally and U-locally.

By and large then, one is impressed with the symmetrical occurrence of *uxorilocality* and *virilocality* (in the broader sense which combines both categories). Thus among 39 couples Banks tells us, there is a fairly close similarity of of incidence of the wife moving to live in the husband's village (23) as the husband moving to the wife's (16). Furthermore there were as many couples living on the wife's property as on the husband's. But the most noteworthy fact of all is that the largest number of couples (85) did not move from the village at all i.e. they married within the village.

Banks writes: 'In Jaffna residence is decided by where there is a house, or where there is a house compound on which a house can be built, and people not infrequently find it to their advantage to move more than once in their lifetime.'

Now how can we make more sense of these facts? First of all we must settle the problem posed by the old Thesawalamai code: sons, we are told, inherited only after the death of their parents, but nevertheless sons may take over the administration of parental property when parents grow old and are looked after by sons. The actual situation in the Jaffna village is that parents (having of course dowried off their daughters) actually tended in their old age to transfer their lands to sons. It was widows or widowers living with their children who tended to do this most. This pre-mortem transference, however, is not formulated as an obligatory rule of behaviour, though empirically it is widespread.

This then in part at least explains why residence can show an equal balance of virilocality and uxorilocality (and shifts between them). Couples may decide to live where it is most convenient, but by the same token, couples have control over property of the husband or the wife that is frequently *located in different villages*, and in villages other than those of their residence.

The fact that properties are dispersed can open the way for a strategy by which they are recombined through marriage: e.g. a man may marry a woman of a villiage where he himself (or his parents) own property with the prospect of adding his wife's to his own. Apparently the Jaffna Tamils do not systematically follow this strategy, though no doubt it occurs in individual cases.

Secondly, we have seen that in fact marriages do not seem to occur over any great distance — there is a high incidence of intra-village marriage and marriage within a collection of nearby villages. But in any case communication within the Jaffna Peninsula is easy. Direct or indirect management of dispersed properties is therefore not difficult.

However, there are many instances in which the couple may live virilocally or neolocally near a man's non-agricultural place of work (e.g. government office, school, etc.), away from the wife's dowry property. In such cases the dowry property remains in the day-to-day management of the wife's father or her brothers. The husband does not demand profits in full nor even an economic rent, but this does not mean that the dowries are notional. For the husband can, with the consent of his wife, sell, lease or rent to whomever he chooses. Such action is resorted to when economic circumstances so demand or when it is not necessary for a man to remain friendly with his wife's family.

In all these respects concerning the dispersion of property and the devices to recombine and manage effectively, the practices of the Jaffna Tamils are not very different from those of the Kandyan Sinhalese which have already been discussed elsewhere (Leach 1961; Tambiah 1965). We are quite clearly confronting problems common to bilateral societies where both men and women have property rights. The resemblance increases when we take marriage patterns and kinship groupings into account.

Marriage patterns and bilateral kin groupings (*sondakarar*). Although marriages are said to be preferred with cross-cousins, above all with the mother's brother's daughter, the actuality is quite different. Similarly, although it is said that one of the advantages in the marriage of cross-cousins is that high dowries need not be given, this is not true − for the dowries given are usually no different from those given in the case of marriage with non-kin, with the difference that among close kin there is less haggling and the amount is reached amicably, even with a show of generosity.

The following table compiled by Banks shows the relationship between spouses in a sample of marriages (one or both spouses being alive);

Relationship of spouse (*wife*)	*Number of marriages*	*% of total number of marriages*
Own cross-cousins	30	24.8
(MBD 14)		
(FZD 16)		
(Bilateral c.c. 0)		
Classificatory cross-cousin	12	9.8
Own cross-cousin's da. and grandda.	8	6.7
Related but not known exactly how; and related and do not know how.	33	27.0
Don't know if related	2 } 38	1.7 } 31.5
Not related	36 }	29.8 }

These figures are interesting because they show a gradient from the marriage of own cross-cousins to classificatory to indeterminate and finally non-kin; also that patrilateral and matrilateral forms are equally distributed and there is no case of bilateral cross-cousin marriage (of the first cousin range). I wish to emphasize that the actors themselves do have concepts of genealogical distance that are superimposed upon the categorical terminological system. Thus *sonda machan* − own cross-cousin and *ondai vitta machan* − cross-cousin once removed (i.e. second cousin), *tai mama* − *mama* on the mother's side as opposed to the father's side, etc. are examples of verbal concepts relating to genealogical connection and distance used widely to differentiate kin. Such distinctions are made when circumstances demand a differentiation between paternal and maternal kin, siblings and parallel cousins, first cousin and second cousin and so on. A most interesting usage is the Jaffna Tamil *English* expression 'cousin brother' for parallel cousin (who is a 'brother' in the Tamil terminology and a cousin by English reckoning)!

By and large, genealogical knowledge is imperfect or inaccurate beyond a certain distance. After the exact knowledge of genealogical links has disappeared the relationship is remembered as being mother's line or father's line (*tai vali, tahappan vaii*), or 'not cross-cousin but related'. Banks says 'The category "not related" is ambiguous: it means in effect that there is said to be no previous relationship, not even a distant one.' But Banks interposes that what is perhaps meant is that 'there is no sociological recollection of such relationship, rather than to say that no biological link exists'. In general, 'memory of relationships extends back for three ascendant generations . . . but the details of the third ascendant generations' collateral descendants are often spotty and contradictory . . .'

I must emphasize the importance of genealogical distance which Tamils (and Sinhalese) superimpose (particularly in relation to 'close' kin) as a grid upon the categorical terminological system. Perhaps the bringing together of the semantic fields of categorical and genealogical reckoning helps to solve some contradictions in Yalman's book which reveals an astounding reversal — it begins with a categorical conception of kinship categories whereby classes of kin are contrasted within a semantic universe, but concludes with the most narrow genealogical argument possible, whereby it is the relation of own brother and sister, their separation and their union through their children, that provides the key to the Sinhalese system! Analysis would be more adequate if both the categorical and genealogical grids were brought together from the very beginning of the analysis, as for instance are the notions of hue and brightness in colour differentiation.

This double referential system ultimately has consequences for the way we view kinship groupings and collectivities among the Jaffna Tamils and the Kandyan Sinhalese.

The concept of sondakarar. *Sondakarar* literally means 'people who are close', 'people of own group' or some such equivalent. In a manner which closely resembles Yalman's characterization of the Kandyan Sinhalese *pavula* as 'micro-caste', Banks elucidates that for the Vellalah of Jaffna, his caste (*sadi*) itself is divided further into grades, levels or 'sub-castes'. But unlike the Indian divisions of castes into named sub-castes, the Jaffna Tamil Vellalah caste does not differentiate into named or fully endogamous 'sub-castes'.

But a remarkable phenomenon among the Jaffna Vellalahs (and I can here confirm Banks's description with my own data) is that the village is divided into named *wards* or neighbourhoods; these wards think of themselves as kin (*sondakarar*); the Vellalah wards of any single village are said to be of unequal 'caste' standing and therefore do not all intermarry;[39] but wards in different villages are thought to marry in endogamous circles. And it is this wider circle of equal status within which marriage takes place which is ideally the 'sondakarar' grouping or 'micro-caste' that Banks isolates: '. . . the sondakara caste is defined in terms of (a) all those with whom one marries, (b) all consanguineal relations, and (c) all who live in particular wards, with the two corollaries that all who live in a given ward are consanguineal kin (irrespective of whether they are also affinal kin); and that marriages only occur (at least in traditional practice) with existing kin, and not with strangers.'

But although the Vellalahs may idealize their sondakarar as a 'closed' status grouping, Banks sees the conception as empirically impossible: 'Although sondakara castes are locally believed to be endogamous, this is not so. The wards with which any one ward marries are themselves marrying other wards which do not marry the first ward, in reference to which the boundaries of the given sondakara caste were originally defined. Thus sondakara castes[40] are not mutually exclusive, but rather, overlapping entities. Each ward is a member of several sondakara castes: its own sondakara caste, and those of the wards with which it intermarries.'

Banks goes further to reveal that there is a second fiction contained in the notion that all members of a ward share the same sondakarar. This notion is not true because a certain number of people who have married into the ward come from families not previously married with. These persons do not share other traditional places of marriage with co-resident ward members. Every ward in fact contains a high proportion of both men and women who were not born there − a result of the ambilocal residence patterns we have already examined. 'Apart from the lack of knowledge of the kinship links connecting its members, it [the ward] is a bilateral unit; many of its residents came originally from other wards and were only introduced as affinals . . .'

Finally it must be remembered that the sondakarar collectivity of kin have differentiated claims on each other which had best be seen as a gradient: 'A man can lay claim for help or wives only on relations close enough to him to know how he is related to them. With the rest of the sondakara caste, either in one's own ward or in other wards, there is the possibility of marriage, but hardly a right, and marriages occur more nearly as strict bargains. Marriages with strangers are the subject of still more extensive bargaining over the dowry and the man's job, and intermediaties are essential, although these are not professional marriage brokers'.

The economic and political factors which cause sondakarar collectivities to differentiate internally by ceasing to inter-marry, and to ally with new collectivities by initiating inter-marriage, the politics of using marriage feasts for declaration of status inequality or fission within the sondakarar, the accentuation of these tendencies in modern times owing to the widening of socio-economic horizons by virtue of increases in clerical/professional occupations enabled by modern education, all these trends so closely parallel accounts given of both Kandyan (Yalman 1967) and Low Country Sinhalese (Obeyesekere 1967) that repetition here is unnecessary.

The purpose of this digression into the constitution of *sondakarar* kindred is this: whether it is imagined in terms of locality or neighbourhood (i.e. a collection of intermarrying localities) or of kinship (persons of same status who have inter-married), its internal structure is bilateral, and its boundaries inevitably not closed. This structure in fact is consonant with and reflects the other principles we have previously examined — property rights allotted to men and women, a symmetrical incidence of uxorilocal and virilocal residence, and the use of dowry not only to repeat marriage with old kin but also to initiate ties with new desirable families.

I shall close this account of the Jaffna Vellalahs by making a brief reference to certain patrilineal features that cast their shadows on the bilateral scene. Banks refers to the presence of *sundadi* which are patrilineal name-bearing collectivities (geographically dispersed); another patrilineal accent is found in the larger number of persons on the paternal side rather than the maternal side subject to pollution observances at death, etc. But it is important to note that the *sundadi* are never corporate or localized groups — the names cycle through the residential wards by virtue of ambilocal residence. It is sufficient here to remind the reader that these non-corporate name-bearing collectivities are no different from the multiple *vasagama* groups occurring today without carrying any weight besides status signification in the low country Sinhalese villages, and in the Kandyan villages of Central Ceylon (with even less status significance).

The Kandyan Sinhalese

There are two basic features that should be constantly kept in view in order to understand the system of kinship and marriage (and their accompanying rules of residence and pattern of property transactions and transmission) among the Kandyan Sinhalese. Both features help us to locate the Kandyan case in relation to the others we have discussed:

(1) The Kandyan system shows a gradient which contains at one end the prestigious or aristocratic form (which in many respects consciously looks to the orthodox Indian traditions) and at the other end the ordinary or the commoner forms which are practised by most ordinary villagers.

(2) By and large the Kandyan system constitutes a 'weakening and 'loosening' of the dominant Indian pattern towards bilateralism.

The prestigious and the ordinary forms of marriage. D'Oyly (1929), documenting Kandyan marriage in the early nineteenth century, gives an account of the following matrimonial transactions 'among superior classes of the Sinhalese'.

D'Oyly's description is recognizable as the 'aristocratic' form among the

Gifts and payments by bridegroom's side	Gifts and payments by brides side
(1) On day of wedding 'Betel, cakes, fruit, etc.' are sent in advance of the bridegroom's procession.	
(2) Before solemnising marriage (a) the bridegroom's mother gives a valuable cloth (as a *killikeda hela*) to the bride's mother, together with another cloth and a set of jewels. (b) The bridegroom ties a gold chain over the bride's neck and 'then presents her with a complete set of apparel and ornaments'.	The bride's father gives 'a suit of apparel to the bridegroom.
	(3) After a lapse of 'some days or months' the wife's parents formally 'bestow, according to their means, a dowry on their daughter, consisting of goods, *land*, etc.' (my italics) (1929: 83)

Kandyan Sinhalese. It is clear that it parallels the pattern of transfers in the standard Indian form, e.g. among the Kallar; apart from reversible prestations, the bridegroom's side among the Kallar give an initial gift of *paricam* and the wife's side reciprocate with the more substantial dowry. What is significantly different in D'Oyly's account is that land figures as a constituent of the dowry among the Kandyan aristocrats.

We must go back in time still further to consult the best ethnographer of the Kandyans – Knox – to see the outlines of orthodox marriage not among the aristocrats but among the ordinary village folk among whom he spent his captivity. The following prestations were in vogue in the late seventeenth century:

(1) The match being made, 'the Man carrieth or sends to the Woman her Wedding Cloths' (1911: 148). This prestation is made before the wedding.

(2) The bridegroom's party then carry to the wedding 'Provisions and Sweet-meats... towards the Charges of the Wedding' (p. 148). This is a reference to the *kat* carried by the bridegroom's side in a formal marriage.

(3) Finally, while commenting on the fact that Kandyan marriages were quite easily terminated, Knox makes a reference to what is obviously a woman's dowry: 'They do give according to their Ability a Portion of Cattle, Slaves and Money with their Daughters; but if they chance to mislike one another and part asunder, this Portion must be returned again, and then she is fit for another man ...' (p. 149).

Knox's account resembles closely the formal marriage transactions an anthropologist is likely to witness today in a Kandyan village. The standard Indian pattern is still visible but *the exchanges are abbreviated*. On the side of the bride the property (which consists of strong forms of *movable* wealth) given her as dowry is reminiscent of the classical notion of *stridhanam:* it is exclusively female property. But we may infer from Knox's account that the transfer of dowry is not an essential part of the marriage ceremony as such.

On the bridegroom's side, the major contributions are made up of the *kat*, which is a food contribution to the cost of the festivities, and the cloth and jacket for the bride. A good description of an elaborate *kat* is to be found in Nevill (1887). Describing the wedding among the 'higher classes' (i.e. the respectable high *goyigama* caste folk), he says that on the day of the wedding, pingos of cloth, plantains, rice and other food are borne to the bride's house by men of the *hakuru* caste. The most important part of this *kat* is the *yeladakada* containing spices, cakes, betel, areca nuts and dried fish 'which is intended to compensate the bride's people for the expenses incurred in entertaining the bridegroom's party'. Significantly Neville noted that the *kat* may be omitted when the bride is a cross-cousin of the bridegroom.

Summing up the historical accounts, we may say this of the forms of marriage among the dominant *goyigama* caste (the 'superior classes' of our authors). The aristocratic or prestigious form among the Kandyan approaches the orthodox form in patrilineal India − with the exception that a woman's dowry may include land among the Kandyans. But the ordinary form among the Kandyan *goyigama* appears to be a *weaker and abbreviated* form of the orthodox Indian version. This weakening of prestation exchange is accompanied by a strengthening of female property rights, which provides the key to the change.

The gradient of marriage customs is complete only when we take into account the marriage forms among the so-called 'lower classes of people', namely the poor members of the *goyigama* caste and the majority of the under privileged lower castes of interior (but not coastal) Ceylon.

Our historical authorities tell us that the common people in contrast to the higher categories, contract marriage in a very simple manner: typically the bridegroom goes, accompanied by a few attendants, to the bride's house carrying with him a cloth, and having performed a minimal ritual (e.g. mutual feeding, tying of fingers together), the bride is dressed in the cloth and is conducted to the bridegroom's house. This ceremonial is even more simplified in the case of cross-cousins. Contemporary fieldwork has reported this amply.

Finally, we come to that form of Kandyan marriage which consists of the public's acceptance of a couple simply living and eating together as valid marriage. In spite of the existence of the Kandyan Marriage Ordinance which recognizes only registered marriage as valid, 'If a man and a woman of the same rank lived together it was sufficient to establish a valid marriage giving their children right to inherit from them, although the parents may not have gone through the regular rituals of marriage.' (H.W. Tambiah 1968: 117).

I shall argue later that this 'laxity' of the marriage tie evidenced not only in the making of marriage but also its easy dissolution is related to the strong and independent property holding rights of both males and females. To appreciate this it is first necessary to view the Kandyan formulation of residence and inheritance.

Diga and binna. The Kandyan forms of *diga* and *binna* marriage strongly recall the classical Indian formulations until we realize, on looking closer, that the Indian principles have been subtly changed and the male/female distinction watered down.

Binna is apparently derived from the Sanskrit term *bhinna* which means broken or separated. Technically *binna* marriage is one in which the husband contracts to go and live in the wife's parental house or in any family residence or property of her family.[41] The children of this marriage may take the family name of their mother's father. The *binna* husband thus begins to look like the classical Indian institution of the uxorilocal son-in-law (e.g. *illatom, gharjamai,* etc.). The nineteenth-century codifiers and commentators tell us that the *binna* son-in-law was in a 'subordinate' position to his affines, and that he was liable to expulsion at any time by them. A famous saying contained in D'Oyly is often cited as evidence — the *binna* husband should take care to have constantly ready at the door of his wife's room a walking stick, a *talpot* (palm leaf umbrella) and a torch so that he can leave at any hour he is asked to quit the house.

The Kandyan official legal theory (when compared with the Indian parallels) somewhat overdoes the inferior position of the uxorilocal son-in-law, but the object is clearly similar to that in the Hindu formulation — to raise up heirs for a man through his daughter's children by virtue of a legal fiction.

Once again the concept of *diga* marriage appears as the counterpart of the classical Indian notion of normal patrilocal marriage: the *diga* marriage implies the conducting of the wife to and living in the husband's house (or in any other family residence).[42] According to Kandyan formulation the *diga* concept places emphasis on the implications of the severance of the daughter from her natal family. It is said that the *diga*-married daughter forfeits her right to inheritance in her father's estate[42] in favour of her brothers, *binna*-married sisters and unmarried sisters. This exclusion of the *diga*-married daughter is on the grounds that she had been given a dowry (*davadde*) at marriage (in the form of jewels, money, movables and even land).

These features of *diga* and *binna* marriage look orthodox judged by the classical Indian formulations but, on closer analysis, we find some customary formulations in Ceylon unknown in India. Thus according to Kandyan law a daughter given away in *diga* marriage can inherit parental property not only if she is the only issue but also if she acquires the same rights as a *binna*-married sister and her brothers — by subsequently returning to her parental house, by keeping in close and constant contact with her parents and their *mulgedera* (ancestral house), by contracting a subsequent *binna* marriage, by rendering assistance and aid to parents, etc. This idea that a virilocally married daughter can subsequently reverse her inheritance rights and make equal claims as her uxorilocal sisters and virilocal brothers is unthinkable in classical Indian law and is evidence of great flexibility.

There is a similar weakening in the bilateral direction and the making of concessions to situational circumstances in the Kandyan concept of *binna* marriage. The main local understanding of *binna* marriage is that a sister has equal rights to parental property as her brothers. But the transformation of the Indian pattern consists in changing what in India was considered an exceptional circumstance created by lack of sons (and grandsons) to a more frequent circumstance in the Kandyan case of letting sisters reside uxorilocally even when brothers were in existence and living patrilocally! And just as a *diga*-married daughter could acquire *binna*-rights by changing her situation, so can a *binna*-woman forfeit her property rights (but not those of her children born while she was in *binna*) by subsequently contracting a *diga*-marriage.

The legal codifiers and interpreters of Kandyan law are in the face of such dynamic flexibility less than illuminating on certain issues. We are never told as to what happens to the dowry of a *diga*-married woman if she subsequently claims' rights equivalent to a *binna*-sister. We are not even definite as to the generality of the practice of giving *davadde* (dowry) at marriage to daughters marrying in *diga*. The commentaries are further confounded by the basic declaration of Kandyan law − which was never accepted in Hindu *shastric* law − that there is a *formal equality of division of patental property among all children.*

It seems to me that just as Kandyan legal theory echoed the literary formulations of the prestigious classical Hindu *shastric* law in the same manner as the Kandyan theory of caste verbally 'initiated' the *varna* model (while in actuality the practices were more flexible and bilateral), so in reverse the British commentators and lawyers sometimes imposed on the Kandyan customary practices a patrilineality which they picked up from the prestigious legal formulations of Indo-Aryan law by authorities such as Mayne, Maine, Jolly, etc![44] In my view my brilliant friend Obeyesekere commits the same fallacy (1967) when, in the interest of establishing a patrilineal base, he wrongly interprets (1) the rule that in the absence of issue the property should revert to the source from which it came as referring to *an agnatic source* (when clearly Kandyan law divides ancestral [*praveni*] property into paternal and maternal sorts thereby stating a duality of source) and (2) the *davadda* (dowry) as 'a conversion of her [daughter's] interest in the landed property into cash, jewellery, and other movable or non-praveni property', when there is no evidence at all that *davadda* categorically excluded the daughter's right to ancestral land. He is however correct that in the context of preferred *diga* marriage (and for other circumstances) the long-run consequence of the rules would be to encourage an aggregation of agnatic kinsmen in a localized area – but this of course was never achieved systematically or enduringly (see Tambiah 1965).

The Kandyan evidence can, as I have suggested before, be made to make coherent sense, if we are prepared to think of a gradient with aristocratic and humble forms as the modalities which channel a theoretical equality of all children regarding property inheritance into two marriage strategies – the use of dowry preferably in movable wealth by the wealthy and high-born at marriage as a vehicle for status mobility and affinal alliance, and the completely informal marriage of the poor, with its lack of frills and dowry, which lets circumstances decide whether women will eventually realise the property rights which they have in theory inherited. The Kandyan Sinhalese thus show a wide latitude as regards marriage – ranging from the giving of substantial dowries among the aristocratic (*radala*) or wealthy categories to the complete ignorance of dowry among the poor and perhaps in the extreme event the dispossession of daughters who have gone away on marriage.

A passage from Yalman (1967) perfectly expresses the point:

> The most important fact about inheritance, which applied also to our discussion of *binna* and *deega*, is that rich and poor families do not act in the same way . . . The most important difference between them concerned the position of women, with regard both to their inheritances and to the freedom of choice they were allowed. The rich, however, actively controlled the property rights of the daughters and used this as a tool in the arrangement of marriage. In contrast, labourers did not control the property rights of the daughters and all siblings shared alike. There was no emphasis of unilineal descent among them (p. 131).

It must also be emphasized that the relations between affines is very closely connected with whether or not property transactions have taken place. The comparison with orthodox Indian expectations of affinity is once again noteworthy.

> In a *deega* marriage, the groom falls under no formal and specific obligations towards his in-laws . . . The connection gains importance if – as often happens – the woman has been given a dowry or if lands have been set aside for her and her children to be used after the decease of her parents. (Yalman 1967: 122, 123).

When there is a promise of property, affinity is a long-term affair and a *deega* husband will not necessarily press his wife's claims and wish to acquire immediate control over her property. In contrast: 'Among the poorest sections with no property to provide the basis for structured obligations between the in-laws it was largely a matter of indifference exactly where the young couple chose to live' (p. 127).

I should like to emphasize that among the Kandyan Sinhalese the giving of *dowry* (*davadda*) – indeed the very conception – is not normal or general as among the Jaffna Tamils, but associated only either with the prestigious form of marriage or with hypergamy and social mobility among the newly rich, and among the urban 'middle classes'. In respect of the dominant Indian pattern, where we saw that a woman's *stridhanam* (dowry) is transferred at marriage and consists of movables, the Kandyan restricted and prestigious practice of dowry deviated in two directions: as among the Jaffna Tamils dowry may include land together with movables (as Yalman says, 'It may be cash only, or a combination of land, houses, and trees as well as cash') and secondly, it may be transferred either at marriage or subsequently (at varying times). The variability of timing in the transfer of dowry — sometimes a mere promise that materializes as succession after the death of the wife's parents — is related to the kinship connection and social position of the son-in-law. If he is a distant relative or non-kinsman, if he is particularly desirable by virtue of his occupation and education and if there is a distinct status difference so that the marriage is hypergamous, then the dowry represents a bargain struck and is likely to be actually paid at the time of marriage, or at least the deeds of transfer actually signed (Yalman 1967: 174-5).

It is abundantly clear — not only from my own fieldwork but in the writings of other anthropologists as well — that the vast majority of ordinary humble Kandyan villagers not only do not practice the giving of dowry in the form discussed above, but indeed exchange very little in the form of prestations or payments at marriage. The taking of *kat* by the bridegroom's party and the attempt to formalize the property rights of the bride (as a definite promise rather than as a right of intestate succession) begins to occur especially when marriage is between members of different villages and of some kinship distance. By and large the property rights of wives are not a matter of negotiation at marriage but are realized either when parents transfer property in their old age or upon their death.

These same variations in the expression of women's property rights as dowry or as intestate succession find another parallel materialization in the incidence of *diga–binna* residence. The legalistic notion of *binna* — which echoes the classical Hindu formulation — that an uxorilocal son-in-law is sought only when parents have no male issue and in order to raise up heirs through a daughter makes sense only in the ideology of the propertied. The *binna/diga* distinction tends to lose all structural significance for the propertyless; among them, although residence is normatively virilocal in practice, it is frequently uxorilocal; not only do both types occur pretty freely but not infrequently there is change from one to the other back and forth according to opportunities and convenience; finally, under certain circumstances there is a greater incidence of uxorilocal residence as one descends the wealth hierarchy. It would appear that this flexibility is intimately connected with the fact that both men and women can inherit equally, and therefore couples suit their residence to the outcome of their actual fortunes, an argument well developed by Leach (1961(d)). In between the extremes stand the middle-range small-propertied villagers who tend to marry *diga* outside the village but mix this with intra-village marriage, and accomodate some of their sisters (or daughters) in *binna* marriage.

There is one more Kandyan feature to be noted. Because men and women can inherit equally the same kinds of property, because they in law hold their properties separately (though in actual fact they merge into a conjugal estate managed by the husband), and because each parent transmits property separately to his or her own blood children (thereby ensuring that multiple marriages do not interfere with unambiguous transmission), we can see how in fact much of Kandyan marriage can be casually made and casually broken, for the parties to it have their rights separately ensured. The distinctiveness of the properties of husband and wife places no grave obstacle in the way of divorce and re-marriage. However, I should underline that this concordance or fit is not necessarily causal, for the Jaffna Tamils who have similar notions of the separate-ness of male and female properties, put their normative emphasis on durable marriage. Though divorce and remarriage take place, their incidence is far less among the Tamils than among the Kandyan Sinhalese.

Our final characterization of the Kandyan kinship system is that it is bilateral internally arranged as a gradient whose upper end approaches but stops far short of the dominant Indian patrilineal pattern. It is now perhaps clearer why I view the codified Kandyan legal system as taking the classical Indian pattern as its ideological model, but seriously watering it down and weakening it, to produce a system shift towards bilaterality. In understanding this shift we should view the formal rights of women to inherit equally with their brothers both movable and immovable properties as the critical transforming agent. For the *binna–diga* distinction, which on the face of it looks like the normal Hindu patrilineal transmission of joint-family property with exceptional transmission through women (who carry with them *stridhanam* in movables upon marriage), is weakened and made flexible by the investiture of equal property rights on sons and daughters. The same move displaces the giving of *stridhanam* at marriage from its central place, and also greatly abbreviates marriage prestations. At a formal level it is apparent that the Kandyan system resembles the Jaffna Tamil system which is also bilateral. But we should take note of the fact that the signposts of the Jaffna Tamil system are somewhat different and it has arrived at bilaterality by a slightly different route. It too is a shift from or transformation of the dominant Indian model. But it begins with the dualistic notion of male property (*mudisam*) and female property (*chidenam*) held and transmitted separately as its basic criterion. Unlike the Kandyan Sinhalese, the Tamils do not pay attention in their ideology to residence rules, nor necessarily prefer virilocal residence; in fact they practice an open virilocal–uxorilocal pattern with the latter being more frequent at the beginning of marriage. Again unlike the Kandyans, the Tamils put great emphasis on a woman's property rights being transferred to her at her marriage or soon afterwards in the form of dowry (*chidenam*). But

Table 5   The Kandyan Sinhalese (*goyigama*) and the Jaffna Tamils (*vellalah*)
compared

Kandyan Sinhalese	Jaffna Tamils
(1) Premarital chastity of girl, though preferred, is not expected.	Chastity absolutely expected and empirically attained to a very high degree.
(2) A gradient of marriages from formal ceremony to informal co-residence.	Though same modalities found, informal co-residence is infrequent.
(3) 'Dravidian' kinship terminology.	'Dravidian' kinship terminology, identical in structure.
(4) Cross-cousin marriage — preference for both patrilateral and matrilateral kinds; the empirical occurrence of first cross-cousin marriage is limited. There is usually a gradient from close to distant to non-kin.	The same preference for cross-cousin marriages, and they seem to occur more frequently; also to be taken into account is marriage with the daughter of a cross-cousin (*machinipillai*). The same gradient occurs.
(5) By and large the majority of marriages are not accompanied by dowry — normal inheritance takes place for both men and women. Dowry becomes important only in prestigious or hypergamous forms of marriage.	Dowry (*chidenam*) is an essential part of most marriages consisting of land, jewels and cash. It is usually given at marriage as a kind of *pre-mortem* inheritance. Hypergamy is not a general value among the Tamils.
(6) Kandyan customary 'law' emphasizes *diga—binna* residence and attaches to them different inheritance rights. Among the propertied the distinction is important, among the poor it is not, and both kinds of residence freely occur. The culturally preferred form is *diga*.	No normative accent on residence, which is open and freely chosen between vililocal and uxorilocal forms. Initial residence tends to be uxorilocal, and this form probably occurs to a greater degree among all segments than is the case with the Kandyan Sinhalese.
(7) Divorce/separation and remarriage are relatively easy; no bar on widow remarriage.	Divorce/separation possible, but remarriage difficult; however no bar on widow remarriage.
(8) Certain patrilineal features (especially associated with 'names') occur, like *vasagama, gedera* but except among landed or aristocratic circles they never achieve a stable or enduring form, let alone corporate character. In actual fact multiple *gedera* and *vasagama* names flow in and out of localities in great dispersion as a result of flexible residence.	There exist patrilineal features, e.g name-lines (*sundadi*) and pollution rules, but no corporate features. By virtue of ambilocal residence, the *sundadi* flow in and out of neighbourhoods.

the strong notion of dowry among the Tamils, which includes land, appears to have abbreviated or made unnecessary the complex pattern of reversible and oriented prestations that is found in the patrilineal concept in India.

Thus in the case of the Jaffna Tamils and the Kandyan Sinhalese we see how although at the level of deep structure they show significant differences yet they generate similar surface forms – a phenomenon that is well known in transformational grammar (Chomsky 1969). With this in mind, it is instructive to compare in tabular form the major features of the Kandyan and Jaffna Tamil systems. It should be noted that the comparison relates only to the high caste *goyigama* and *vellalahs* who are strict counterparts in the two societies.

A central analytic assumption in this essay has been that history, direction of cultural transmission, the genesis of central ideology and its spread to peripheries dictate that one should cross the Palk Straits from India to Ceylon and not *vice versa*. It is only then that we can clearly understand the Ceylonese systems both as variants of a classical Indian model and as a systematic transformation of that model.

The dominant Indian pattern itself has its remarkable transformation in South India as for example among the matrilineal-matrilocal Nangudi Vellalar whose women share the land and property rights equally with their men.

The Jaffna Tamil and Kandyan systems agree in their bilaterality, but the former is a *direct* and *immediate* variant of the South Indian Nangudi Vellalar whereas the Kandyan system is a *weakened* form of the dominant classical patrilineal form. But travelling on different routes they achieve a similarity in certain features which is unmistakable.

The structural forms we have discussed for India and Ceylon with special reference to female property rights, dowry and inheritance are summarized below. Both in India and Ceylon women have noticeable property rights. But the shift from unilineality and unilocal residence in India to bilaterality and ambilocal residence in Ceylon appears to be related to the strengthening of female rights to property in Ceylon.

INDIA

(1) *Dominant Indian Pattern*: Patrilineal descent, plus patrilocal residence, plus patrilineal transmission of land (but exceptionally and discontinuously through daughters), plus female *stridhanam* rights to dowry in movables. The occurrence of matrilineal descent and avunculocal residence has the same accompaniments.

(2) *Variant South Indian pattern* (Nangudi Vellalar): Matrilineal descent, plus matrilocal (or duolocal residence), plus female *stridhanam* rights to dowry in movables and land (i.e. bilateral transmission of land and property).

CEYLON

(1) *Vellalahs of Jaffna*: Bilateral kinship, plus ambilocal residence, plus *chidenam* rights to dowry in movables and land (i.e. bilateral transmission of land and property).

(2) *Kandyan Sinhalese*: Bilateral kinship, plus ambilocal residence (*diga/binna* with an accent on the former), plus *davadde* rights to dowry in movables and land (which is the prestigious form) or normal bilateral inheritance to land and property (which is the common form).

Dumont is probably right in stressing that in South India the twin axes are unilineal descent and alliance (affinity): although lineages exist, alliance is *not a group phenomenon* but is confined to particular families or lines. Yalman is probably correct to work towards a concept of *pavula* (kindred/micro-caste) among the Kandyan Sinhalese — which are correlates of bilaterality and affinity. The same we have seen to occur among the Jaffna Tamils' concept of *sondakarar*. The moral of this essay is that it would be unwise to follow any of these courses: to allow the more defined South Indian forms to encompass the Ceylonese forms, or to reject the Ceylonese forms as 'non-Indian', or to extrapolate from the Ceylon experience to the mainland of India and impose the Ceylonese grid upon it. The correct journey is from India to Ceylon, to see the latter as representing a shift from the former, and to acknowledge also that India and Ceylon stand as dominant and variant within the same family. The same conclusion should hold for other institutions such as caste.

PART FIVE

The Burmese design

If the relation of India to the southern island of Ceylon is that of dominant to weakened and transformed variants, then can we say the same of Burma which is situated on India's eastern periphery?

Indeed Burma should constitute a crucial test of our principal arguments: on the one hand, since historically Indian culture and social influence flowed, by and large, from India to Burma and not *vice versa* (as was also the case with Ceylon), Burmese society should show some evidence of this contact in the field of family and kinship. But on the other hand, since Burma (like Ceylon) lies on India's periphery, it ought also to stand in a dialectical contrast or a relation of transformation to the centre. It is this double relation of Burma to India, as well as its relationship to a third point in the triangle, Ceylon (specifically Buddhist Sinhalese), that will be briefly considered in this final section.

Let us first see what features Sinhalese-Ceylon and Burma both share and do not share with India. Their major common possession is Theravada Buddhism which, as is well known, they share through historical contacts and exchanges at various points of time since at least the 11th century. The dialectical contrast between India and its peripheries (to south, east and north east) is the latter's espousal of Buddhism while Hinduism remained entrenched in the centre. We are not concerned here with the Mahayana Buddhism of Tibet, Nepal, Sikkim, Bhutan, and elsewhere; but, at least in respect of Burma and Ceylon (and other Southeast Asian countries), it has been suggested that it is their very espousal of Theravada Buddhism that in large part 'explains' various aspects of their social structure and organization, including such matters as family and kinship structure, inheritance customs, the secular nature of marriage, the degree of equality between the sexes, the permissibility of divorce, etc. Indeed, it could be seriously suggested that the 'liberalization' of Sinhalese and Burmese society as for instance evidenced by greater property rights given women, the loosening of social forms such as unilinearity and joint family towards bilaterality and conjugal family is directly related to two features of Buddhism. Firstly unlike Hinduism and its prime officiants, the Brahmans, there is little 'religious' legislation by Buddhism and its monks on, and ritual concern with, family and kinship practices and norms; secondly, since the destination of the Buddist search is said to be *individual* salvation, the religion is alleged to encourage a weakening of social groupings like the joint family, to emphasize the distribution of property to all children of both sexes alike, to devalue ancestor worship and the preoccupation with male heirs. It would take us too far afield if we investigated in detail the relation between Hinduism and Buddhism to their respective social structures, but what can be conceded here (without suggesting a causal link) is that there certainly is a fit between the structure of Theravada Buddhism and the social organization of the societies in which it

138

prevails, especially when we keep in view the contrasting relation between Hindu religion and the society which it informs.

In terms of the narrower interests of this essay we can take the following as the broad dialectical relation (with exceptions already noted) between India on the one hand and the Kandyan Sinhalese and the Burmese on the other. All these societies fall within a belt of double transmission of property to males and females, but the Sinhalese and Burmese go a step further from India in general and give females equal rights with males in regard to inheritance of patrimonial property, including land.[45]

While the Burmese and the Sinhalese share Buddhism, there are also differences between them with regard to details of kinship, marriage, and property transmission. These differences may in part relate to certain different relations they have with India itself. We should note that while the Sinhalese and other peoples of Ceylon are ethnically Indian in origin, and speak languages that are derived from the major Indian Indo-Aryan or Dravidian languages, the majority of Burmese are, being Tibeto-Burman in origin, ethnically different from the majority of Indians and speak a language that is once again distinct from the *major* Indian languages. The greater closeness of the Sinhalese to Indian peoples is reflected in the fact that they possess a caste system which is a less rigid version of the Indian model. The Burmese for their part do not possess a caste system at all (though they have some degraded groups).

Nevertheless, Brahmanical influence has not been lacking in Burma. It is well known that 'Brahmans' imported from India acted as court functionaries well into the late nineteenth century when upper Burma ultimately fell to the British. They performed the rituals of kingship from installation (*abhiseka* ceremony) to making the kings divine. Being the *literati*, the Brahmans in Burma (and elsewhere in Southeast Asia) were also entrusted with judical and clerical duties – preparing legal treatises, interpreting laws, etc. – once again as functionaries in the employ of the king. Curiously enough in Ceylon, while there is evidence that Brahmans performed similar functions in the Anuradhapura and Polonnaruwa periods they seem to have disappeared from the palace and from the major deity shrines in the Kandyan period, at least from the seventeenth century onwards. How do we explain this curious circumstance? Paradoxically the progressive elimination of the Brahmans from the Kandyan patrimonial-cum-feudalistic society must be attributed to the very existence of the Sinhalese version of the caste system, in which the dominant caste was the *goyigama* from whose upper reaches (the *radala* subcaste/grades) were drawn the kings and aristocats. From the same caste were also recruited the monks of the established monastic chapter, the Siyam Nikaya. Thus the hierarchical purity and power structure of Sinhalese society would always be threatened by the presence of Brahmans, who if they were allowed to exist would be pre-eminent in status, and therefore had to be eliminated in order to preserve the integrity of the Kandyan caste and feudal polity. In time lay functionaries (*kapuralas*), drawn principally from the *goyigama* caste, officiated in the major deity temples (*devales*).

139

It is my thesis that in Burma (as in Siam and Cambodia, etc.) the Brahmans could continue to function as 'court officials' focused on the King, without creating problems for the wider society, because these societies were not caste-structured. The Brahmans could not therefore have the same status-significance for the stratification system of the society as a whole.

The absence of court and temple Brahmans in Kandyan society in the centuries immediately preceding British conquest of Ceylon, and their presence in Burma well into the nineteenth century, may throw light on the curious circumstance that there appears to have been no lively tradition of written legal treatises in Ceylon[46] while there was an almost excessively luxuriant one in Burma.

On first sight the Brahmanical influence on formal Burmese law seems indisputable when one notes that the Burmese 'legal' treatises are called *Dhammathat* (i.e. *Dharmashastra*) and the discoverer of the Burmese usages and their first codifier is said to have been the sage Manu himself. Lingat (1950) has commented on the dissemination of the Hindu conception of law (especially *dharma*, a moral law coeval with cosmic law) into Southeast Asia – most importantly to the Champa and Cambodian polities of the eighth – thirteenth centuries, but also later in time in modified form to the Buddhist kingdoms of Burma and Siam.

The Mons were the crucial transmitters of this 'legal' tradition to the upstart Burmese and Siamese polities: borrowing the Indian *dharmashastric* tradition, the Mons made important adaptations and transformations to suit local conditions and a Buddhist, not Hindu, faith. In other words, it is clear that the authoritative Hindu cultural influence of the Brahmanical tradition was used as a veneer for prestige reasons, but beneath this thin veneer were embedded the customs of frontier societies quite different from those prevailing on the mainland.

While the Mons who were committed to Pali Buddhism appear to have developed their legal tradition around the seventh century, it was much later, during the Pagan period (twelfth century onwards) that the Mons, apparently at the request of Burmese kings, first composed Pali books, equivalent to the Hindu sanskritic *dharmashastra*. These Pali treatises were called *dhammasattham*.

Lingat (1950: 14) describes the Mon transformation of the Brahmanical texts as follows:

In composing this literature, Mon writers took for their model Hindu *dharmasastras*, and this is why many provisions of the new codes may be found in the Indian Manu code or other similar works. But *dhammasatthams* are quite different from Sanskrit *dharmasastras*. First of all their authors left aside every matter which, in Hindu codes, was connected with Brahmanical religion or traditions. They were Buddhist people, and their codes were first to be applied to Buddhist people . . . Consequently the aims of *dhammasatthams* was very small compared with that of *dharmasastras*. They dealt only with the eighteen types of lawsuits expounded by Manu and used them as headings of chapters. The substance of law was not entirely taken from Hindu codes. They introduced, as was natural, a few customary rules prevalent among the indigenous population ...

The result was that the new legal literature was completely deprived of religious support, and was therefore a secular code. But the Mon authors wanted the name of Manu, associated in all Indian-influenced nations with the origin of law, to give legitimacy to their work. Thus a myth of a Buddhist Manu in the service of King Mahathammata, first ruler of the world inhabitants was forged — but of this more later. As Maung Maung puts it (1963: 5): '... It was not Hindu law that the wise Manu expounded in the Burmese texts, it was Burmese law and custom, and Manu was the convenient and prestigious mouthpiece'.

The *dhammathat* tradition of the Mon-Burmese (and Siamese) has proved to be prolix and lush; several treatises have been produced over time, as copies, syntheses, and permutations of one another. Thus U Gaung's Digest (see Mootham 1938: 140) listed 36 works, the earliest attributed to A.D. 727, the vast majority being compiled in the seventeenth and eighteenth centuries, and continuing to be produced in the nineteenth. And it is noteworthy that during this long passage of time Pali versions were translated into the Burmese language and modified; portions of preceding works were deleted, new legal usages to suit changing circumstances were interpolated with or without deletion of previous contradictory usages. In the seventeenth century writers of the Alaungpaya dynasty actively began to provide for the first time Buddhist scriptural legitimation for the law of Manu — by citing Buddhist precedents as for example from the Jataka stories. Two processes can be deciphered here: on the one hand the giving of old *dhammasatham* usages a Buddhist validation, and on the other the updating of current customary rules, giving them Buddhist canonical support, and then incorporating them into the *dhammasatham*.

Matters were not made easier when during British rule Sir John Jardine, Judicial Commissioner of Upper Burma, decided that one of the *dhammathat* versions, the *Manugye*, composed in Burmese prose around 1752, was 'fuller than most' and should be used as the standard reference in the administration of justice, a decision confirmed by the Privy Council. It was this text that had been translated into English by Dr Richardson in 1847.[47] However, the British accepted in the words of Sir Arthur Page that 'the Dhammathats are not the sole repository of Burmese customary law, which is also to be ascertained from decided cases and the prevailing customs and practices of Burma' (Maung 1963: 10). And the new colonial rulers, themselves acting as codifiers, no doubt attempted to give Burmese customary usages a greater coherence and form than they had enjoyed in the past. Lord Macaulay's dictum was the guiding light: 'uniformity when you can have it, diversity when you must have it; but, in all cases, certainty'.

In looking at the organic evolution of the alleged Burmese customary law, we ought to recognize the wave of British cultural influence in the nineteenth century, succeeding the Brahmanical wave many centuries earlier. Codes of law which the British developed for India on the basis of British common law to fill 'the vast gaps and interspaces in the [local] substantive law' were imported wholesale into Burma. Thus Burma received for some time *via* India elements of British common law second hand.

Finally, modern Burma since Independence, while viewing the *dhammathat* literature as traditional law, has not baulked at changing it to suit current circumstances on the principle that 'Burmese are not doomed to live forever under the rulings and customs by which they were governed in the days of King Alaunpaya.' As Maung Maung asserts, without mincing his words: 'Much of this ancient law has become anachronistic, and the courts from time to time have restated the common law of Burma in the light of new conditions of life that have come into being, discarding as obsolete ancient rules that no longer accord with the modern outlooks or the habits of the people' (p. 105).

Having given due consideration to the flux of history which has continually affected Burmese 'traditional custom', yet I am impressed by the continuity in basic family and kinship principles that appears to have persited through time. I shall try and demonstrate this continuity by first considering some features of the *Manugye* version (1752) translated by Richardson in 1847, and subsequently by bringing into relief, certain features of Burmese 'customary law' as elucidated by some contemporary legal experts.

The Manugye as translated by Richardson

This mid-eighteenth century document, based on older versions of *dhammathat*, will be used by me to make three kinds of statements. The first to show how at the level of *myth* there is a transformation of the Hindu myth of Manu to the Burmese (Buddhist) version of Manu; the second to show how the male/female relations in respect of property rights show a shift in Burma in the direction of bilaterality (as in Ceylon); and lastly how certain classical Indian concepts have been taken over by the Burmese and transformed in meaning.

The Brahmanical and Buddhist Manus. The reader is directed to the myth of world creation and the role of Manu the lawgiver at the begining of *Laws of Manu*, [48] and the origin myth of the world, especially that part relating to King Mahathammata and his minister Manu as reported in Richardson (1896: 1-25).

The shift in myth revolves around a central point: in Hindu society the Brahman is 'superior' to the King, legitimates his power, and interprets law (*dharma*); in the Mon-Burmese (and Siamese) version, it is the King who, if not the maker of laws, is still the fountain of justice and a Bodhisattva himself; and the Brahman works for the Buddhist King as his subordinate functionary. Herein lies a basic difference in the ideological armatures of Indian and Southeast Asian polities.

In the Indian myth we are told that the self-existent (*svayambhu*) created the universe; and in order to clearly settle his duties and those of other castes according to their order, wise Manu, 'sprung from the self-existent,' composed institutes of the sacred Law, which, we may note, cover all fields of social order — castes,

142

sacraments, marriage, inheritance, occupations, and, most important, 'the whole duty of a King and the manner of deciding lawsuits'. Furthermore, Manu's successors are to be found in the *brahmana* who sprang from the Brahmans' mouth, the first born and the possessor of the Veda. As a later passage says: 'A Brahmana, coming into existence, is born as the highest on earth, the lord of all created beings, for the protection of the treasury of the law' (Manu I: 99). The Brahmanas are given the authority to restrain overbearing Kshatriyas 'for the Kshatriyas sprang from the Brahmanas' (Manu IX: 321).

Now consider the Burmese version, especially the relation between King Mahathammata and Manu. Mahathammata was elected the first king by the people because he was a *para-laung* (an embryo Buddha), 'just in all his proportions beyond all men'. He was given the title of Yaza 'because he was capable of instructing men according to the laws'; he was also the lineal descendant of the sun, who habitually performs works of the purest benevolence.[49]

In comparison to this royal figure of divine proportions, Menoo (Manu) was born a cowherd, who because of his flair for adjudicating disputes was made the King's minister while still a child. But when Manu gave a wrong decision over the ownership of a cucumber, he decided to become an ascetic in search of infallible truth, practising both meditation and austerities, which in classical belief enable a man to gain special spiritual powers. Thus Manu became *yathe* or a *rahan*, and at the stone cave in the hill near Mandagini Lake, 'here he remained subduing his lust and other passions', and thereby ascended to the heaven and there found the *dhammathat* laws engraven on the boundary wall of the solar system. He brought back the divine laws to his King. Thus Manu introduced more just and perfect laws into a situation in which the law of the king and his legal procedures and institutions, however imperfect, had pre-existed. The contrast with the Indian version is remarkable here.

In the sum then the Burmese myth (which is also to be found in Ceylon and in Siam, reflecting a transformation common to Theravada Buddhist countries)[50] makes two points about the relation between 'king' and 'brahman',

(1) Mahathammata, although 'elected' king, is at the same time an embryo Buddha, and an embodiment of justice.

(2) Menoo is a cowherd boy-wonder who, because of his judicial acumen, is appointed minister by the King and who then, by the practice of austerities and meditation, discovers the divine writ and brings it back to the world in his capacity as a wise ascetic and holy man in the service of his king.

The laws of the Manugye. Let us now briefly consider the content of Manu's laws, particularly those portions relating to the areas of interest to this essay (Richardson 1896, Vol III, IV, V, VI, and X). Let us keep in mind the main articulating principle of Hindu *shastric* law and the Kandyan Sinhalese usages which we have already discussed. The *Manugye* appears to portray the following features and preoccupations:

(1) Bilateral inheritance of both sons and daughters to parental property is well established; however the text also shows a graduation of inheritance rights according to relative age and sex, the eldest son and eldest daughter being the largest beneficiaries. Residence with parents or away from them is also taken into account.

The following passages serve as examples:

(1)   In the case of the death of both father and mother, and their leaving only sons: After the eldest son has taken the clothes and ornaments of the father, let all the residue of the property, animate and inanimate with the mother's clothes and ornaments, be divided into ten parts, and let the eldest son have one; let the residue be again divided into ten, and let the second have one share; let the remainder be again divided into ten, and let the other children each have a share; and let the rest be divided equally amongst all. In this case also it had been laid down that the division into ten shall be repeated seven times, and here also some must be set apart for religious offerings.

       If the father and mother both die, leaving male and female children, let the eldest son have the clothes and ornaments of the father, and the eldest daughter the clothes and ornaments of the mother; the residue of the property, animate, and inanimate, shall be divided into fifteen shares, and let each take one according to age; having added them together and divided them three times, let the residue then be divided equally. In this case also, seven divisions have been ordered prior to the equal distribution of the residue (Richardson 1896: 276).

(2)   A father and mother, after having five daughters, shall have one son: if any parents after having had five daughters, shall by the means of their prayers have a son, let him inherit his father's clothes, ornaments, personal slaves, house, sword, goblet, water and betel bearer, according to his class in society, in the first instance; then let the eldest daughter have her mother's clothes and ornaments, and of all the remaining property, animate and inanimate, let the eldest sister and the youngest (son) have equal shares let the other sisters share according to their ages in the share which falls to the sister, and pay the debts in the same proportions. (p. 286).

The law of inheritance as regards three brothers and sisters:

       If the three be living together on the death of the parents, let the brother have the father's clothes and ornaments, and the elder sister the clothes and ornaments of the mother, and of the remaining property let the brother have one-third share more than the elder sister, and the younger sister one-third share less; this is when the brother is the eldest. Should the sister be the eldest and the brother the youngest, let them share the clothes and ornaments as above laid down; and of the remaining property let the eldest sister and the brothers share alike, and the younger have one-third less share, and if there be debts, let them pay them in the same proportions. If they be living separately, let the partition be the same. If one was living with the parents at the time of their death, let that one have twice the share he (or she) would otherwise have been entitled to. This double share is not laid down with reference to the others, but twice what the one so remaining with the parents would otherwise have had, and let them pay the debts in the same proportion. Thus the lord hermit ordered (pp. 299-300).

(2) However, unlike in India and Ceylon, the Manugye does not contain any well defined or clear cut discussion of marriage payments and gifts at marriage. Concepts analoguous to dowry and brideprice as such are missing. However there are passing references to such things as property given to a man by his bride's parents at the daughter's marriage, a bride's personal possessions and gifts made to her at marriage, etc. Finally, and most importantly, it is clear that marriage did not disqualify a woman from *prospective inheritance from her parents* (e.g. pp. 282, 283, 284, 286).

Therefore one is tempted to infer that the major part of a woman's property rights were not negotiated at marriage (in the form of dowry), and that marriage payments were not of critical importance. It would seem that man and wife realized their major property rights through inheritance after their marriage. Consider for instance this passage which weaves-in many themes:

If the daughter dies before she has any family, let the son-in-law have all the property, animate or inanimate, which was given to him at the time of marriage; let him also have her personal chattels, and all property actually in possession . . . nor shall the son-in-law though he demands the wife's inheritance of her parents, have any right to obtain it. Besides this, he shall not recover any of his wife's property actually in the possession or keeping of her parents; they shall retain it. But if it has been placed in their charge after marriage; the parents and son-in-law shall share it equally between them; this is said when the (young couple) have no family . . . (pp. 282-3.)

(3) There are also indications in the Manugye of the occurence of uxorilocal marriage and the incoming son-in-law, and of ambilocal residence (p. 162). This again reflects a bilateral kinship system. However these possibilities are not codified in terms of residential-cum-property rules such as *diga/binna* in Kandyan Ceylon, or in terms of the 'appointed daughter' 'incoming son-in-law', the *putrika putra*, etc., as in India.

(4) The customary formulations show some preoccupations with the rights and privileges and differential excellence of stratified levels of society. But the all important *varna* scheme of India articulated around the *brahman, kshatriya, vaisya*

and *shudra* is replaced by the following classes instituted at the first establishment of the world: 'the class of Chiefs, of Brahmans, of the Wealthy and the Poor' (p. 9). Indeed expressions such as *bayama* (or Brahman) class, or *khattiya* class (*kshatriya*), or *waythee* (*vaisya*) class, and alleged differential privileges of these strata are found here and there in the text, but it is clear that this was more a borrowing of Indian terms rather than a representation of the actual hierarchy in the society.[51]

(5) But a more convincing preoccupation of the Manugye — and here we feel that it touches a core traditional Burmese concern is that concerning polygyny, the ranking of wives into senior and inferior wives, concubines, slave wives, etc., and correspondingly the ranking of different kinds of children and their associated inheritance rights. For instance consider this passage (see also previous references in introduction):

Regarding children who are entitled to inherit, and those who are not.

There are twelve kinds of children, and of these, six are entitled to inherit.

1st. All children, male and female, old and young, born to a couple given in marriage by their parents, commencing with the *au-ra-tha*, (son and heir).

2nd. The children of another person, adopted publicly with a promise that they shall inherit, which is a matter of public notoriety, these are called *kiek-tee-ma*.

3rd. When there is a superior and inferior wife, a woman who is publicly cohabited with, but who does not eat out of the same dish, is called *a-pyoung*; the children of this concubine are called *hayt-tee-ma*, because they are 'inferior' to the children of the head wives.

4th. The children by a slave who was in the possession of the husband or of the wife, at the time of marriage, or a slave bought by the couple; these children are slave, and a male and female are called *khayt-ta-za*.

5th. Children, male or female, of a wife by a former husband, or of a husband by a former wife; these are called *dway-pop-pa-ka-ra*.

6th. Children, male or female, who have no parents, or whose parents or relations are known, who have been casually taken charge of and brought up, are called *teek-tee-ka*. (Richardson 1896: 314).

The question arises as to the exact relevance of these fine legalistic discriminations for actual events and everyday affairs. These discriminations between superior and inferior wives and children may be expected to reach Byzantine complexity in the palace and court circles. King Mindohn for example is alleged to have had fifty-three recognized wives, and one hundred and ten children by them (besides children by numerous concubines). I have already on p. 65 reported the alleged classification of royal wives and concubines in the Burmese court. But the curious fact is that succession to the throne was always contentious, and the winner who was rarely if ever the eldest son of the chief wife, usually murdered all his half-brothers and their immediate relatives. 'The sovereign always marries at least one

146

half-sister to ensure the purity of the royal blood, but rather illogically, the issue of this union is not by any means necessarily heir to the throne' (Shway Yoe 1896: 59). The son who most often succeeded was the son who could take and maintain the kingship by force. To understand why for instance the same Burmese dynasty which wielded control from the middle of the eighteenth century to the end of the nineteenth century did not manage its succession according to the theoretical rules we have to look deeper into the inherent political instability of these traditional kingdoms which experienced endemic rebellions despite the divinization of their kings. However, an oblique comparison can perhaps be useful. The Thai monarchy which traditionally manifested the same rules and practical inconsistencies, managed to observe orderly succession since the present Chakkri dynasty established and stabilized itself at the end of the eighteenth century. This stabilization corresponds to the growing strength and viability of the wider polity itself during the nineteenth century. Moreover, the rights of superior and inferior wives (and their respective children), of aristocrats, of officals and of wealthy men in Thailand have in the same period been adjudicated on similar principles of discrimination manifested in Burma. But as we shall indicate later we should bear in mind that polygamy was inevitably of small incidence, though like other fabulous doings of the great, it had high social visibility wherever it occured.

(6) A clearly specified feature of husband—wife relations is the tradition-sanctioned possibility of divorce by mutual consent, the granting of equal rights to initiate divorce to the wife and husband, and an equitable division of properties consequent on divorce. The following passage is an egalitarian bilateral formulation:

> It is not only when the one has taken a paramour, or the other a lesser wife, or uses violence towards the other that there is the right to separate: and though the person whose habits are bad should say he does not wish to separate, it shall be considered as a separation by mutual consent and let all the property common to both be divided equally between them, and let them have the right to separate ... (Richardson 1896: 147-8).

We should, however note that the Manugye also contains not so much contradictory as alternative formulations, as when it declares that when there is unilaterally initiated divorce the offending party, whether male or female, loses all rights to the conjugal estate to the injured spouse (pp. 142-3). It is difficult to see how such a ruling could have been implemented as it stands. (The ruling however does not violate the equality of the sexes.)

(7) Adoption was a recognized institution in the Dhammathat literature. The provisions in Manugye focus on the inheritance rights of an adopted child *vis-à-vis* a natural child; and on the adopted child's property rights being related to the fact of co-residence with the new parents, performance of filial duties and the like. (Richardson p. 281). Unlike the Indian *shastric* literature there is no discussion of the aims of adoption (such Hindu preoccupations as having a male heir to carry on the line, to make religious offerings to the dead ancestors, etc. being irrelevant and

therefore absent), and of the preferred kinship status of the adoptee to the adopting parents. Indeed Burmese adoption, pertaining to a child of either sex, is related to supplementing the family labour force or simply adopting a child of either sex in the absence of issue. And how different the spirit of the Burmese institution is from the Indian one be gauged from the provisions which discuss the possibility of parents taking back children they have given away in adoption, of the adopted child's right to express his (or her) choice whether he wishes to continue to stay with the adopted parents, etc. Indeed these discussions seem to indicate that we are in the Burmese context dealing in some instances with 'fosterage' rather than formal adoption. And we are led to infer that formal adoption as such could not have been an important institution in Burmese family life.

Contemporary customary law

In many ways the *dhammathats* are still alive in modern Burma. In the nineteenth century the British rulers tried to establish what the Burmese customary laws were: the works of Richardson, Jardine, Sparks, Forchhammer, Sandford attest to this effort. And the effort to build on the past as well as modify and transform it has gone on uninterrupted. In this section I shall rely primarily on contemporary legal works such as Lahiri (1951), Mootham (1939) and Maung (1963). One quickly finds how much the past is woven into their expositions of the present, despite new legislation.[52]

Curiously, Burmese refer to their law as 'Burmese Buddhist Law' in an attempt to mark off their legal usages from those of the non-Buddhist hill tribes like the Kachin, Chin, etc., and from aliens, particularly Indians and Chinese, living in Burma. What is conveyed by the label is not so much that Burmese customary civil and criminal law is derived from or laid down by Buddhism, but that its relevant application is to Burmese Buddhists, the major ethnic-cum-religious category in the country. Note that the customary law also does not necessarily apply to the Shan provinces, though the Shans may come within the Buddhist label. However, as mentioned earlier, Burmese do tend to attribute the design of their society to Buddhist influence, and sometimes talk as if their law is Buddhist-inspired.

Burmese writers are self-consciously aware of the particularities of Burmese conjugal family relations. Thus Maung Maung (1963) attributing to Buddhism (which is alleged to inspire 'individualism') the main features of Burmese family structure writes in a comparative vein:

Since nothing is permanent on this earth, the Burmese family does not trouble itself with its perpetuation. In the Chinese family of old 'there are four things which are unfilial, and the greatest of them is not to have posterity' [Mencius IV, A.27]. In the Hindu family too it was important to have certain rites and rituals performed by male heirs; mere women being inadequate, and marriage and adoption were institutions which often had the purpose of bringing males into the family. In the Burmese family rituals are absent, there is equality between husband, wife, sons and daughters, and as for perpertuating, why, the Buddha himself had to die (p. 48).

A more incisive statement of the Burmese configuration is made by Mi Mi Khaing who pointed out that despite the formal social precedence given men yet 'in the all-important matters of money, of divorce, inheritance, of freedom of movement, the right of giving advice of transacting business . . . women admit of no inferiority'.

In the home the wife is by custom and law, a sharer . . . Her rights to her own property, which she brought to the marital home or acquires later, are well defined; her share in the husband's and joint earnings is a vested right. When the husband is away, or dies, the headship of the family passes to her, not to the eldest son.[53]

Mi Mi Khaing presents the same argument with greater clarity in another place when she comments on the rulings of Burmese Buddhist Law in regard to the property rights of women:

She retains sole ownership of whatever property she brings to the marriage, and on the dissolution of the marriage is entitled to half of all the additions of wealth since the marriage . . . On the death of one parent the surviving parent still has sole ownership of half the property. The other half is open to division among the children, but it is only a black sheep which will insist on division while one parent is still alive. (Mi Mi Khaing 1946: 123).

Mi Mi Khaing's assertions could well act as the text for the elucidation of customary law, which I shall now outline.

Marriage. This is a civil institution into which the religious element does not enter. Although parents may arrange marriage, a woman's right to choose her partner is well attested in the Dhammathat texts. Manugye lists three kinds of marriages — that effected by parents, that contracted through a go-between, and marriage by mutual consent.

Burmese traditional marriage ritual is similar to that enacted in Kandyan villages in Ceylon. 'The hands of bride and groom are joined and bound together with a silk scarf. They partake of food from the same bowls and make obeisance together. The guests bring gifts of money to help in setting up the household' (Maung 1963: 55). Shway Yoe, writing towards the end of the last century, reported a similar ritual and commented that this old custom 'has in many cases died out' (1896: 57).

Reviewing the relatively sparse literature I find it somewhat difficult to establish what precisely were and are the marriage customs, particularly those relating

149

to payments, residence and the like. It could of course very well be that the essence of Burmese marriage is this imprecise and flexible formulation.

Let us attempt to construct a picture by dipping into the recent past. The Italian priest, Sangermano described the Burmese customs prevailing at the close of the eighteenth century in terms which suggest that a young man took with him some 'dower' and spent the early part of his marriage living with his wife's parents, but possessed the rights of wife-removal subsequently:

> In concluding a marriage the customs of the Burmsee are somewhat different from ours. With us it is the woman who brings the dowry, and she goes to live in the house of the husband; but in this country the man, on the contrary, goes to the house of his bride's parents, and must take with him a dower according to the resources of his family, . . . If [the girl's parents] and their daughter consent to the match, the contract is immediately made, and the bridegroom, accompanied by his friends and relations goes to the house of his father-in-law where he continues to reside for three years. If at the end of this time he is discontented with his situation, he may then take his wife and go to live somewhere else (Jardine 1893: 165).

Shway Yoe writing precisely a century later confirms Sangermano, both in respect of the bridegroom taking some goods with him and of his uxorilocal residence. He described the bridegroom as coming 'in procession with all his friends, carrying the greater portion of the belongings with which he intends to set up house; a bundle of mats, a long arm-chair, a teak box, mattresses, pillows, besides materials for the feast and presents for the bride' (p. 57). 'After marriage the couple almost always live for two or three years in the house of the bride's parents, the son-in-law becoming one of the family and contributing to its support' (p. 59).

Now two points are in order regarding these accounts. Shway Yoe's account of what the bridegroom takes with him leaves us in no doubt that (leaving aside the food for the feast) they constitute the bedding and furniture, etc. for the young couple to set up house plus presents for the wife; in other words they constitute not brideprice (paid to parents) but the nucleus of a conjugal estate (to be used by the couple). Shway Yoe also refers to the fixing of a 'dowry' (p. 57) as part of the formal marriage proceedings which would suggest that the bride's parents reciprocally contributed goods to the couple's conjugal estate.

How general might have been the initial uxorilocal residence reported by these authors? It is noteworthy that Sangermano proceeds to inform us: 'Frequently marriages are contracted without the consent of parents of either party, and even in direct opposition to their wishes. For the Burmese law allows of no restraint in these matters, but leaves young people to follow their own inclinations . . .' (Jardine 1893: 165). And Shway Yoe reports that 'runaway marriages are common enough' and the couple soon enough 'come and ask for pardon and a house to live in' (p. 55). Clearly this would suggest that in this lax atmosphere of elopements definite payments on both sides could not be insisted upon, and residence was probably chosen according to convenience and according to the circumstances of both sets of parents.

We may summarize our inferences from the above authors and our reading of other authors as follows: By and large marriage was effected by the consent of the young couple; while some of them were arranged by parents and proceeded according to formal requirements, many others were simply runaway marriages or simple cohabitation. In such a context the transmission of property by one or both sets of parents to the couple (or to each other) could not have been a principal issue. However, there is evidence that while marriage payments themselves are conspicuous by their unstructured nature, parents and kin of the couple may give gifts to the young couple which enables them to begin life with a conjugal estate. There are references to betrothal gifts given by a man to his wife's parents (Mootham 1928: 24) and to gifts of the nature of 'dowry'; but these are clearly optional. Maung's account of marriage payments is apt; 'The flow of gifts was not a one-way traffic; there was no rigid requirement of dowry, though parents on both sides would give what they could, often announcing the gifts at the ceremony itself, if there was one, or a meeting of the elders' (1963: 53). It is clear that whatever property was transferred was in the form of *movables* rather than land. As I have suggested before, the critical fact is that it is not at marriage but later through normal inheritance that men and women acquire rights to parental property including land.

We note then in the Burmese instance unformalized traces and aspects of marriage transactions which we noted for India and Ceylon. The Burmese general form corresponds to the non-aristocratic ordinary form of the Kandyan Sinhalese where it is not the abbreviated gift transactions but subsequent bilateral inheritance that regulates property transmission. Next, the Burmese uxorilocal marriage echoes aspects of the Kandyan *binna* marriage. Thirdly, as in most of India (and Kandyan Ceylon) if both parental sides to the marriage make gifts, these take the form of movables (household effects, jewellery and clothing) and are meant to be contributions to the conjugal estate of the couple.

In all stratified societies the aristocrats, the elite, the propertied elements of the population deviate from the general norm, and Burma appears to be no exception. In South Asia, this deviation as far as it relates to marriage expresses itself in inflated dowries that accompany brides in search of desirable husbands. We have previously noted how the institution of dowry has assumed astronomical proportions among the 'middle classes', and the bureaucratic and professional segments in India and Ceylon. Burma too evolved under British rule its corresponding English-educated administrative and professional elite, with a corresponding accentuation of dowry as a vital component of their marriage. Mi Mi Khaing's family and its peers is an excellent illustration. She describes how among the circle of Burmese government officals there was deviation from the tradition of 'the man's family asking fot the hand of the girl with presents of money and jewellery' towards the opposite of eligible husbands seeking dowries from their wives, thus confirming our view that in contemporary times a young man's holding of a prestigious salaried (or income generating) job by virtue of his educational attainments puts him in a position to attract a dowry from equally ambitious and aspiring parents of daughters (1946: 74)[54]. Such a man is in a different situation from a young farmer who must await his inheritance from his parents and for whom a wife is an economic asset as a worker in the fields and as a 'means of support instead of being a burden to a husband'. It is within the same class of affluent families that the conspicuous display of jewellery develops: it is deemed necessary that a woman be adorned with expensive jewellery, which is displayed on social occasions and taken with her into marriage. Mi Mi Khaing describes in detail the diamond and gem-studded hairpins, combs, necklaces, ear-studs, bracelets and anklets with which the beautiful women of her class were bedecked, and which parents felt obliged to provide for their daughters and husbands for their wives (1946: 47).

To return again to general problems. Marriage prohibitions and preferences are once again not a focus of rigid definition in Burma. For instance consider this passage:

> As regards cousins, generally speaking, union with agnates is strongly deprecated, while that with other cognates is not looked upon with disfavour, provided the woman is on the same line as the man or below it. No case has arisen in which the validity of a marriage had been questioned on the ground of consanguinity or of affinity and, when one does, a considerable body of evidence will have to be led to prove prevailing customs (Maung 1963: 57; see also Lahiri 1951: 15 and Shway Yoe 1896: 59).

The Dhammathats themselves are conspicuously silent on marriage prohibitions and the range of 'incest'.

Divorce can be brought about by mutual consent.[55] The grounds for divorce action can be cruelty, desertion, adultery, etc. How close the Burmese situation is to much of Kandyan Sinhalese village practice can be gauged from this statement:

> Just as a man and woman can come together, set up house as husband and wife and establish their status as such, without any ceremony or entertainment of friends, without recourse to the courts or the administrative authorities, so they can end marriage (Maung 1963: 72).

'The liberty of divorce' reported Shway Yoe (1896: 59) 'is practically unrestricted, except by the elaborate laws respecting the division of property.'

The property of marriage and its partition on divorce. The Burmese husband and wife are alleged to have a 'community of property', a principle that is supposed to flow from the equal status accorded to women. The attempt of British judges to understand the Burmese conventions as regards the conjugal estate is instructive: there was much debate among them whether the husband and wife constituted a 'partnership', 'joint tenants' or 'tenants in common'. Apparently ultimately the decision was reached that they were 'tenants in common' either party being competent to alienate or dispose of his or her own share in the joint property, but not to alienate the interest of the other without the latter's consent. The term 'partnership' (once favoured by Jardine) is inappropriate because one spouse is not automatically jointly responsible for the debts and contracts made by the other. And as for the other two concepts, Lahiri (1951: 64) clearly enunciates the difference between them: 'where they are *joint tenants*, the estate on the death of one of them passes to the survivor; where they are *tenants in common*, they are entitled to rents and profits in proportion to their shares, but on the death of one his interest in that estate passes not to the survivor but to his heirs'.

As a matter of fact our task can be simplified and also made more exact if we can decompose the 'property of the family' or the 'conjugal estate' into its explicitly recognized components, and see what rights husband and wife enjoy in relation to them during marriage and at divorce (in particular divorce by mutual consent). This is what Table 6 attempts to do.[56] We see in the table that spouses in general share equally in the gifts received at marriage (*kanwin*). Varying degrees of separateness are recognized as regards property which spouses owned *before* marriage (*payin/atetpa*). As regards property acquired after marriage, a distinction is observed between property which one or both spouses acquired by joint or individual effort (in which case it is shared equally) and property which either spouse inherited, or received as gifts (in which case the spouse succeeding to it has major but not exclusive rights at divorce).

Thus it would be a mistake to infer that husband and wife have a simple and equal 'community of property'. But in a comparative context, it is evident that a Burmese man's or woman's rights in the conjugal estate at divorce are greater than that enjoyed by Sinhalese or most Indian counterparts. This is because *complete* separateness of properties owned before marriage, or received at marriage, or even inherited after marriage, is *not* recognized, so that the poorer spouse benefits by receiving a share of the other's property (as well as share equally in the property acquired by joint or individual effort).

We may also conveniently allude here to the division of children at divorce. Generally it is left to the parting parents to agree which children should go with them. Apparently the girls generally go with the mother, and the boys with the father. It was previously ruled (on the basis of a misreading of the *Manugye*) that such parental agreements leading to a division into two separate families deprived the children going with one parent of inheritance rights in the other's estate. The Supreme Court has subsequently decided that this rule of exclusion was not to be strictly applied.

Whatever the outcome in each particular instance of divorce, still it might be surmised that the theoretical principle of the division of children according to sex consonant with the sex of each parent can only be envisaged in a society where bilateral inheritance rights exist, and where neither dowry nor brideprice are significant payments. For in a dowry situation female children are an economic burden, and sons are needed to recoup; brideprice we have noted, is usually

Table 6   Categories of property of the family and rights of spouses in them

Categories of property	Rights of spouses in property of marriage (conjugal estate)	Partition rights on divorce (by mutual consent)
(1) *Kanwin*: marriage 'portion' or gifts received by the bride and bridegroom from parents (and relatives) at marriage. Also includes property given by bridegroom to bride at time of marriage for their joint use.	Owned jointly and equally by husband and wife.	Shared equally.
(2) Property owned before marriage by either spouse and brought to marriage. This divides into two categories:		
(a) *Payin*: property brought by spouses previously unmarried.	Retains some separate identity during marriage; husband and wife have each a one-third share in the *payin* brought by the other.	Normally on divorce by mutual consent the spouses take back their *payin* and *atetpa* properties, unless the rule of dependency applies, wherein the spouse who is the richer and the supporter (*nissaya*) takes a two-thirds share and the poorer and dependent spouse (*nissita*) takes a one-third share.
(b) *Atetpa*: property brought by spouses who have been previously married (*eindaunggyi*).	Property usually held separately and disposed of separately, in order to ensure rights of children by previous marriage.	
(3) Property acquired during marriage. This again divides into two categories:		
(a) *Lettetpwa*: property accruing during marriage to husband or wife individually either by succession or individual exertion.	Generally spouses have equal interest, except in property inherited or received by gift by either spouse.	On divorce shared equally, except where property is acquired through inheritance (or gift) by one spouse, in which case the recipient of the inheritance is entitled to two-thirds and the other one-third share.
(b) *Hnapazon*: property acquired during marriage by joint exertion of husband and wife.	Husband and wife each have half share, i.e. equal interest.	Shared equally.

154

associated with unilineal descent groups in which case the rights over children often belong exclusively to the patrilineal or matrilineal descent group concerned; where division of children does take place in a unilineal or non-unilineal society the best strategy is for parents to divide the children equally as regards sex and number, the paired brother and sister making the best economic sense.[57]

Inheritance and succession. While a Burmese may make gifts *inter vivos*, or make a family compact orally or in writing when alive, he does not have the right to dispose of his property by means of a will. Inheritance is most commonly by intestate succession only, and it is the major rules associated with this succession that need concern us here.

The following are the general principles that appear to be the prevailing rulings of the courts (as discussed by our authorities), which themselves have taken into account principles enunciated in the Dhammathats.

(1) Inheritance shall not ascend when it can descend. (Thus a remoter descendant gets preference over a closer ascendant; and if the deceased has no surviving spouse or issue his or her younger siblings inherit before the older siblings and parents.)

(2) In the event of collateral succession, the nearer excludes the more remote. Thus if A, B, C are brothers, and if A dies before B, A's children are excluded from B's property by C; again, relatives of full blood are preferred to those of half blood; and finally collaterals of a lower level exclude those of a higher level.

(3) Now we come to the most critical rule, the order of succession to the estate of a deceased person (Maung 1963: 107): the *surviving spouse*, subject to the share of the *orasa*; the descendants (children and grandchildren);[58] the first line of collaterals (brothers and sisters); the parents; the second line of collaterals (uncles aunts); etc.

The right of the surviving spouse. The remarkable feature of Burmese law is that the surviving spouse becomes the *absolute* owner (until her remarriage) of the whole estate of the deceased spouse, to the exclusion of all children of the marriage except the *orasa* child (who will be discussed shortly).

This provision is remarkable, especially if we reflect on the rights vested in a woman elsewhere. Compared with India and Kandyan Ceylon, the Burmese spouse has the greatest advantages: in the patrilineal parts of India, according to *shastric* law, a woman who normally only takes with her movable property as dowry with no rights to patrimonial land (except exceptionally), is entitled on the death of her husband to only a share in his property equal to that of any one son (the quantity of property diminishing according to the number of sons); in Kandyan Ceylon where by virtue of bilateral inheritance women can own both land and movables, the separateness of the properties of wife and husband are recognized to the degree that the surviving spouse in the more usual *diga* virilocal marriage only has the usufruct of the deceased spouse's *praveni* (inherited) property, which in due course she must transmit entire to the children of the deceased.[59] In the Burmese situation it would seem that not only does bilateral inheritance vest her with strong property rights but also, on the death of a spouse the survivor gains control of that spouse's property until he or she dies or remarries. And even when the surviving parent remarries he or she can lay claim to half the deceased spouse's property; while the children of the former marriage receive the other remaining half which they share *per capita*.[60]

We may also briefly refer to the succession rights of the multiple wives of a deceased. The wives of equal standing with the husband inherit equally; but a superior wife *vis-à-vis* an inferior wife also who lived with the husband gets three-fifths as opposed to the latter's two-fifths. But an inferior wife who was not in co-residence but was merely visited by the husband is not entitled to anything more than the property which he had already given her during his life time.

The rights of children. While in general bilateral inheritance prevails, there is a special place assigned to the *orasa* son or daughter. The *orasa* (Skt = *aurasa*) means in its classical sense a true or natural child of the body; but in successive Dhammathat interpretations the meaning has been transformed in Burma to the eldest born child — male or female — who is capable of undertaking the responsibilities of a deceased father or mother respectively. The child should have attained majority and should be capable of discharging a dead parent's responsibilities in the control and management of family property and household. Such an *orasa* child is in Burmese law vested with a right to one-fourth of the estate left to the surviving parent by the deceased parent.

Children other than *orasa* sons and daughters share equally regardless of age when they inherit. Equality is the rule between them today, the finer distinctions attempted by the Dhammathats within the general scope of bilateral inheritance which I previously cited being ignored.

Thus one might sum up the pattern of devolution thus: the rights of children can be enforced, except that of the *orasa*, only when the surviving parent re-marries or dies. The surviving parent at re-marriage can claim half the dead spouse's property, the *orasa* (or the eldest surviving child) one-fourth, and the remaining children one-fourth.

We should also briefly describe the rights of grandchildren. If an individual has no surviving children his or her property goes to the grandchildren of both sexes. It would appear that the children of a deceased person do not exclude his grandchildren born to another pre-deceased child. (Lahiri 1951: 183). Mootham (1939: 79) refers to them as 'out of time grandchildren,' i.e. whose father or mother die before their grandparents, and says that such grandchildren receive one-quarter of the share of the surviving grandparent's estate that would have gone to his father or mother had she or his survived the grandparent. The 'out of time' grandchildren inherit in their own right and not by right of representation of their deceased parent. There is nothing in these provisions that are not consistent with a bilateral

156

system of distribution.

Burmese adoption is interesting in comparison with the Indian counterpart. The concepts used are:

(a) *kittima* adoption with a view to inheritance, the adopted child being given the same rights as a natural child;

(b) *appatittha* casual adoption (verging on fosterage) in which that intention is absent and therefore the individual has only a limited right of inheritance.

Keeping these distinctions in mind, let us now bring into view a shift of meanings in some classical Indian concepts when transplanted to Burma. In the Indian literature a set of three concepts are contrasted thus: *aurasa* as natural born son and heir is contrasted with *dattaka* a son and heir adopted in the absence of the former. And again a *dattaka* adoption is contrasted with a *kritima* adoption: a *dattaka* adoption usually is of a minor, he undergoes a ceremony of adoption, adopts the new father's name and performs rites for him and his ancestors when he dies and loses property rights in his natal family and gains rights in his adopted parents' property, while a *kritima* adoption is inferior in that the person adopted is usually an adult whose consent to adoption is required; he undergoes no ceremony, he does not take the name of the adopting parent and he does not lose inheritance rights in his natal family while gaining rights in his new family.

The Burmese set of contrastive terms are *orasa, kitima,* and *appatitha*. The Burmese *orasa* (*aurasa*) refers not so much to a 'natural' child, but to the eldest child male or female within a set of 'natural' children. In the Burmese context when all children inherit and the Hindu problems of male heir and his religious obligations do not obtain, the borrowed term is used to *stress* eldest child *vis-à-vis* the other *unstressed* children.

Similarly, in Burma, the classical Indian adoption in its full blown character does not obtain; Burmese adoption is a weaker form closer to the *kritima* form rather than the *dattaka* form: minor children, unmarried adults and orphans, of both sexes, might be adopted; there is no ceremony of adoption that is performed (though the adoption must be a matter of publicity), and, most importantly, the adoption can be terminated by the natural parents (until the child reaches maturity) or by the adopted child itself when it comes of age. Moreover, since traditionally Burmese had no transmitted *family* names, there is no question of the adopted child assuming a new surname. One is tempted to surmise therefore that there are good reasons why the Burmese borrowed the looser *kritima* concept to label their own adoption institution rather than the more restrictive and particularized *dattaka* concept.[61]

Within adoption the Burmese contrast is really between a 'weak' kind of adoption (*kittima*) and a still weaker form, *appattha*, a 'casual adoption' (including the care of poor relatives), without view to inheritance, which is more correctly described as *fosterage*, a common enough practice in Burma and Thailand, both being bilateral societies and where patron—client relationships are crucial.

I alluded a moment ago to the striking fact that the Burmese (as was the case with the Thai) traditionally had no surnames or patronymics of any kind. From a man's personal name it was (and is) quite impossible to infer what his social class or family affiliation is. But frequently especially among those participating in the network of political office, the title assumed or conferred gave information regarding status and office. And such a man's 'name' changed as he was promoted and invested with new titles. It follows that in this context genealogies were necessarily shallow indeed and that corporate estates tied to kinship groups were non-existent.[62] The naming system thus fits in with other features of cognatic social organization we have already highlighted.

One institution remains to be commented upon. Polygyny, the marrying of multiple wives, seems to be a somewhat more marked in Burma than in India or Ceylon, though among the Burmese too it is a luxury limited to the upper reaches of the society.[63] We have already noted that the Burmese devised an elaborate ranking of wives into senior, junior, and slave wives, concubines, etc. The difference from India and Ceylon is that in these countries the restrictions of caste status limit the 'hypergamous range' of women one can publicly cohabit with; and the ideals of a virgin gift preferably combined with dowry do not altogether prevent though they restrain a full elaboration of polygyny, except among martial Rajput-type groups whose 'dominance' relation to inferiors permits intercourse without serious threat to their status (Tod 1832, Mayer 1960). In Burma we can see that because of the absence of caste there is no bar on men consorting with women of the same as well as much lower status; and the ranking of wives is inevitably closely correlated with their economic (and other social) status, and the magnitude of their own property assets. While in a formal sense all women are entitled to property rights, in actual fact women differ in the amounts of property they inherit, for the society itself is not egalitarian. Superior men marry equal wives with property and make them senior wives; but when it comes to inferior wives, one suspects the superior man not only receives them as tribute but also frequently 'purchases' them; such wives by virtue of their depressed economic and social status tend to be in a dependency relation. Now we see more clearly than at the beginning of this essay why in a situation where there is double transmission of property and where women possess significant property rights, polygamy does paradoxically generate a ranking of wives and their children. Such a ranking pattern cannot emerge in a definitive and elaborate manner in societies where men are the primary owners of property and are also acquiring wives through brideprice payments; the children under these circumstances tend to be assimilated equally to the status of their fathers, irrespective of the status of their mothers.

This account of Burma has restricted itself to the legal literature. I need merely mention in conclusion that Manning Nash's characterisation of a contemporary Upper Burma village confirms the scaffolding I have erected. We are told that 'presumptive inheritance rights (are) equally distributed among all the members, both male and female' (1965: 49); that the kinship system is not only bilateral, it is also the optional variety; that the rich may 'arrange' marriage while the poor may not; that parents may settle gifts on a couple at marriage; that uxorilocal marriage does occur. Finally, 'The kinship system of Nondwin is cognatic. Kinsmen are of equal status on both the mother's and on the father's side . . . The depth of kinship is not great . . . Kinship is wide in collateral relation . . . ' (p. 59). There is no doubt that this Burmese design is old and manifests a remarkable continuity.

The discussion of Burma abundantly confirms the two general propositions that have guided this essay: (a) that India, Ceylon and Burma can be considered as constituting a kind of 'topological structure' held together by similarities and continuities that mark some kind of 'boundary' or 'neighbourhood'; (b) and that within that totality one can move from the 'stronger' and dominant structure represented by India to the 'weaker' structures represented by Ceylon and Burma by transforming a restrictive condition regarding the property rights of women. A summary of the basic features of the Burmese kinship system clearly shows that this system is to be located as an even more flexible version of the Kandyan Sinhalese system: bilateral kinship plus ambilocal residence (without defined residence-cum-inheritance rules) plus flexible and unformalized optional marriage gifts constituting the nucleus of a conjugal estate, but more importantly, the operation of normal bilateral inheritance to property subsequent to marriage. Among the elite bureaucratic-professional class, however, the dowry system becomes accented as in India and Ceylon.

Final comment: the limits of this study

In these concluding paragraphs I do not wish so much to recapitulate my hypotheses and conclusions as to indicate their limits and to allude to an alternative way of.understanding some of the material. I am also conscious at this stage of Gödel's proof that no system of propositions can be complete in itself and not lead to contradiction . . .

I have for instance sought to illuminate the lowland Burmese institutions of kinship and marriage in relation to the classical models of India and Ceylon in terms of a dominant—variant, centre—periphery scheme. But there is also another perspective possible which illuminates the same Burmese institutions. This perspective entails their comparison with those of the hill tribes of Upper Burma (and northeast India), a comparison which will highlight the differences and dialectical *contrasts* between the valley peoples on the one hand who are class stratified, have usually, except among the royalty, no lineages or houses, and whose marriages are the concern of individual families and not groups, and on the other the 'hill tribes', many of whom have lineages, and some of whom have prescriptive marriage systems usually linked with elaborate bridewealth payments.[64] Although this pattern of contrast between the peoples of the valleys and the hills would have added a new dimension to the dowry—bridewealth comparison, I have, save for touching upon it in Part One, excluded a detailed treatment because it has already been done so excellently by Leach in *Political Systems of Highland Burma* (and also Lehman 1963). Leach pointed out (1964 Ch. VII) that while there were marriage links between Kachin and Shans, for inherent structural reasons they had 'a different significance according to the class status of the parties concerned and according to whether the informant is a Kachin or a Shan' (1964: 219). It is fundamentally because the Kachin *mayu—dama* relationship, in which the wife giver is superior to the wife taker, is at loggerheads with the aristrocratic Shan notion of marriage where the polygamous chief takes women from his subject-inferiors that the attempted imitation of Kachin chiefs of Shan princes is ultimately unsuccessful. Thus though linked, the Shan and Kachin models are dialectically opposed, as would be those of the lowland Burmese and many of their neighbouring hill peoples.

I hope it can be seen how the perspectives adopted by Leach and myself in relation to Burma illustrate how the same phenomena can be illuminated in more than one way, in a complementary rather than inconsistent manner.

The last question I have to answer is why I have drawn the territorial boundaries of my subject matter as I have done. Why stop with Ceylon and Burma and go no further? It is certainly true that Thailand for instance can be brought within the same compass. It is precisely because Thailand is in matters of marriage and kinship so similar to Burma and in its classical legal literature so influenced by Mon-Burmese models that I saw no point in writing an additional section which would have appeared redundant, producing as it were diminishing marginal returns to an unprofitable point. Anyway the sort of relationship to India and Ceylon that I developed for Burma might serve as a plausible model for other southeast Asian Buddhist countries.

But now looking in the opposite direction, why have I left out the northwest regions of India and Pakistan? Barth (1960) and Dumont (1970) have taken rival positions as to how the system of social stratification of the Swat Pathans relates to the Hindu caste system. But we shall have to await more investigation and data before we can attempt to see how legal concepts of marriage and kinship practices, and the position of women in the Northwest relate to the dominant ruling castes of North India (Rajputs, Jats, etc.) in particular, and to India in general.

DOWRY, BRIDEWEALTH AND WOMEN'S PROPERTY RIGHTS

NOTES

1. Blunt appears to have sensed this when he wrote: 'The bridegroom price takes the form of a dowry with the bride and is usual among the better classes. It is, partly at all events, the result of hypergamy.' (1931: 70). The custom of hypergamy itself was described by Blunt thus: 'Where it prevails, the exogamous groups are classified according to their social position; and whilst a group of higher rank will take brides, it will not give brides to a group of lower rank. The law is found most highly developed among Rajputs, but it is observed by many other castes, such as the Bhat, Byar, Dharkar, Gujar, Jat, Kanaujiya and Jhijhotiya Brahmans, Kharwar, Khattri and Patwa. Indeed amongst all Hindus there is probably a tendency towards hypergamy.' (p. 46). Our knowledge of the details of hypergamy is not much advanced. Pocock (1957) has discussed the institution among the Pattidar; also see H.S. Morris 1968).

2. Banerjee (1879 pp. 235-8) gives examples of some ruling groups in India practising multiple marriages with the associated gradation of wives and sons. A case in point is the 'Uriya Rajahs and Chiefs' among whom the sons of the first wife, 'Pat Ranee', are preferred to the sons of other Ranees, and the sons of inferior 'phulbibahi' wives succeed in default of sons of Ranees.

3. Also see Karve 1953: 116 and Dumont 1970: 120.

4. These eight forms were not unique to Manu but are repeated in many other *dharmasutras* and *smrtis*, e.g. Gautama, Narada, Vishnu, Kautiliya, etc. (See Kane, vol. II, pt 1, 1941: 516.) They all reflect the same moral approbation of the *kanya dana* and the Brahma (and Daiva, Arsha and Pragapatya forms) and condemn the *asura* form as sale of a girl. The remaining tenuous forms of are course even more condemned as in Manu.

5. Thus while castes such as Ahir, Chamar, Dom are listed as brideprice givers, the Brahman and Rajputs, the Gujar, Kayastha have the institution of dowry. The Jats are described as sometimes paying a brideprice, sometimes a dowry.

6. Madan comments that 'In practice parents-in-law show immense interest in her *stridhan*, and may take away the best of her personal possessions to give to their own daughters' (p. 158). But this is certainly not customary or publicly condoned.

7. There are possibly further differentiations such as the Mayukha School which holds sway in Gujarat and North Konkan, and is far more liberal about the claims of women than any other school.

8. The difference between the legal and the social definition is seen from the assertion that 'The joint Hindu family consists at any one time of at least two related persons within the circle . . .'; even two widows who are co-owners of the property of the same deceased co-parcener, or a mother-in-law and a daughter-in-law may constitute a joint family (Derrett 1963: 244); Kane (vol. III, 1946: 562) differentiates between Mitakshara and Dayabhaga law thus: ' . . . under the Mitakshara the birth of a son starts a coparcenary. Under the Dayabhaga there is no coparcenary between father and sons as the latter acquire no rights by birth even in ancestral property but it may subsist between brothers of uncles and nephews.'

9. It is appropriate to indicate here that the *taravad* of Kerala (of old Malabar and Canara) does not fit the *Mitakshar* prototype. In theory each member of the *taravad* is simply entitled to reside and be maintanied in the family house; partition is not a right vested in the members. In theory the property is indissoluble and members have rights out of the property rather than rights to the property. But in actual fact as Kathleen Gough has pointed out (1961) partition of *taravad* property occured when the local lineage became large. The same pattern appears to be true of the patrilineal *okka* of Coorg where of course only the males were the owners, but the right of partition was not explicit (Srinivas 1952).

10. 'A coparcener's interest is fluctuating, is capable of being enlarged by deaths and is liable to be diminished by births.' (Kane, vol. III, 1946, p. 561).

11. According to the Mitakshara this automatic right of sons, grandsons and great-grandsons to shares in ancestral wealth was described as *apratibandha* (unobstructible), in contrast to obstructible rights (*sapratibandha*) which are essentially those of reversion and therefore conditional. (Kane, vol. III, 1946, p. 56). Another dichotomy is between the rights arising from birth in the Mitakshara system called *janmasvatvavda* and ownership rights that arise only on death (*uparamasvatvavada*) as operative under Dayabhaga.

12. Of course this is consonant with the Dayabhaga law which denies that the son can partition against the father's wishes, and, more importantly, denies that the son and father have equal rights in ancestral property.

13. The case for adoption was (1) securing spiritual benefit from the *pindas* and water offered by the adopted son and (2) the perpetuation of the family name of the adopter.

14. The requirements in current law are that the child must be a Hindu, must not previously have been adopted, must be under 15, and must be unmarried unless a special custom permits the adoption of children over 15 and of married persons (see Hindu Adoptions and Maintenance Act 78 of 1956, section 10).

15. *Niyoga* refers to the 'appointment of a wife or widow to procreate a son from intercourse with an appointed male' (Kane). It appears to cover a range of arrangements — from true levirate, to a temporary 'widow inheritance' in order to produce children to simply hiring a man to procreate a son for the legitimate husband. All these practices are anathema to later Brahmanical morality!

16. The primary right to give in adoption is that of the father who can do so without consulting the mother. The mother cannot give away without the father's permission if he is alive and capable of giving consent. The mother alone can give away a son if the father is dead.

17. This classical Indian ruling throws light on a puzzle about adoption in certain other societies, e.g. the Eskimo disallow the adoption of an orphan and the *raison d'être* may be similar.

18. If such living issue are subject to serious inpediments, adoption is allowed.

19. For example, can the adopted son of a widow upset the parition of property made after the death of her husband and before he was adopted?

20. I shall also render this as *stridhana*, especially when I cite Kane.

21. In addition to Kane whom I cite, the reader may consult with profit Banerjee (particularly pp. 283-349). on the differences between Mitakshara and Dayabhaga conceptions of *stridhana*. Commentators discussed various issues of this order: was all property and gifts received by a woman *stridhana* or only that over which she enjoyed absolute rights of alienation?; are the rights over property received by a woman at marriage or by gift afterwards from parents, siblings, or husband different from those pertaining to property inherited by her from the

same persons?; was the property received from kin at marriage different from that received from strangers?; what kind of dominion did a husband enjoy over the wife's earnings from her own labour during marriage?

22. I shall use both forms – *sulkam* and *sulka* – the appearance of each in the text being dictated by the author I quote.

23. Jack Goody appropriately refers to this as 'indirect dowry'.

24. Banerjee (1879: 296) gives Vyasa's definition of *sulka* as 'what is given to bring the bride to her husband's house.'

25. The link between brother and sister is also underlined in the rule that (under Mitakshara and Dayabhaga) the property of an unmarried girl goes *first* to brothers of the whole blood (uterine brothers), then to her parents, etc.

26. Manu makes other statements as well, e.g. the property received by a woman after marriage goes equally to all the uterine brothers and (unmarried) uterine sisters – a principle consonant with the Bombay school already cited.

27. An example of the first is that ego's father's mother's lineage may secure a girl from ego's mother's lineage. Although ego cannot, say, marry into his father's mother's lineage, his son or daughter can do so and thereby renew the marriage link: if the daughter does so then the hypergamous direction has been reversed. Karve (1953: 122) clearly shows how among the Jat of Punjab and U.P. it is perfectly possible for a man to marry into the *gotra* of his father's father's mother or mother's father's mother's mother, thereby renewing antecedent affinal links, if not reversing the direction of that link.

28. Raṁkheri is not being discussed in this essay, as representing Central India as such, for we know from Karve's work (1953 Ch. IV) that Rajputana and Maharashtra, for example, show variations around the four axes of exogamous clans, cross-cousin marriage (both asymmetrical-matrilateral and bilateral forms), brideprice versus dowry, and hypergamy. Where, for instance, in some parts of Maharashtra there is hypergamous matrilateral cross-cousin marriage among ranked clans accompanied by dowry the realtions between affines and the pattern of prestations will look somewhat similar to the northern pattern.

Dube's Indian Village (1955), which is located further south in the old state of Hyderadad, does not appear in the matter of marriage – e.g. cross-cousin preference, marriage payments (especially the bridegroom's side presenting the bride with ornaments and the bride's parents giving her dowry) – to differ from the general patrilineal South-Indian pattern to be dealt with in the next section. Dube presents too few facts on such matters to be able to help us materially.

29. The devices of adoption, of having a resident 'incorporated' son-in-law who produces children to the wife's *okka* (*okka parije*) and an unincorporated non-resident son-in-law who does the same (*makka parije*), are possible when there were no male heirs to the *okka*. Note how close the last device is to the Nayar *sambandham*; the first two are classical devices.

30. Lest this statement be misunderstood we should note that inheritance among the 'matrilineal' Irava of the north is from the mother's brother to sister's son, i.e. a girl has no inheritance rights in her paternal property either.

31. Obeyesekere (1968), though it deals with a 'low country' village has much of interest to Kandyan traditional law and customs.

32. An exception might be the *Niti-Nighanduva*, reference to which will be made later.

33. I am in a position to confirm much of Banks' ethnography through my own field acquaintance with a Tamil community near Point Pedro which I briefly studied in 1950.

34. But their meanings were changed during British rule by Ordinance No. 1 of 1911.

35. The clause is worth quoting. 'The daughters must content themselves with the dowry given them by the act or *doty ola*, and are not at liberty to make any further claim on the estate after the death of their parents, unless there be no more children, in which case the daughters succeed to the whole estate.'

36. This has been suggested by H.W. Tambiah and before him by V. Cormaraswamy (H.W. Tambiah n.d.), and has been also conjectured by Derrett (see *University of Ceylon Review*, XIV, Nos. 3 and 4.).

37. But the Hindu joint family also says something similar in a weaker manner – girls should ideally marry before their brothers, and the gifts girls receive at marriage and afterwards constitute property they derive long before their brothers actually partition patrimonial property (in which of course they have always held rights since brith according to the Mitakshara).

38. For Chiruppiddi village, Banks found that dowries were composed of the following: excluding rocky waste, paddy land, garden land and compound land figured in that order with respect to acreage.

The actual proportions of each depends of course partly on ecological factors – in the southern half of the peninsula coconut gardens are a more dominant form of property than in the northern half.

39. The criteria used competitively for the ranking of *sondakarar* groups are possession by tradition of inferior caste servants, especially of Koviyar caste to serve them, the holding of offices such as *udayar*, *maniyagar* (headmen at village, district levels), documents, sumptuary privileges, the use of certain rituals, possession of wealth and land, etc. Modern criteria added on to the traditional are western education and white-collar jobs.

40. In my view it is better to describe *sondakarar* as alleged status-bearing 'kin collectivities' than 'castes' but I shall here continue to use Banks' terminology.

41. In a *binna*-marriage the husband is brought to the house of the wife or her relatives and resides on the property belonging to the wife's ancestral house (*mulgedera*), although the house where he resides need not necessarily be that of his bride's father.

42. The Niti-Nighanduva considers even neolocal residence *diga* marriage because the wife has been conducted away from her family.

43. The right of *diga* married daughters to maternal property is a matter of dispute and uncertainty. According to some sources she has equal rights with other siblings, according to others not.

44. A case in point is the ruling by British courts that a *diga*-married daughter cannot inherit *maternal* property.

45 Obviously this broad contrast has to be refined. First of all we should note the strong rights females have to patrimonial property in some South Indian groups such as the Nangudi Vellalar. Next, as far as the Buddhist fit with social organization is concerned, any attempt at a 'casual' argument should take into account that in Ceylon the Jaffna Tamils for example (as indeed the Ceylon Moors) while espousing Hinduism or Islam also invest their women with strong property rights. Thus, this 'bilateralization has something more than simply Theravada Buddhism as its distinguishing feature.

46 Thus when the British attempted to codify in writing Kandyan customs, they had to resort to oral traditions and to testimonies from native chiefs and the like. Various compilations and digests were made notably by D'Oyly, Sawers, Armour, Lawrie, etc. There is one interesting work – the *Niti-Nighanduwa* – the origins of

which are obscure: it is still not altogether clear whether it was compiled from oral testimony in the nineteenth century or whether indeed it is a copy of an older written treatise. The text, in form and arrangement and in its citation of cosmology and myths certainly has the flavour of an older tradition, and corresponds well with the Burmese written tradition of *Dhammathat* (*Dharmashastra*) in certain features, particularly the mythical and cosmological elements, Buddhistic and otherwise. It would appear that although early British codifiers such as D'Oyly and Sawers did not know the Niti-Nighanduwa in its present form they were probably acquainted with an earlier work, on which it was probably based (see Pieris 1956). Apart from such 'internal' evidence, my view is that 'external evidence' (especially the affinity of the style of the Niti-Nighanduwa with the Mon-Burmese-Thai *Dhammathat* tradition) supports the view that it is based on an old written tradition.

47 Jardine in a long footnote (pp. 220-3) in the translation of Father Sangermano's work (Jardine 1893) gives an account of the English translations of *Dhammathat* texts in the nineteenth century. Sangermano who was in Burma from 1783-1808 made the first translation (in Italian); Forchhammer translated the Code of King Wagaru of Martaban (whose reign began in A.D. 1280). Jardine's *Notes on Buddhist Law* contains other translations. Modern Burmese writers do not have the same respect for the *Manugye* as the British did. They point out that it is confused. and borrows from different sources; furthermore Richardson's translation is not without errors. (See Maung 1963). Nevertheless, it is still the most quoted version.

48 Sacred Books of the East, Vol. XXV.

49 In fact in the myth Mahathammata is conflated with Manu who is described as 'the first among all rulers' (Richardson 1896: 8-9).

50 The Niti-Nighanduwa, a Ceylonese document, gives the same kind of myth of human fall from pristine grace, which leads to anatomical and social differentiation, and the election of King Maha Sammata. It however, also adapts itself to local conditions by tracing the origin of the Sinhalese caste system (which is absent in Burma and Thailand) to the same processes of degeneration and differentiation, *The Law of the Three Seals*, first codified under Rama 1 in Thailand, begins with a similar Manu myth, obviously derived from Mon-Burmese sources. All these versions have their ultimate Buddhist canonical link in the *Aganna Sutta* (*The Dialogues of the Buddha* III vol. IV of *Sacred Books*, p. 77).

51 There is even an imitation of the Indian formulation of *pratiloma* when the Manugye talks of men of low class cohabiting with women of higher classes and the ensuing offence. (Richardson 1896: 173).

52 Such as, for example, *The Special Marriage Act of 1872* (which legislated on age of marriage, the consent of parents to marriage, marriage prohibitions, etc.), *The Burmese Women's Special Marriage and Succession Act* of 1940 which protects the rights of Buddhist women married to non-Buddhist men — Chinese, Hindus, Sikhs, Jains, etc.

53 Quoted by Maung Maung 1963: 48.

54 'Mothers of daughters want their daughters to have *gon* [prestige] and *ausa* [authority] and be big of face as the wife of a senior government officer in town, and mothers of sons want to get the most . . . out of having such a golden goose' (1964: 74).

55 According to the Manugye, if a husband leaves his wife and does not support her for three years, or if a wife leaves her husband and he does not support her for one year, then both can remarry after the specified period.

56 Table 6 is based on Lahiri, Mootham and Maung Maung. It is devised not so much to represent current legal accuracy as to convey some idea of the tendencies.

The chart also excludes from consideration a category called *thinthi*, which was in the past surmised to refer to personal property like clothes, jewellery and ornaments held separately by husband and wife. The reason for its exclusion is that it does not seem to figure in modern Burmese family law (See Maung 1963: 92).

57 The point being that although at first sight the more daughters possessed the more bridewealth received, yet sons are needed by parents for reasons of labour and to work the land. The uxorilocal son-in-law who also pays a large brideprice is a rare bird.

58 The rights of grandchildren are discussed later.

59 All legal authorities agree that a woman has no absolute interest in the *praveni* (inherited) property of her deceased husband, though she may enjoy usufruct until her death or *diga* remarriage, but this latter too is contestable. The same exclusion did not apply to property acquired during marriage (see Obeyesekere 1967: 42-3).

60 There are complex rules as regards the rights of children by different marriages made by the deceased, which we need not go into here.

61 It is clear that the Kandyan Sinhalese concept of adoption is similarly a 'weaker' form than the classical Hindu: adoption is for secular purposes, there is no formal rite of adoption, and the adopted child does not necessarily lose his property rights in his natal family. But being a caste society earlier Kandyan law did restrict the adopted child to the same 'caste' as the adopter. And also being a society with firmer kinship formulations such as preferred marriage, and with transmitted *vasagama* and *gedera* names, it is not surprising that early Kandyan law preferred to restrict adoption to close kin especially nephews and nieces. This was later rescinded.

62 In Burmese (as well as Thai) traditional kingdoms royal patronage consisted of distributing tax rights to officials and clients. In Burma, an official became a *myo-sa*, the 'eater of the town', and this entitled him to extract tribute from his domain. 'Kinship groups' were probably clusters of relatives associated with such privileged officials. Although in theory offices (and assoicated tax rights) were in the gift of the crown and the offices were non-hereditary, if one goes by Thai experience, it is doubtful if some important families of nobles and officials did not become entrenched and amass wealth and independent control over land and trading rights. But obviously in a situation of political instability the rise and fall of great families like that of kings must have been rapid, and the fortunes of important families ephemeral.

63 As Forbes (1878: 64) remarked: '(Polygamy) is legal, but except among officials and the wealthy is seldom practised. In ordinary life a man with more than one wife is talked of as not being a respectable person. This seems also to have struck the early European travellers in Burma, for we find many of them, like Nicolo Conti in 1430, remarking 'This people take only one wife.' Jardine points out (1893: 164) that 'Polygamy is now rare, and the numbers of married males and females almost exactly balance each other, being 1,306,722 husbands to 1,307,292 wives', and Shway Yoe (Scott) writing in 1896 reported that polygamy though recognized and permitted 'practically does not exist now in British territory' and that 'In native territory the right to have several wives was equally little used in practice' (1896: 59).

64 In North Thailand, for example, there are hill peoples like the Lua', Karen, Lahu, Thai Lue, who have cognatic systems, non-prescriptive marriage, marriage payments that are not elaborate, etc. (Kunstadter, *Tribesmen and Peasants*, 1967).

BIBLIOGRAPHY

Aiyappan, A. 1945. *Iravas and Culture Change*, Madras Government Museum
Bulletin.

Armour, J.A. 1860. *Grammar of Kandyan Law*, Colombo.

Barth, Frederick. 1960. 'The System of Social Stratification in Swat, North
Pakistan', in *Aspects of Caste* (Ed. E.R. Leach), C.U.P.

Banks, M.Y. *The Social Organization of the Jaffna Tamils of North Ceylon with
Special reference to Kinship, Marriage and Inheritance,* Cambridge University
Ph.D. dissertation, unpublished.

'Caste in Jaffna', in *Aspects of Caste in South India, Ceylon and North-west
Pakistan,* Cambridge Papers in Social Anthropology 2, (Ed. E.R. Leach),
1960.

Banerjee, Gooroodass. 1879. *The Hindu Law of Marriage and Stridhan,* Calcutta.

Blunt, E.A.H. 1931. *The Caste System of Northern India,* C.U.P.

Chomsky, Noam. 1969. *Aspects of the Theory of Syntax.* (1965) Cambridge, Mass.

Derrett, J.D.M. 1963. *Introduction to Modern Hindu Law,* C.U.P.

'The History of the Juridical Framework of the Hindu Joint Family', *Contributions to Indian Sociology,* no. VI., Dec.

'The Origins of the Laws of the Kandyans' *University of Ceylon Review,*
vol. XIV, nos. 3 and 4.

D'Oyly, Sir John. 1929. *The Sketch of the Constitution of the Kandyan Kingdom,*
Ceylon Government Press.

Dube, S.C. 1955. *Indian Village,* London.

Dumont, L. 1957a. *Hierarchy and Marriage Alliance in South Indian Kinship,*
London, R.A.I. Occasional Papers, no. 12.

1970. *Homo\Hierarchicus,* London, (Paris 1966).

'Marriage in India, the Present State of the Question', *Contributions to Indian
Sociology,* V, 1961; VII, 1964; IX, 1966.

'Les mariages Nayar comme faits indiens', *L'Homme,* vol. I, no. 1, 1961.

*Une Sous-Caste De L'Inde Du Sud: Organisation et Religion Des Pramalai
Kallar,* The Hague.

Freedman, Maurice. 1966. *Chinese Lineage and Society: Fukien and Kwantung,*
L.S.E. Monographs on Social Anthropology No. 33, London.

Forbes, C.J.F.S. 1878. *Burma and Its People,* London.

Goody, Jack. 1969. *'Adoption in Cross-cultural Perspective'* in *Comparative
Studies in Sociology and History,* vol. II,

Gough, K. 1955. 'Female Initiation Rites on the Malabar Coast', J.R.A.I. vol. 85
pt. 2.

Gray, R.F. 1960. 'Sonjo Bride-price and the Question of African "Wife Purchase"',
American Anthropologist, vol. 62.

Hayley, F.A. 1923. *A Treatise on the Laws and Customs of the Sinhalese,*
Colombo.

Hutton, J.H. 1957. *Caste in India,* C.U.P. (2nd ed.).

Iyer, L.K.A.K. 1909-12. *The Cochin Tribes and Castes* (2 vols.), Madras.

Jardine, John. 1893. *The Burmese Empire, A Hundred Years Ago as described by Father Sangermano,* London.

Junod, H.A. 1927. *The Life of a South African Tribe* (2nd ed.; 2 vols.), London.

Kane, P.V. 1941. *History of Dharmasastra,* vol. II, p. 1, Government Oriental Series, Poona.

1946. *History of Dharmasastra,* vol. III, Government Oriental Series, Poona.

Karve, Irawati. 1953. *Kinship Organisation in India,* Poona.

Khaing, Mi Mi. 1946. *Burmese Family,* London.

Knox, Robert (1681). 1911. *An Historical Relation of Ceylon,* London.

Kolenda, Pauline M. 1969. 'Region, Caste, and Family Structure: A Comparative Study of the Indian Joint Family', *Structure and Change in Indian Society,* Viking Fund Publications in Anthropology, no. 47.

Krige, E.J. and J.D. Krige. 1943. *The Realm of a Rain-Queen: A Study of the Pattern of Lovedu Society,* C.U.P.

Kunstadter, P. (ed.) 1967. *Southeast Asian Tribes,* Minorities and Nations, Princeton Univ. Press.

Lahiri, S.C. 1951. *Principles of Modern Burmese Buddhist Law* (5th ed.), Calcutta.

Leach, E.R. 1961a. 'Aspects of Bridewealth and Marriage Stability among the Kachin and Lakher' in *Rethinking Anthropology,* L.S.E. Monographs in Social Anthropology, no. 22.

1961b. 'Polyandry, Inheritance and the Definition of Marriage,' in *Rethinking Anthropology,* L.S.E. Monographs in Social Anthropology, no. 22.

1961c. 'The Structural Implications of Matrilateral Cross-Cousin Marriage,' in *Rethinking Anthropology,* L.S.E. Monographs in Social Anthropology, no. 22 London.

1961d. *Pul Eliya, A Village in Ceylon: A Study in Land Tenure and Kinship,* C.U.P.

1964. *Political Systems of Highland Burma,* London. (First published 1954.)

Lehman, F.K. 1963. *The Structure of Chin Society,* University of Illinois Press.

de Le Mesurier, C.J.R. and T.B. Panabokke 1880. *Niti Nighanduwa or The Vocabulary of Law as it Existed in the Last Days of the Kandyan Kingdom,* Colombo.

Lévi-Strauss, Claude. 1969. *The Elementary Structures of Kinship,* London.

Lewis, Oscar. 1958. *Village Life in Northern India: Studies in a Delhi Village.*

Lingat, R. 1950. 'Evolution of the Conception of Law in Burma and Siam' in *Journal of the Siam Society,* pt. 1, pp. 9-31.

Logan, W. 1887. *Malabar,* Madras.

Madan, T.N. 1965. *Family and Kinship: A Study of the Pandits of Rural Kashmir,* Bombay.

Maung, Maung. 1963. *Law and Custom in Burma and the Burmese Family,* The Hague.

Mayer, Adrian C. 1960. *Caste and Kinship in Central India: A Village and its Region,* London.

Mayer, Philip. 1950. *Gusii Bridewealth Law and Custom,* The Rhodes—Livingstone Papers, no. 18, C.U.P.

Mayne, J.D. 1883. *A Treatise on Hindu Law and Usage* (3rd ed.) Madras.

Modder, F. 1914. *The Principles of Kandyan Law,* London.

Mootham, O.H. 1938. *Burmese Buddist Law,* C.U.P. (Indian Branch).

Morris, H.S. 1968. *The Indians in Uganda,* London.

Nash, Manning. 1965. *The Golden Road to Modernity: Village Life in Contemporary Burma,* New York.